Unexpected Encounters

To Alison Tokita

Unexpected encounters
Neglected histories behind the Australia–Japan relationship

Edited by Michael Ackland and Pam Oliver

Monash Asia Institute
Clayton

Monash University Press
Monash University
Victoria 3800, Australia
www.monash.edu.au/mai

© Monash Asia Institute 2007

National Library of Australia cataloguing-in-publication data:

Unexpected encounters : neglected histories behind the Australia–Japan relationship.

ISBN 9781876924508.
Bibliography

1. Australia - Relations - Japan - History. 2. Japan - Relations - Australia - History. I. Ackland, Michael, 1951– . II. Oliver, Pamela M.

327.94052

Cover design by Emma Fisher.
Printed by BPA Books, Burwood, Victoria, Australia.

contents

Preface vii

About the authors viii

Introduction xi

1   Henry Black: consummate Meiji man 1
    Ian McArthur

2   Harold S Williams and his Japan 29
    Keiko Tamura

3   Frank A Nankivell's Japan: from means to marker 51
    Ron Stewart

4   Peter Russo and Japan: a controversial relationship 73
    Prue Torney

5   Paths of wrath and reconciliation:
    homophobia, Japan and the life-work of Harold Stewart 89
    Michael Ackland

6   A matter of perspective: two Australian-Japanese
    families' encounters with white Australia, 1888–1946 113
    Pam Oliver

7   The Hirodo story: a three generational family
    case study of bi-cultural living 135
    Graham Eccles

8   Ten years in a Victorian jail: the convict as the 'other' 155
    Hideko Nakamura

9   Theatres of discipline in the age of consensual euphoria:
    performing globalisation and 'empire' in recent
    contemporary performance in Australia and Japan 171
    Peter Eckersall

Bibliography 191

Preface
Michael Ackland and Pam Oliver

Work on this volume was begun at the instigation of Associate Professor Alison Tokita in the final year of her ten years as Director of the Japanese Studies Centre at Monash University. She oversaw its early stages and offered crucial advice on its shape and contents, while a number of the essays had their beginnings as papers given at symposiums she had organised. The volume is dedicated to her as a mark of respect for this contribution and, more importantly, in recognition of her outstanding work over many years in promoting research on the Australia–Japan relationship. Herself the author of many essays on various aspects of the relationship, she has been instrumental in highlighting key issues and profitably bringing together experts from a range of disciplines. Her enthusiasm, energy and generous sharing of her knowledge have been of untold benefit to her students and many researchers in the field.

Our work was saddened, however, by the sudden death of Dr Prue Torney just before this volume went to press. She will be missed both as a friend and colleague. We wish here to extend our sympathy to her family and her colleagues at the Department of History, University of Melbourne.

About the contributors

Dr Michael Ackland is Reader in English at Monash University and teaches English and Comparative Literature. His most recent monograph is *Henry Handel Richardson: a life* (Cambridge University Press, 2004). He is currently working on a book-length study of Christina Stead.

Graham Eccles began his writing career as a newspaper reporter in Sydney. He spent almost 30 years as a journalist with the Melbourne *Herald*, where he worked as European correspondent for the *Herald* and *Weekly Times* group and later as Chief of Staff of the *Herald*. He held several senior executive positions within the *Herald* and *Weekly Times* organisation before serving as Press Secretary to a leading federal politician and later as a public relations executive. In semi-retirement he continues to write articles for magazines and recently has completed a biography on the Hirodo family's involvement in the Australian wool trade.

Dr Peter Eckersall is Senior Lecturer in Theatre Studies at the University of Melbourne. Recent publications include *Theorising the angura space: avant-garde performance and politics in Japan 1960–2000* (Brill, 2006) and, as co-editor, *Alternatives: debating theatre culture in an age of confusion* (Peter Lang, 2004). He is co-editor of the journal *Performance Paradigm* and dramaturge for the Not Yet It's Difficult performance group.

Dr Ian McArthur teaches Japanese language and Japanese studies at the University of New South Wales. During his 14 years in Japan, he studied at Keio University and worked as an English teacher, a journalist for *Kyodo News* and a correspondent for the Melbourne-based *Herald* and *Weekly Times* group of newspapers. It was in the 1980s as the *Herald* and *Weekly Times* Tokyo correspondent that Ian first became aware of the story of Henry Black, the Adelaide-born man who worked in Japan as a *rakugoka* (oral storyteller). In 1992, while at *Kyodo News*, Ian authored a Japanese-language semi-fictionalised book about Black. He later settled in Sydney where he wrote his PhD dissertation on Black's contribution to the reform debate in Meiji-period Japan.

Dr Hideko Nakamura is a Japanese-born freelance writer and researcher. Her PhD on Japanese women in the peace movement was completed at the University of Melbourne. Her interests are Japan's responsibility for the war and issues about human rights, sexual violence against women in war situations and the minority. She regularly writes for various periodicals of women's non-government organisations and peace organisations of Japan. In March 2005, together with her 'peace concerned' friends, she founded a group called 'Japanese for peace'. Also, she has been acting as Vice-President of Hope Connection Inc, a Melbourne-based Japanese welfare organisation, since 1996. The research on the Melbourne Case formed part of her work as an Honorary Research Associate at the Japanese Studies Centre at Monash University. She is currently a Research Assistant to Associate Professor Alison Tokita at Monash University.

Dr Pam Oliver is an Honorary Research Associate of the School of History, Monash University. She completed her PhD in History at the University of Melbourne and holds a Master of Arts in Japanese Studies from Monash University. She has written many articles and chapters on her specialty, the history of the Japanese presence in Australia, and is preparing a monograph on this subject. Her books include *Changing histories: Australia and Japan* (co-edited with Paul Jones, Monash Asia Institute, 2001), *Allies, enemies, trading partners: records on Australia and Japan* (National Archives of Australia, 2004) and *Empty north: the Japanese presence and Australian reactions* (Charles Darwin University Press, 2006).

Ron Stewart studied Japanese, printmaking and education at the University of Wollongong. Since 1995 he has spent eight and a half years studying in Japan on scholarships from the Yokoyama Foundation, Rotary International and Monbusho. Ron has studied at Sophia University, Tokyo University and Nagoya University, where he completed his Masters in 2001 on representations of nation, race and ethnicity in late-Meiji period cartoon magazines. He is currently a PhD candidate at the same university, working on a dissertation titled 'Contextualizing Nankivell'. Papers by Ron have been published in Japanese in the journals *Manga Kenkyu, Tagen Bunka* and *The Community*. He was also one of *Yomiuri shinbun*'s 'Manga saito' columnists from April 2002 to October 2003. Ron began working as an instructor at Ritsumeikan University in April 2005.

Dr Keiko Tamura was born and raised in Osaka, Japan. She graduated in English from Kobe College and then undertook postgraduate studies in anthropology at the Australian National University, where she was awarded her PhD in 2000 on the Japanese war brides. In 2002 she was a Harold White Fellow at the National Library of Australia, where she carried out research on Westerners in Japan based on the Harold White Collection. She has held positions at the Australian War Memorial, where she is currently a Senior Research Officer in the Australia–Japan Research Project. She is also a Visiting Fellow at the Australian National University. Her publications include *Michi's memories: a story of a Japanese war bride* (Pandanus Books, 2001).

Dr Prue Torney was a Research Fellow of the Department of History, University of Melbourne. She held a PhD from the University of Melbourne. She published articles on aspects of Australian journalism history and had a particular interest in Australia–Japan relations. She published two monographs, *Somewhere in Asia: war, journalism and Australia's neighbours, 1941–75* (University of New South Wales Press, 2000) and a biography of Peter Russo, *Behind the news* (University of Western Australia Press, 2005). Sadly, she died suddenly in May 2006

Introduction

Michael Ackland and Pam Oliver

Unlike many studies that focus on official, bilateral transactions and large-scale engagements, this volume explores the less publicised experiences of individuals and non-government groups within the Australia–Japan relationship. It represents diverse areas of involvement of men and women who moved geographically and vocationally as they pursued their special interests in the creative arts, media, business and international trade. It encompasses many aspects of personal life, such as travel, marriage, family dynamics and the experiences of children. It spans 150 years of peace, war, globalisation and terrorism, and examines how these issues have affected individuals. Rather than concentrating on the familiar chronicle dominated by military, political and trade milestones, these essays investigate how personal space and alien customs were negotiated, how foreign cultures were drawn on and selectively recast in accordance with particular needs, and how competing codes and loyalties have sometimes generated great emotional and psychological dilemmas in these little-known participants.

A similar diversity characterises the contributors to the volume, who are based in Australia and Japan. Like the individual subjects of their research, some are expatriates, others are writing from the country of their birth. They include academics and non-academic researchers from history, cultural studies, social research, journalism, English and communications, arts and media studies.

Taking the individual as our central focus raises a number of issues that are tested in successive case studies. Most obviously there is the question of the extent to which people, although shaped by their times and circumstances, can exert some influence on the course of events and the contours of their own landscapes, in ways often unremarked by conventional history. Of special interest to this inquiry are unexpected, unscripted encounters within the Australia–Japan relationship. For this reason the volume has excluded some obvious and well-known subjects who were influential politically and diplomatically. Instead it concentrates on those without power to make policy or to dictate governmental and cultural directions. Nevertheless, they made contributions that fed, in small but often significant ways, into mainstream historical and artistic developments. They also demonstrate in diverse ways how, as Cynthia Enloe argues, the international becomes the personal. The essays of the present volume strongly support her viewpoint (Mackie & Jones 2001:4).

The background context of individual encounters

The Australia–Japan relationship, on official and personal levels, affords a longstanding and diversely lit drama, stretching from before the Meiji Restoration of 1868 to the post-modern age. The historical focus has invariably fallen on landmark events that affected the lives of the individuals represented in this volume. Nevertheless, our understanding of even these key scenes and their actors is arguably often episodic and far from objective. The experiences of the Second World War, as well as wartime propaganda, indelibly marked successive generations of men and women who lived through the turmoil and uncertainty that characterised the period from the late 1930s to the mid-1950s. Issues of internment, the treatment of prisoners of war, occupation and repatriation put further strain on relations and public perceptions in both nations. More recently, however, political and trade alliances have dominated media coverage and perceptions. Increasing economic interdependence has provided an important impetus for initiatives to promote mutual understanding. The year of exchange in 2006 marks the 30th anniversary of the Treaty of Friendship and Co-operation. English is now the most widely taught foreign language in Japan, while in Australia Japanese language education thrives and supports interaction at many levels. Both Australians and Japanese are familiar with the trade, tourism, cultural and student exchange programs that have dominated the relationship since the 1950s. These developments are well represented in recent research.[1]

This deeply fractured and uneven public knowledge has, not surprisingly, fostered stereotypes and produced shifting as well as selective perceptions of the respective nations. By the middle of the 20th century, the sword and cannon had eclipsed the pagoda and cherry blossom as stock associations with the exotic, once-forbidden kingdom of *Dai Nippon* in Australian minds. These leitmotifs have given way, in turn, to commercial images that have shifted as Japanese products moved up the scale of consumer recognition, from the inexpensive to the technologically sophisticated, while Australian awareness of Japan's arts has evolved from woodblocks of the floating world to *manga*, innovative theatre and the post-modern wedding of traditional and contemporary art forms, as in Yasumasa Morimura's reworking of Goya's *Caprichos*. From the Japanese perspective Australia has been successively engaged as a rural cornucopia, as a bountiful source of raw materials and, most recently, as a highly desirable tourist destination. But the record of interaction at a personal level is undeservedly far less explored and less well known. As Mackie and Jones observe, international relations between the two nations are not the exclusive realm of intergovernmental negotiations—they are also forged through individual contacts. This is further underscored by the essays in this volume; however, first we need to sketch in crucial aspects of the macro-picture in which our subjects found themselves encountering the other (Mackie & Jones 2001:introduction).

Japan's interest in the outside world predates white settlement in Australia by many centuries. Its long engagement with China and the Asian mainland has been thoroughly documented. Less well known is the story of its contact with the West. This began, as Henry Frei, Christopher Howe and Harold Williams argue, long before the Tokugawa seclusion of 1639–1853. Williams maintains that it was Queen Elizabeth I who initially encouraged English trade with Japan in 1599. Japan also traded with Portuguese, Dutch and other European traders who visited its ports. Japan in its turn, as a successful seafaring nation, traded beyond its shores with the far-flung islands and archipelagos to its south, particularly with modern-day Indonesia, where tens of thousands of Japanese settled and established trading concerns. What these transactions, in defiance of oceans, borders, foreign tongues and baffling conventions, meant for the individuals involved in those early centuries of encounter is largely lost. None the less their impact can be surmised from later case studies, where the categories of self and other, normative and deviant, citizen and foreigner, often blur, warp or are otherwise challenged.[2]

At the end of the seclusion period, with the forced opening of Japan's ports and sea lanes by Commodore Perry's 'black ships' in 1853, talented, highly motivated foreigners were permitted to enter Japan, and Japanese nationals could again travel overseas. From this time onwards the historical record becomes more detailed, as disparate individuals and identifiable groups took advantage of Japan's new accessibility and its desire to acquire foreign skills. From the 1850s Australian men such as Alexander Marks and TA Tallermann travelled to Yokohama to establish trading businesses, to be followed by figures with more diverse interests, who are represented in this volume by Henry Black and Harold Williams. The foreign population of the compounds of the treaty ports swelled quickly in the 1850s and 1860s (Barr 1967; Sissons 1988), as did the number of Japanese subjects who voyaged southwards on passports from the 1860s. This wave of *minami e* (southward ho!) fever provided an opportunity for young men like Muramatsu, Nakashiba and Hirodo (represented in this volume) and thousands of others to explore the possibilities awaiting them in other countries.

The stage was set for the opening acts of the Australia–Japan relationship, which passed through discernible phases marked initially by reciprocal interest, then by growing suspicion and hostility. Japanese officials assiduously promoted overseas, fact-finding missions, as well as their nation's changing image. Unlike their Eurocentric Australian counterparts, they made expert use of international exhibitions in Britain, Europe and the Australian colonies of Victoria and New South Wales to display the goods Japan had to offer. These displays, particularly at Australian international exhibitions, unfailingly attracted huge visitor numbers (Meaney 1999:43ff), while Australians shared Anglo-European interest in the East, as testified to by the widespread vogues of chinoiserie and 'Japonisme'. Prejudice, however, as well as language and cultural barriers, helped obscure the fact that both the Australian colonies and *Dai Nippon*, in spite of vast differences in the histories of their settlement and development, had much in common as they strove to attain the status of independent, modern nation states during the latter part of the 19th century. This shared endeavour produced shifting but parallel experiences (Meaney 1999).

Japan's rapid development generated initial strains in the fledgling relationship. For, whereas the 19th century Australian economy played the role of resource and market for the finished goods of the British mercantile system, Japan pursued an accelerated path to industrialisation and modernisation. Its highly successful acquisition of manufacturing technologies and heavy industry soon enabled local products to be substituted for imported goods. The next step was to manufacture sufficient quantities to compete in international markets and challenge the dominance of market leaders like Britain which, as Howe has documented, it did between 1899 and the 1930s (Howe 1996:part 1). The development of banking, shipping and large trading companies assisted the rise of a modern competitive nation. Additional causes of potential concern to the Anglophone world were Japan's desire for a world-class navy and overseas territory. Colonies or their equivalent, it was argued, were necessary to supply the raw materials needed for a modern industrial state. These immense changes came at a time when Australia was still a handful of colonies, economically under-developed and heavily reliant on Britain for defence.

The colonies' defence concerns escalated after the withdrawal of British troops in 1870, but not initially in response to a resurgent Japan. Thompson, investigating Australian imperial ambitions in the Pacific region, argues persuasively that the major cause of anxiety in the colonies, after 1870, was the annexation of territory by European powers, not threats from Asia: the Crimean War and French and German annexation of Pacific islands, especially those close to Australia's northern borders in New Caledonia, the New Hebrides and New Guinea, unnerved Australian colonial governments (Thompson 1980). La Nauze (1965) has underlined how the need to develop potent defence forces was a persistent theme at Federation, articulated forcefully by Alfred Deakin, first as Minister for External Affairs, then as Prime Minister. But the millennium ushered in a new menace. Although China posed little military concern to the West, Japan did. First it achieved notable successes in the Sino–Japanese War (1894–95). Then the full extent of its advance from an essentially medieval to a modern fighting force became apparent during the Russo–Japanese War (1904–05). Japanese victories on land and sea shocked Australia, as well as the traditional great powers of Europe (La Nauze 1965:517–18; Sissons 1956).

The Australian response to Japan's defeat of Russia at the Battle of Tsushima in 1905 was immediate. Deakin, in the *Herald* (1905), argued strongly for the pressing need to establish a separate defence force and a navy. The growth of three new naval powers, the United States of America, Germany and Japan, he maintained, jeopardised Britain's mastery of the seas. From July 1905 to April 1910, Deakin lobbied for an Australian naval force. England's increasing reliance on the goodwill of Japan for the safety of British interests in Asia and the Pacific led Australia to believe that it was in a perilous position and to foresee an impending crisis. Deakin also feared possible Japanese interference in Commonwealth affairs should a substantial minority of Japanese reside in Australia. Japan, for instance, might press for modification of immigration laws. Australia also feared Japanese southward expansion into the islands to Australia's immediate north. The worse case scenario of invasion was often discussed and, after Tsushima, the intended targets of fortified batteries, which guarded Australia's main waterways, were not exclusively Caucasian. The existence of formal agreements between Britain and Japan, like the Commercial Treaty of 1894 and its successor, the Anglo–Japanese Alliance of 1902, did not remove the unease felt in Australia over Japan's growing naval and military power.

Race was destined to remain a vexatious issue between Australia and Japan. Neither had a tradition of incorporating the ethnic 'other', and both set considerable store on racial homogeneity. Also, both shared the desire to restrict the residence and involvement of the racial 'other' in their national affairs. But neither the closed kingdom of Tokugawa Japan, nor the 'quarantined colonies' of white Australia could entirely fend off officially undesirable foreigners. Creating special enclaves for *gaijin* was one way Edo attempted to control the pressure from abroad; however, the system gradually crumbled and, following the Meiji Restoration, racial intermingling became more widespread. Porous conditions existed in Australia as well. Although the six colonies, and later the Federation, publicly pursued policies aimed at deterrence, such as the Immigration Restriction Acts, governments of the day responded flexibly to individual situations and specific economic needs.

Australia's measures to establish and preserve a white British nation, though not specifically aimed at Japan, nevertheless affected its nationals adversely. Japanese residents who arrived before 1902 were granted 'domicile', or residence, on condition that they obtained a Certificate of Domicile before leaving and re-entering Australia. This exemption provided some stability for Japanese residents. But white racist notions and discriminatory legal proceedings surrounding the *Immigration Restriction Act 1901*, or 'white Australia' policy, strained personal and governmental relations. In addition to official protests, the Japanese government sought practical solutions to this rhetorical and ideological impasse, as the archival record attests and Murakami and others have argued (Murakami 2001:45ff).[3] The 1904 agreement with Japan permitted merchants, tourists and students to enter Australia on a passport for 12 months. Thereafter individuals could apply for a Certificate of Exemption from the Dictation Test, valid for a period of between three months and three years, with multiple three-year extensions possible for those engaged in business (Oliver 2004).

The restrictive provisions both nations placed on the racial 'other' were products of an age when theories of racial hierarchy were widely accepted. Australians viewed themselves as southern heirs to the mantle of the superior white man, destined eventually to found a local empire and, perhaps, to bear the torch of progress if ever British might was to wane. This was the traditional course of empire: a concept implicit in the writings of historians and theorists from Thucydides and Gibbon through to Spengler, and directly evoked by Australian colonial poets such as Michael Massey Robinson and William Charles Wentworth. This prospect, however, demanded the preservation of the colonies' core stock and, in the year of Federation, parliamentary debates on the Dictation Test referred to racial theorists such as Charles Pearson (Pearson 1893). Japan, on the other hand, expected respect as a nation at the pinnacle of development among Asian countries. It had long prided itself on its stable institutions and advanced civilisation. Concentrated efforts had seen it throw off the designation of barbarian, conferred on it by a haughty China, with a vigour reduplicated by its determined embrace of Western customs and technology in the Meiji period. It also learned from, and prepared to follow, the European practice of gunboat diplomacy, or foreign policy imposed through force of arms. Old dreams of a foothold in Korea were rekindled. The ebb and flow of invasion between the Asian mainland and the island kingdom would soon resume.

The literary record

The call for a white Australia and fear of invasion by a great power were strongly represented in the literature of the late 19th and early 20th centuries. Many of the colonial and early-Federation works were variations on a relatively new form of fiction: the projection of future wars, whose literary prototype, entitled 'The battle of Dorking', had appeared in 1871 in *Blackwood*'s magazine. This story, by Lieutenant Colonel Sir George Tomkyns Chesney, set the pattern until 1914 for most futuristic war stories, which often highlighted the effect of technological developments, such as new or improved weaponry, on warfare, and implicitly warned readers of the dangers of remaining unprepared in a belligerent, strife-torn world. European, American and Australian writers adopted the theme. Prior to Federation, when the actual sense of threat was amorphous and its source a matter for speculation, different nationalities featured as potential invaders in these vivid narratives. In *The battle of the Yarra* in 1883 it is the Russians, while in William Lane's novel, *White or yellow? A story of race-war in AD 1908*, which appeared in serial form in the *Boomerang*, the plot turns on a projected Asian aggressor.

The local social and psychological wellsprings of this literature have been thoroughly explored. Dixon (1995), for example, argues that writings about an imagined invasion of Australia reflected a mood of crisis that characterised the pre- and immediate post-Federation eras—a view confirmed by Docker (1991). Another aspect of this fear, directed towards the nation's northern borders, was the concept of the land beyond Australia as uninscribed earth, or empty 'no-man's-land', ready for the taking, and so posing a threat to the Australian colonies. The rivalry of colonial powers such as Germany, France, Britain and the United States of America for that 'no-man's-land' in the Pacific in the late 19th century was of urgent concern to Australians. If good harbours in the Pacific Ocean were established by foreign powers, Australia was at risk from naval attack. Stories of adventure in the South Seas, such as those of Marcus Clarke and Louis Becke, are often sinister and gruesome rather than idyllic. Others dealing with invasions, or the establishment of unknown colonies of 'Asiatics' deep in the unexplored regions of the north of Australia, show the nation, Dixon (1995:ch 8) contends, at its most strident and paranoid (see also Clarke 1966).

Post-Tsushima, the stock 'hordes to the north' theme of the invasion literature was supplemented by specific fears of Japanese spies and intelligence activities, particularly along the Queensland coast.[4] Espionage became an important component of the demonising of Japan, as in the September 1908 issue of *The lone hand*. There the serialised adventure episodes of 'The big five' were followed by Walter Kirton's article 'A Jap school for spies'. This featured information about and pictures of students especially selected for covert operations. From this school in Shanghai had allegedly come the Japanese agents who had engaged in such effective work during the Russo–Japanese War. The new threat of Japanese espionage was underscored when AK Shearston

May (1911) asserted that Japanese spies from New Caledonia made periodic visits to Queensland and other states. Twelve months before, for example, so-called Japanese emissaries had visited Maitland and Newcastle in New South Wales and inquired about the extent and output of mine deposits and the price of minerals. The message of such articles was clear. Australia needed to wake from its slumber. Later that year Arnold White stressed the importance of including spying in any plan to counter a future invasion. Japan, he claimed, had a wonderful system of espionage and would know the location of mines and submarines before attempting to land: 'The secretive capacities of the Japanese [are] so highly developed that the preparation and dispatch of a raiding force of twelve thousand picked men might easily take place without any Australians or any European Power being any the wiser' (White 1911:41). The need for greater preparedness and improved intelligence was strongly urged. Espionage and invasion became paired themes in the literature of the time, as well as within defence and intelligence circles in Australia before 1914.

This evidence of paranoia and the demonisation of Asiatics must, however, be treated with circumspection. Though true for selected strands of popular literature and defence thinking, these blood-chilling scenarios were not widely accepted across the political spectrum or by society in general, as has sometimes been claimed. Examination of individual experiences and relationships between Australians and Japanese in this volume supports the need for caution, and shows that Australians were far from constituting, en masse, the xenophobic nation catered to by many 'ripping yarns' and jingoistic press releases.

A related complexity has been established in contemporaneous discourses on race and national identity. Far from there being a united chorus in favour of white supremacy, David Walker, for instance, has identified conflicting views of Australia's racial future. Some visionaries imagined the elimination of the white race from the Australian continent, others the development of a powerful nation with strong trading and cultural links with Asia. Moreover, Walker argues that almost every possibility between the two extremes of white ascendancy and eclipse was canvassed. 'Asia', in the discourse of the day, often functioned as a rhetorical device to force Australians to behave responsibly on matters of concern, such as population growth and defence. As an example, Walker (1999:6,10,102,107) cites William Lane's pillorying of the Australian male for being passionate about horseracing but indifferent to matters of defence. Similarly, the issues of the ideal constituents of the Coming Man and Coming Woman were hotly debated. On this question, too, the voice of the *Bulletin* was long held to be representative, whereas more recent feminist studies have recuperated a counter discourse, closely linked to women's concerns (for example, Grimshaw et al 1994). Moreover, in women's literature of the early

1900s the Japanese could be presented not as imminent violators of the fair sex but as well mannered and gentlemanly; hence, Rosa Praed's *Madame Izan* can portray them as potentially more desirable husbands than rough Australian males. Similarly, the grace and handsomeness of Japanese officers on visiting ships were admitted, and feelings of excitement and wonder were more likely to be stirred in the minds of young Australian women by the arrival of a Japanese training squadron than by the xenophobic sentiments and fear of miscegenation tirelessly propagated by the *Bulletin*. Some comparable evidence of Japanese attitudes to Australia is evident in two of the chapters of this volume.[5]

Interwar years

Trade, a recurrent theme of this volume, is a good barometer of the Australia–Japan relationship from the Edwardian period through to Pearl Harbour. Initially it boomed. Japanese exports to Australia increased almost tenfold from £1 million in 1913 to over £9 million by 1918, partly because of the difficulty of importing cotton piece goods from Britain under wartime conditions. Japanese purchases of wheat and metals from Australia increased fivefold during the war. But the surge in trade was strongly in Japan's favour. By the 1930s, for instance, it had made serious inroads into Britain's trade with both Australia and India, as Howe has demonstrated. Further *zaibatsu*[6] firms established branches in Australian capital cities as the Japanese trading company network expanded. Mitsui & Co, F Kanematsu (Australia) Ltd, Mitsubishi Shoji Kaisha and Okura Trading Co supplied Australia's department stores and assisted the retail boom of the 1920s.[7] Australia, on the other hand, was slow to make use of opportunities in Asian markets, except where individuals had longstanding company ties. Although government advisers such as HW Gepp recommended increased involvement in Asian trade, and especially better trade representation and delegations, official drives into Asia were short-lived, as Oliver and Walker have shown.

Economic issues came to a head at the Ottawa Conference in 1932. Political opposition to trade with Japan, fuelled by increasing imbalances, had been growing during the 1930s (Gepp 1932). These developments encouraged the establishment of a system of preferential tariffs among British dominions, officially to help them overcome the Great Depression. Japan felt itself unfairly targeted. None the less Sir John Latham, faced with opposition from Chambers of Commerce throughout Australia, led a goodwill mission to Japan in 1934, and Special Minister Katsuji Debuchi returned the mission with a visit in 1935. But a new low point was reached in 1936, when Australia's decision to divert trade away from Japan to Britain was answered with a Japanese decree that import licences were required for Australian wool, wheat and flour. Both

Australian and Japanese firms in Sydney worked to resolve the damaging situation, and key events from these years resonate in the life-stories discussed in chapters three, six and seven.

Apart from trade inequities, there were serious tensions between Australia and Japan. Despite the Anglo–Japanese Alliance and Japan's assistance to the Allies during the First World War, Australian anxieties had increased with Tokyo's strides towards parity with Europe and the United States. The Pacific nations clashed diplomatically over Japan's support of a racial equality clause in the League of Nations charter at the Washington Conference in 1922 and again over its successful claim to former German territories in the Pacific (Jones 2001:25–48). Then came the tariff dispute that seriously impaired trade. Even after its resolution, trade levels never returned to those of the early 1930s and did not improve substantially until war broke out in 1939, when some Japanese firms gained contracts from the Australian Army (see NAA: SP1096/6). Meanwhile international hostilities were straining the bilateral relationship. The Manchurian Incident of 1931, the war with China from 1937 on and the signing of the Axis treaty in 1940 all caused official alarm in Australia. Although international condemnation and sanctions proved ineffectual as a deterrent to military campaigns on the Asian mainland, they did make Japan's elite feel that war with the United States was inevitable. Fearing America's wealth, resources and industrial capacity, Japanese military leaders argued that they could only be sure of winning a short conflict, and called for a surprise strike, like that which had been so successful at Tsushima. The attack on Pearl Harbour on 7 December 1941 ushered in the Pacific War. It climaxed with the dropping of an atomic bomb, code-named 'Little Boy', on 6 August 1945 on Hiroshima. Decades would be required for Japan to recover from the nuclear holocaust, to redress many of the stereotypes of wartime propaganda and for a young 'school' of Japanese artists, headed by Mirokami, to win international acclaim for works that overtly alluded to, and creatively appropriated, the 'Little Boy' iconography.

These difficult global experiences, however, did not entirely overshadow positive individual interaction, which provided an affirmative, unprejudiced basis for the post-war resumption of relationships. Since then, trade and commercial exchange, as well as artistic and cultural influences, have often worked to blur national boundaries in favour of global perspectives, while individuals have moved comfortably between formerly warring nation states to create new personal spaces and co-operative situations of mutual benefit to themselves and their countries of origin.

Individual encounters—race and identity

Common sense would suggest that the attractions exercised by one country on the nationals of another are likely to be almost as varied as the number of individuals involved. In reality, however, the allure of particular nations is more limited and tends to be a recurrent feature of emigrant stories. Prominent in the case of Japan has been the appeal of its aesthetic and artistic traditions. During the 19th century the vogue of chinoiserie was gradually supplanted among Western connoisseurs by an appreciation of traditional Japanese arts and handicrafts. Exquisite detailing, refined lacquer work and the accoutrements of *bushido*[8] had attracted attention in the Australian colonies by the time of Federation (Broinowski 1996). Meanwhile Western painting, and hidebound Western academies, were about to be revolutionised by the Japanese woodblock. It challenged the dominance of perspective and encouraged, among the transatlantic avant-garde, bold experimentation with colour and abstract patterning. In due course Australian painting was transformed by these changes, while gifted individuals, from Henry Black to Harold Stewart, immersed themselves on the spot in Japanese arts and popular culture. Each man created his own distinctive interblending of the two cultures and became, over time, an emissary either of Anglo-European enlightenment to Japan, or of Eastern spiritual lore to a benighted Western world.

For Japanese, beginning with the *minami e* (southward ho!) movement, Australia was a land of diverse opportunities. The contribution of Japanese nationals to pearling centres, cane-cutting operations and in import–export trading areas was crucial. It also encouraged an unsuspected level of intermingling between the two communities. Recently available records of Japanese trading companies, opened by the National Archives of Australia and described in its 2004 guide to records on the relationship between Australia and Japan, provide new evidence of communities in Sydney and Melbourne that rivalled those of pearling centres in size and importance.[9] Japanese married Australian women. Children, either born in Australia, like Kenji Hirodo in chapter seven, or arriving in Australia in their early years, like Muramatsu and Nakashiba in chapter six, integrated into Australian society. Other Japanese families became part of local suburban life. Rich records now enable a detailed examination of individual encounters of Australians and Japanese in business, social and family life (*Asia Pacific Focus* 2004).

These individual encounters raise a host of questions that sit uncomfortably with pre-war notions of identity and race. Before the Second World War, racial and cultural identity were often considered to be fixed, and the biological theory of race was accepted as scientific truth. But in practice these monolithic notions were far from unassailable, as the administration of the white Australia legislation showed. Though official policy distinguished rigidly between self and other, the difficulties of interpreting and applying it to a particular group or circumstance to decide who was 'one of us', or 'other', were recognised. Furthermore, the definition of terms and their usage did not constitute an exact science. The white/non-white binary referred principally to skin colour. However, it is evident from the following case studies that culture played a large part in defining whiteness (Oliver 2002). As chapter six demonstrates, a white person with white parents could be classed as Japanese. A Japanese could be considered British, a term customarily used to refer to white Australians whose origins lay in the British Isles, while the designation 'Australian' usually denoted a person whose cultural orientation was Australian more than anything else. Similarly, 'British subject' could refer to non-white or white citizens born in the British Empire.

In instances where Australians or Japanese lived most of their working lives in respectively Japan or Australia, often with their families, it is sometimes difficult to define precisely the space to which they belonged, or in which they predominantly forged their personal identities. Potentially, then, traditional binaries of self and other, local and foreign, white and non-white are far from absolute, their boundaries porous. Few studies, however, have addressed the question of the shifting identity of Japanese in Australia, or Australians in Japan. This permeability is repeatedly evident in the life-stories discussed in this volume. In most cases of long-term residency in an alien land, people embraced the host country in various ways; the possibility of entirely cutting themselves off from its influence was virtually impossible.

Consider, for example, the position of the Japanese residents in white Australia, who occupied an unusual space. The laws controlling entry to Australia defined Japanese identity from an official perspective. This perspective is, however, misleading, as it suggests the existence of an immutable position not subject to interpretation. A much more complex and, in some respects, unexpected picture of relations between Japanese and white Australia emerges when the stories of individual encounters are examined. As Nagata notes, we lack adequate words to describe Japanese people who live in Australia in a way that places them within a meaningful socio-cultural context. The term 'Japanese-Australian' is almost never heard in Australia. Designations used, such as 'Japanese in Australia', fail to convey the layering of culture and experience behind their identity. Chapter six of this volume expands on the useful insights provided by the exploratory work of Jones on Japanese in Western Australia, and Tamura on war brides (Jones 2002; Nagata 1999; 2001; Tamura 2003:81–2). In addition, chapter seven, on the Hirodo family, raises questions of how to categorise families that embraced both Australia and Japan. Their lives were neither totally Australian nor totally Japanese because they could shift comfortably within the geographic and cultural space that encompassed the two nations. Their wartime encounters as residents in Japan, where some of the family were Australian-born and some held Japanese citizenship, raise further dilemmas concerning identity.

Post-modern theories have heightened awareness of identity as multivalent, fractured and self-dramatising—insights supported by the individual stories dealt with in this volume. Identities, according to Hall, are constituted from within representations. They involve a certain suturing together of perceptions. At issue are how we are represented and the ways in which that bears on how we represent ourselves. Hall's notion of suturing or articulation, moreover, leaves the self with a very fragile identity and a consequent risk of dissolution, reflected diversely in Henry Black's attempted suicide, Harold Stewart's rigidly compartmentalised existence or the shifting confessional stances of Japanese prisoners in Australian jails. Alternatively Powell calls for a reconfiguring of identity that acknowledges a multiplicity of cultural influences and the 'lived perplexity' of peoples' lives. The notion of hybridity captures aspects of this condition. So does the metaphor of border crossings, which acknowledges both boundary limitations, or 'originary characteristics', and psychological as well as geographical and intellectual mobility. The relevance of these conceptions is repeatedly underscored by our specific case studies, as is the need to move beyond notions of identity as biologically or racially given to embrace such issues of background, class, nurture and trans-nationality (Hall & du Gay 1996 91–2; Powell 1999; Malik 1996:2–7).

In addition, each of our subjects has been called on to stage his or her existence before a critical, alien audience. While this is, of course, a condition of individuality, as Stephen Greenblatt has eloquently argued (see in particular Greenblatt 1980), it is so to a heightened extent in this bilateral relationship. For here distinctive racial characteristics mark the Japanese in Australia, and Australians in Japan, as always and irremediable 'other'. He or she is perpetually on stage and constantly subject to critical scrutiny. There is little chance to blend in indistinguishably with the local crowd, to assume local colour. And this is often a key feature of the lives investigated here where, for example, some tried to embrace it to their advantage, while others cocooned themselves in private or separate worlds. The last essay of the volume encompasses the issues involved in individual participation in a group context and closes the theatrical trajectory begun with Henry Black's career as a performer. Through its analysis of two case studies, it examines how contemporary theatre deals with topical issues, from global terror to human displacement. In addition, it is concerned with matters close to Black's heart, for example, how theatre may renew itself as it responds to and, in some cases, resists global forces. In addition, it investigates how such forces intersect with resurgent nationalism, which excludes the outside, the 'other', a point also explored in other chapters.

What lies ahead for the bilateral relationship is unclear, though some of the effects of living in an era marked as much by terrorism as by globalisation and post-modern conceptions are shown here. Recently, emphasis on the strategic and economic imperative for the Australia–Japan relationship has weakened. But there has been little perceptible lessening in personal contacts. Instead, within the broad framework of political, diplomatic, cultural, trade and military co-operation, the real strength of the relationship can be seen in the burgeoning informal exchanges between individuals, far surpassing in volume anything in the pre-Hiroshima era. Presumably, these and future encounters will continue to throw doubt on the concept of a static and unitary identity, and reconfirm the role played by personal movement within the Australia–Japan relationship as a crucial catalyst in reshaping, and often in crystallising, individual identity and careers.

Finally, these life studies have not been selected to illustrate a theoretical position, or to serve a polemical end. Essentially they are acts of recuperation, which afford insights into neglected existences, incidents and exchanges, and more generally throw light on the role of individuals in the complex web of relationships that have long linked Australia and Japan. They add detail and colour to the broad, and often crude, brushstrokes of historical narratives; they are, to borrow Ezra Pound's evocative description of striking faces materialising from the hurly-burly of the Paris Metro, 'petals on the wet, black bough' of history. Personal interaction between cultures and countries cannot be prescribed, or trammelled up in a single, resonant phrase. It varies according to the circumstances of the day, the needs of individuals and the nature of the contact. As these essays show, defining and negotiating personal space along the many continuums of the Australia–Japan relationship was a task undertaken in as many different ways as there were individuals engaged in it, with the global and international ultimately promoting particular, often challenging and highly personal, experiences then perhaps as much as they do today.

Notes

1. Some notable examples include Rix (1998) and Meaney (1976; 1996; 1999). The introduction to Meaney (1999) provides the general background not specifically noted here.
2. For Williams, see chapter two of this volume. See also Frei (1984; 1991); Howe (1995); Saxonhouse (1974); Wray (1984).
3. For an overview of Japanese immigration to Australia and legal provisions, see the introduction to Oliver (2004).
4. For an understanding of the relationship between the literature and suspected Japanese spying in Australia, see Oliver (2003b).
5. See *The new idea* for 1903–11, where Japan and Japanese cultural mores are featured in almost every issue.
6. The term *zaibatsu* refers to large, family-owned companies established after 1868 in Japan that had diverse trading arms in areas of endeavour such as shipping, mining, banking, commodity trading and importing and exporting particularly in primary areas such as silk, cotton, rayon and wool in return for manufactured goods.
7. References pertaining to the interwar years include Murphy (1980); Nish (1982); Sissons (1976); Tsokhas (1989; 1994); Howe (1996:228–9).
8. The term *bushido* refers to Japanese samurai or warrior culture.
9. These are found in NAA: SP11/4, Japanese A–Z; NAA: MT33/1, WOS; NAA: B13/0, WOS. See also work by Sissons (1977; 1979a; 1979b).

UNEXPECTED ENCOUNTERS

1

Henry Black: consummate Meiji man

Ian McArthur

When the 561-ton *Granada* anchored off Yokohama on 8 November 1865 (Asaoka 1987:11–14), a seven-year-old, Adelaide-born boy called Henry James Black stood on the deck with his mother, Elizabeth, to survey the bustling new port town with its Chinese coolies and substantial buildings. The boy's father, John Reddie Black, already worked in the town as a newspaper editor. For John and Elizabeth Black, Japan represented the geographic end point of a journey. It had earlier taken them from London, in 1854, to the British colony of South Australia and the goldfields of Victoria. But for their eldest son, Henry James Black, born in North Adelaide on 22 December 1858,[1] Yokohama was the beginning of a cultural journey during which he became a celebrated storyteller, *kabuki* actor and hypnotist, and, with hindsight, an example of what could be achieved by individual Westerners during a period when Japan had rediscovered its hunger for, and curiosity about, the West.

Black disembarked at a time when relations between Japan and the West were arguably at their most open and undefined, and his life and career would benefit from this early period of extreme fluidity. His arrival in 1865 came just three years before a coalition of former samurai, from the southwest, overthrew the military government (*bakufu*) and installed the new boy-emperor Meiji in Tokyo. The new government was impelled to establish an order capable of matching the West. Little did Henry Black know in 1865 that, apart from a brief trip to China, he was to spend the rest of his life in Japan, becoming a Japanese citizen in 1893. After Black died on 19 September 1923 in the family home of his adopted Japanese son, he was buried in the Foreigners' Cemetery in Yokohama, on the side of a hill overlooking the port where the *Granada* had once anchored. Born British in the British colony of South Australia, Black became a Japanese citizen, only to be buried as British by his sister in a grave he shared with his parents.

His was, in important ways, a hybrid identity. The contradiction implied in situating the grave of a Japanese in a cemetery for foreigners bespeaks the ambivalence that surrounded his identity. For, in the eyes of many Japanese observers and certainly those who commented on his talents in the newspapers, the Australian-born Black was forever 'British'. As a creative outlet for his talents, the theatre had its apparent attractions. Newspaper accounts attest to his popularity. However, life was not always straightforward for an outspoken storyteller (*rakugoka*) with a drinking habit, a male lover, occasional debts and a large household to look after. There were times during his career when Black faced interference from zealous police, who administered laws pertaining to the assembly and movement of foreigners. He also had to contend with family displeasure over his chosen career. And at least on one occasion the inner tensions inspired by his hybrid identity, as a naturalised Japanese stage performer of foreign origin, were the likely motive for a suicide attempt.

Black always overcame these problems and succeeded in making a lasting contribution to Meiji popular culture through literature, drama and the ideas purveyed in his writings, rather than through introducing technological innovation. Much of his work reads like an extension of the ideas of his father, who, as an editor and Freemason, held the conviction that his work contributed to a mission to civilise the Japanese (Black 1968), a belief shared with many other European advisors to the Japanese government. Henry Black imbibed from his father a faith in science, a belief in equality before the law and strong support for freedom of expression. These ideals found expression in the stories that he narrated to audiences in the 1880s and 1890s as critical comments on reform and warnings about the results of unimpeded modernisation. Some of the stories were adaptations of European writers, including Charles Dickens and Mary Braddon; others were original compositions. Many were published in book form. A small plaque, belatedly placed by Black's grave in 1983, acknowledges this contribution. But Black was arguably more than a multi-talented artist. As a man who effortlessly straddled and interwove two cultures, and who used his productions as conduits for new ideas from the West, and who adopted Japan as his chosen homeland, he was a consummate Meiji man.

Thanks to his family, Black, from an early age, was exposed to two cultures. The Blacks became members of a large British expatriate community in Yokohama. Their presence was a consequence of Japan's entry to the world trade system at a time when Britain's rate of economic growth was at a peak and its industrial revolution was powering trade expansion (Jansen 1995:174). In Yokohama, the Blacks lived 'quite a luxurious life' typified by John Black's fondness for 'a large joint of meat on a dish', which he would carve for the family (Hanazono 1926:78). British residents staged fox hunts, using mongrel dogs, as well as wild geese hunts, although this was officially discouraged because of sensitivities toward the Japanese. A foreign circus or acrobat troupe occasionally visited but, otherwise, the foreign community provided its own entertainment.[2] As he grew older, Black's exposure to the Japanese community broadened to embrace not only government and domestic staff, but also newspaper staff, political activists, theatre personnel, orators and storytellers.

Black's interest in performance art may have originated in his father's participation in expatriate gatherings. A cartoon in the September 1873 issue of *Japan Punch* (Morioka & Sasaki 1983:137), depicting John Black as a kilted Bonnie Prince Charlie at St Andrew's Day commemorations, attests to his penchant for amateur entertainment. The Scottish diarist John Francis Campbell (1822–86), on a visit in 1874, mentioned John Black's ability to 'jingle Japanese ditties on a piano and denounce them' (Campbell 1876:247). In December 1901 a contributor to the *Kobe Weekly Chronicle* also recalled how John Black 'possessed a fine personality and commanding presence on the stage, with a powerful, clear and sonorous voice'. The same writer remarked that Henry Black had 'inherited his father's gift for public readings' (*Kobe Weekly Chronicle* 1901b). This passage confirms that, by 1901, Henry was known within the foreign community as a storyteller.

Campbell supplies the earliest extant, English-language evidence of a possible nascent interest by Henry in storytelling. In a diary entry covering several days prior to 4 December 1874, Campbell recorded a visit to John Black's printing press, which by then was in the Zōjōji temple precinct in Tokyo (Campbell 1876:245). Campbell refers to Henry Black as 'Harry', an appellation his family members also used.

> One of these mornings Mr. Harry Black conducted me to the office of the Japanese newspaper, of which his father is editor.
>
> My guide carried a magnificent hunting hawk on his wrist. It had no hood and gazed about composedly at the sun and the crowds of people. The falconer followed. He was a Japanese gentleman and looked like it. We were seeking a professional storyteller. He was off his beat, so we went on, hawk and all, to the editor's room, and the equivalent of the Queen's Printers (Campbell 1876:242).

Henry Black was almost 16 years old. Campbell does not identify the storyteller, but the reference to the hawk is indicative of an early interest in samurai culture.

This sign of split cultural affiliation is typical of the Meiji period (1868–1912), which became synonymous with rapid and far-reaching change, instigated by men such as John and Henry Black. They, and hundreds of foreign experts (*oyatoi*),[3] were imported by the Japanese government to assist in the modernisation of the country[4] as a result of recommendations made after a series of investigative missions to Western capitals. One of the most important was the Iwakura Mission to the United States and Europe between 1871 and 1873. What impressed the mission were recent developments in Western nations, such as national education systems, large-scale mechanised factories, constitutional forms of government, centrally organised bureaucracies and conscripted military forces. The findings of such missions shaped a program of modernisation, whose planks included bureaucratic efficiency, industrialisation, mass education, networks of efficient communication and transportation, a stable currency and strengthening of the country's military and technical prowess. But admitting Westerners also ushered in unexpected influences, as well as mixed responses. Reactions to foreigners, during Henry Black's childhood years, ranged from curiosity to hostility and fear of cultural violation (Irokawa 1985:38). Such feelings translated into differences over how Japan should be opened to foreign influence, making the foreign presence a litmus test of government control over progress toward modernity.

Black's writing skills and his interest in an enlightenment agenda were both promoted by working on his father's newspaper, the *Nisshin shinjishi*. Henry became acquainted with news-gathering from an early age, frequently commuting on horseback between Tokyo and Yokohama on newspaper errands. Here, too, he learned how to compile a story—a skill that was to serve him well in later years—and he gained first-hand knowledge of events and prominent Meiji period personalities.

> Around that time, my father was on familiar terms with Saigō Takamori, Count Itagaki, Count Gotō, Count Kawamura, and other well-known Chōya figures. Etō Shinpei and others used to come quite often to our place, and he even came for dinner the night before he returned to Saga (Campbell 1876:242).[5]

John Black's proximity to these figures eventually cost him his job as editor of the newspaper, when the government manoeuvred him into a post in the bureaucracy only to sack him in 1875. Disappointed, he left for Shanghai. He returned to Japan in 1879 for health reasons.

His father's fall from grace was the catalyst for Black's move to the theatre. The timing of his early stage performances suggests that he remained in Japan throughout his father's absence. In July 1876 Black gave his first stage performance at the Yoshikawa Theatre in Asakusa. It was a performance of magic. In its report of the performance, the *Yūbin hōchi shinbun* stated that Black would appear with Yanagawa Ichōsai to perform conjuring tricks (*tejina*). He also performed at the Seizōin Hall in 1876, but this reportedly did not meet with the success of the previous performance.[6] Henry Black did not mention these performances when, in interviews, he discussed how he commenced his career as a storyteller. According to Black, he came to public speaking through one of his father's acquaintances, the retired naval officer Hori Ryūta, who was himself a speechmaker.

He [Horī] said to me; 'you're used to Japanese. Why don't you make a speech?' I was young and foolish at the time, so devoid of political thoughts or opinions as I was, I said I would, and took on the task. So I made a speech before the public and that was at the Yūraku Theatre, which no longer exists, in Kōjimachi (Nishūbashi 1905:296).

The date of the Yūraku Theatre performance is unclear, but it appears to have been during his father's stay in China.

Black was to become an important cultural mediator because of his celebrated prowess as a storyteller in the Japanese tradition. Through the theatre he apparently met Shōrin Hakuen (1831–1905), an exponent of the *kōdan* style of storytelling, who coached him in the art. Afterwards the 20-year-old Black appeared in December 1878 at Tomitake Theatre in Yokohama's main entertainment and theatre street of Bashamichi. Black spoke about Joan of Arc and the exiled pretender to the Scottish throne, Charles Edward Stuart.[7] The stories of two mythologised nationalist heroes fit well with the didactic *kōdan* style, which in the early Meiji years was more popular than *rakugo*. *Kōdan* drew from a tradition that included stories of the lives of Buddhist saints, 'tales of heroic protectors of the common people', and tales of military prowess (Morioka & Sasaki 1990:5). The choice of Charles Stuart and Joan of Arc, two prototypical nationalist heroes, suggests that Black was sensitive to nationalism as one of the attributes of the ideal 19th-century European nation-state to which many Japanese aspired.

In this new role Black benefited from his intimate understanding of European and Japanese culture. He knew which topics would resonate with a Japanese audience, and that his foreign-born status was one reason for his early appeal to audiences (Nyorai 1896b:1). In reference to his presentation of Charles Stuart and Joan of Arc, Black attributed the 'full house' to the novel (*mezurashii*) nature of the topic and the speaker (Nishūbashi 1905:296). No other narrator combined European ancestry with a mastery of the Japanese language and an ability to tell a tale. Black had become a sought-after commodity. His Western history stories (*seiyō no rekishi banashi*) made him 'quite popular' (*jūbun ninki ga yoku nariyashita*) (Nyorai 1896a).

Between May and November 1879, following John Black's return from Shanghai, John and Henry Black addressed meetings organised by their associates within the Freedom and People's Rights Movement (*jiyū minken undō*). They addressed the meetings on the subjects of law and prison reform, extraterritoriality and the relative merits of opening Japan (*nihon kaika*) to trade with the West (see Oizuru 1986:10–11). The topics show a preoccupation with the practical aspects of social and legal reform and, more generally, modernisation, reflected in the government's own popular slogan 'civilisation and enlightenment' (*bunmei kaika*). As they and their associates in the movement understood it, the slogan stood in the early Meiji years for the Westernisation of many aspects of administrative and daily life in Japan. The movement was part of the struggle among educated former samurai for control over definitions of modernity.

While his father was busy compiling a history of his time (Black 1968), Henry Black pursued his reformist interests by embarking in April 1880 on a speaking tour to Kanagawa Prefecture. The tour included Odawara, 70 kilometres south-west of Tokyo, where the Tōkaidō, the main trunk route between Tokyo and the Kansai region, passes through the foothills of Mount Fuji. There police, in response to newly gazetted regulations restricting public gatherings, intervened to prevent Henry from speaking. The *Japan Daily Herald* on 28 April 1880 gave an account of the incident:

> Mr Black had delivered lectures in several places, and at one time he proceeded to Odawara, where he lectured upon the effects of a national convention, and upon the subjects respecting the laws of conscription. On the third day of his lecture, he was officially ordered by the police authorities to abstain from lecturing, but in opposition to this order, he again announced his work. This time again, on the third day, a similar order was given him. Utterly disgusted at the proceedings of the officials, he immediately set out for Hakone, and after having taken the baths there for a few days, he quitted that place on the 19th instant. It is said that soon after his arrival in the metropolis, he will bring an action against the chief of police at Odawara for having suspended his lecture.

The same willingness to take on the authorities assisted Black as a storyteller. He circumvented restrictions on public gatherings by joining a military stories (*gundan*) group under Hogyūsha Tōrin.[8] *Gundan* originated in the early Edo period, when masterless samurai read war tales to audiences in towns (Morioka & Sasaki 1990:5). Black later told a journalist that, after his father's death on 11 June 1880, he, then aged 21, 'did not know what to do', so he became a storyteller 'on the advice and persuasion' of his father's colleague, Numa Morikazu, who edited the *Mainichi shinbun* (Hanazono 1926:75).[9] The *Asahi shinbun* of 7 September 1883 confirms this move with a report of him giving *gundan* performances with his mentor Shōrin Hakuen in Osaka (Morioka & Sasaki 1983:139). The *Jiji shinpō*, 7 March 1884, also mentioned Black appearing in a number of *rakugo* theatres, known as *yose*, as well as 'taking detailed notes' at the Tokyo Court of Petty Sessions (Tōkyō keizai saibanjo) 'with a view to producing one or two narrations' (Kurata 1982:81).

John Black's sudden death was a watershed for his family, forcing them to reappraise their options. They chose to remain in Japan. Two years later, traveller Arthur H Crow recorded in his diary a visit with English diplomat Ernest Satow (1843–1929) to Henry's mother, Elizabeth. She lived in 'a purely Japanese house, but with, of course, European furniture', outside the foreign concession of Tsukiji 'by special favour of the Government' (Crow 1883:26–7).[10] Crow does not mention Henry, but by May 1885 he was living in Tsukiji. Now dependent on his own resources for a living, he was reportedly engaged in illegal sake brewing (*Japan Weekly Mail* 1885). The venture was probably designed to earn money, but it may also have met his own needs, as in later years Black was known as a heavy drinker. In a letter to the British consul, Black apologised for the sake brewing and promised 'that in future I will have nothing to do with any such business'.[11] In February 1886 he temporarily ceased storytelling to teach English at an institution known as Tōkyō Gakkan, having listened to a friend who argued that being a *yose geinin* (performer) was 'disreputable' (*gaibun ga warui*) and would bring shame on his father (Nishūbashi 1905:297). At the time *yose* entertainers were regarded as 'low class' (Morioka & Sasaki 1990:3).[12]

Work as an English teacher provided the energetic Black with new outlets and contacts. It probably facilitated an association with the young Miyatake Gaikotsu (1993:989), later to become a prominent journalist and cultural historian. Gaikotsu's elder brother, Miyatake Nanbai, ran the school. Black was 29 and Gaikotsu 19. In November 1886 Gaikotsu began *E-iri kōkoku shinbun*, the first of his satirical newspapers and magazines. The first issue claimed endorsement from *rakugo* luminaries, including Black, and the prominent *rakugoka* San'yūtei Enchō, head of the San'yū school of storytelling. This is apparently the first printed indication of an association between Black and his future mentor. The most enduring testament to Black's involvement in language teaching, however, was his authorship of a 100-page English grammar book in 1887 (Burakku 1886). The book's 14 lessons cover topics including relationships, parts of the body and the weather. Its didactic comparisons of Western and Japanese customs are consistent with Black's mission to civilise. References to *kabuki* actors and differences in style between English and Japanese drama presage Black's later *kabuki* performances (Burakku 1886).

Black also had to respond nimbly to a rapidly changing social environment. By late 1886 interest in learning English was temporarily waning. Foreigners and their cultures were resented, owing to postponement of the hoped-for revision of the Ansei treaties concluded with Western powers in the 1850s and 1860s. With support from the San'yūha, Black reverted to storytelling. The move coincided with the advent of stenography and its application to publication in book form (*sokkibon*).[13] In another stroke of good fortune, this also enabled newspapers and magazines to begin to serialise verbatim stories by professional storytellers. The sudden popularity of *rakugo* stories in the mass media facilitated Black's storytelling career. It also extended his participation in the debate over definitions of modernity, carrying it beyond the gatherings organised by elite political pressure groups to a wider, national audience.

Narrating modernity

Black's first major narrative was his 1886 adaptation of *Flower and weed*, a novelette by Mary Braddon, the British sensation fiction author. This was published as *Kusaba no tsuyu* (*Dew by the graveside*). By this time the precondition for his success—an audience receptive toward a foreigner and involved in the reform debate—was in place. Now, however, the debate was shaped by different political imperatives, including a promised new constitution, which was in place by 1889, while the first general election was due in 1890. In Tokyo and major cities, modern forms of communication, such as the telephone and telegraph, and faster forms of transport, such as the railway and horse-drawn omnibus, as well as incorporation of Western styles in housing, had begun to transform people's ways of life. New job opportunities began to change the way people related to each other. New laws changed their understanding of justice, inheritance, marriage and even of their place in the family and modern state.

The government's reform agenda also impacted on the demographic composition and topography of Tokyo, and so directly changed the nature of Black's audiences. Formerly named Edo, Tokyo was undergoing a social, political and architectural metamorphosis that accompanied its transformation from the seat of the shōgun to the capital city of a modern nation-state. Large urban swathes were razed to make way for open vistas and boulevards along which the new Meiji emperor could parade. The model for these changes was Haussmann's redesigned Paris, which had become a prototype of the 'grand, permanent, and monumental' city (Smith 1978:50). An influx of new residents, including students and new-style bureaucrats, altered the composition of *yose* audiences and led to an increase in venues. Soon *yose*, each accommodating between 100 and 300 people, were in every district of Tokyo, and each provincial city had at least one or more. *Yose* numbers in Tokyo stood at 163 in 1880, 120 in 1884, 199 in 1885 and 230 in 1886, the year Black performed *Kusaba no tsuyu* (Morioka & Sasaki 1990:251–2), making *rakugo* one of the most prevalent forms of entertainment then available.

The early Meiji years were 'a golden age' for storytelling in Japan (Miller 1997:582). Although a popular art form, *rakugo* was satisfying a demand for entertainment and information among the city's population, giving theatres an educative function. *Yose* developed as places for Tokyo's newer residents to socialise and to be socialised by learning the ways of the world, as well as local forms of speech from the stories they heard (Katsura 1976:86). Accounts of attendance by intellectuals, such as Fukuzawa Yukichi and Arahata Kanson (Arahata 1965:20),[14] and acknowledgment of its influence on writers such as Natsume Sōseki (Nobuhiro 1986:20), testify to the broad popularity of *rakugo*.

There were various reasons for this wide appeal. The siting of much of the classic *rakugo* repertoire among the lower class, 'lower city' (*shitamachi*) parts of Edo, or the licensed prostitution quarters, and its frequent lampooning of samurai and the priesthood added to its appeal among the newly enfranchised and upwardly mobile population. *Rakugo*, with its low cost and absence of written instructions and rules (Balkenhol & Sasaki 1979:156), had sufficient flexibility to withstand censorship and cultural ossification. Mass appeal and flexibility made it an ideal form of cross-cultural communication for Black, in an era when reform frequently meant the introduction of Western themes and methods, even in the entertainment industry.

Rakugo reflected the old and the new. By the Meiji period, *rakugo* stories had acquired a characteristic structure consisting of a preface (*makura*), a main story (*hanashi*) and a cathartic punch line (*ochi*).[15] *Yose* audiences removed their shoes at the entrance and sat on *zabuton* (large cushions) on the floor. A *rakugo* performance involved the lone narrator sitting centre stage on a *zabuton*. Although narrators were the mainstay, jugglers, magicians, mimics, acrobats and musicians also performed. Popular *rakugoka*, including Black, performed at more than one *yose* during the day, relying on rickshaw drivers to speed them to the next venue. Some illustrations of Black performing show him seated on a chair behind a table, upon which were a glass cup and a water decanter. Black sometimes wore Western clothing during performances. This departure from tradition fitted the reform mood. Francis McCullagh, who witnessed Black's performances, claimed that the popularity of *rakugoka* was due to their ability to survive censorship and adapt to demands for reform.

In the first place the class is large, and, instead of sweeping it away with other mediaeval relics, the new civilisation seems to have given it a new lease of life. The reason of this survival seems to be that which has caused the survival of Japan herself as an independent country; as Japan not only saved herself from extinction but attained a higher pitch of power than she had ever reached before by timely modernisation, so the story-teller became in like manner a greater power in the land than ever owing to his judiciously identifying himself with the reform movement (McCullagh 1902:207).

Symptomatic of the reform debate's impact on *rakugoka* was the second issue of *Kōdan zasshi* (1897), which declared that there was a 'pressing need' (*kyūmu*) for reform in *yose*. After explaining that storytellers were 'in a vocation in which they are duty bound to offer guidance' (*kyōdō*),[16] it cautioned against debasing the art 'as mere light entertainment'. It also called on the 'storytelling community in general to appraise highly the popularity of stenography', and concluded that if performances could attract more women and children, audiences and storytellers would benefit and a contribution would be made to society (*Kōdan zasshi* 1897:1–2).

Black's entry to *rakugo* signalled that the reform debate had reached the top ranks of *rakugoka*. He formally affiliated with the San'yūha in September 1890 at the age of 31.[17] According to Black, the *rakugoka* Gorin Ennosuke officially approached him on behalf of the San'yūha, arguing that 'a Western *rakugoka* is unusual' (*seiyōjin no rakugoka wa mezurashii*) (Nishūbashi 1905:298). *Rakugoka* responded

Henry Black (left), possibly posing as Omiwa in the kabuki play *Imoseyama* (Mt Imo and Mt Se), with unidentified Japanese actor. The tale involves thwarted love and mistaken identity. Reports of the performance appear in the 17 September 1890 edition of *Asahi shinbun*. Photo printed on an undated postcard sent to Black as a new year greeting, probably from an admirer. Photo courtesy of Mr Hisashi Kanō.

in a number of ways to the reform debate, experimenting with story contents, the style of presentation and even the use of props. The head of the San'yūha, San'yūtei Enchō I, responded by adapting principally from French sources.[18] Although their sources are not always traceable, other *rakugoka* followed suit. But it was Black who became the pre-eminent adaptor of foreign material, claiming by 1901 to have 'translated no fewer than 14 English novels into Japanese' for narration (*Kobe Weekly Chronicle* 1901b:623).[19]

Black's transformation into an officially recognised *rakugoka* took place in March 1891 when he took the professional name of Kairakutei Burakku on achieving principal performer (*shin'uchi*) status.[20] On 24 March

Studio portrait of Henry Black posing as Banzuin Chōbei in the kabuki play *Suzugamori*. Probably around 1892, when Black is known to have played the role. Photo from 'The story teller in Japan', *East Asia Magazine* (1902:212). Reproduced with permission of Mrs Harold S Williams.

1891 the *Yamato shinbun* (Kurata 1984:97) noted that Black, 'who is promoting the fact that he is someone with different colored hair,[21] has an increasing number of disciples, and it is becoming inconvenient not to have a professional name under the auspices of a school [of *rakugo*]'. Despite the new name, it took several years for newspapers, particularly those in the country, to begin using it.

Black's attempts at innovation made him a pacesetter in the art. He saw reform as a matter of survival for *rakugo*. In 1896 an outspoken Black complained to the *Yomiuri* that the majority of *rakugoka* merely paid lip service to calls for reform. Black complained that, despite the 'enlightenment' of society in everyday life (*yo no naka wa hibi ni hirakete mairiyasu*):

rakugo does not advance one iota. The telegraph, the railway, agriculture and technology all advance on a daily basis, but the reform of drama and society, well, we hear about it, but there is nothing that amounts to reform of *rakugo*. There are none among the majority of the *rakugoka* who do not call for reform, but they do it in name only. They do not get together and discuss the pros and cons.

There might be some 180 *rakugoka* in Tokyo now, but I dare say there is not a single one among the younger generation of them who will become a shin'uchi. All of them are good at *hauta*, *dodoitsu*, dance (*mai*), and *tedori*, but these are just accomplishments that please the audience when they get onto the stage and they won't last for long at all.

Will *Koen'yū* succeed to *En'yū*? *Ryūma* and *Kinma*, even though they become shin'uchi, they are all-so-rounds, none of them rate enough to make the big time. So who will follow *En'yū*? When *Enshō* and *Enkyō* die, who will follow them? There's not a soul in sight. If things go on like this, then the world of *rakugo* will be in a sorry state (Nyorai 1896d:1).

His main contribution to the reform of this art form was to introduce adaptations of European novels to the repertoire. In the eight years between 1886 and 1894, Black produced at least ten full-length, serialised narrations, the majority of which appear to have had European origins. Black's debut use of a Braddon novel had established him as a successful adaptor of foreign material, as well as a *rakugoka* of note. He also benefited from the publication of Japan's first *sokkibon*, *Enchō's botan dōrō* (*The peony lantern*), which prompted newspapers to publish serialised stories by prominent *rakugoka* to boost circulation. The year 1891 was one of his most prolific. *Nagare no akatsuki* (*Dawn at the river*) (Morioka & Sasaki 1983:161)[22] and *Eikoko no otoshibanashi* (*The beer drinking contest*) were the first of seven new stories that year. The other five were a murder mystery, *Setsunaru tsumi* (*The pitiful sin*); an adaptation of Braddon's 1876 short story *Her last appearance* as *Eikoku Rondon gekijō miyage* (*Story from a London theatre*); the detective mystery *Bara musume* (*The rose girl*); *Shachū no dokubari* (*The poisoned pin in the coach*), which begins with the discovery of a mysterious woman dead on arrival in a coach; and *Iwade ginkō chishio no tegata* (*The bloodstained handprint in the Iwade Bank*), in which Black pioneered the use of a handprint to solve a murder. The first six of these became *sokkibon* that year. *Iwade ginkō chishio no tegata* was printed in the third issue of the *kōdan* and *rakugo* magazine; *Azuma nishiki*, in June the following year (Shogei 1977:1).

Links between these adaptations and the wider reform movement were diverse. With the exception of the first story, his adaptation of *Flower and weed* as *Kusaba no tsuyu* (*Dew by the graveside*), the printed versions of Black's stories bear a linguistic affinity with novels inspired by the movement for the promotion of the vernacular in prose (*gen'bun itchi*). The plots adhere to standard Victorian sensation or crime fiction forms. In theme, structure and frequency of digressions, devoted to explanations of Western customs, the narrations dating from 1891 are the creation of an artist confident that he was supplying a product that was much in demand. In his stories Black blended familiarity with the exotic in hybrid worlds. Characters could just as easily read the *Yamato shinbun* as attend the Paris opera. As such, they provided a blueprint for survival in the newly Westernising Japan.

Black's last major serialised work appears to have been *Minashigo*, his 1893 adaptation of Charles Dickens's *Oliver Twist*. *Minashigo* tells of the orphan Seikichi who longs for love and a hot bowl of miso soup, but finds fear and betrayal at the hands of a pickpocket gang in London. It was published in 57 installments from May 1893 in the *Yamato shinbun* (Morioka & Sasaki 1983:145), and as a *sokkibon* in 1896 (Burakku 1896). The urge for social justice, on the part of the middle class portrayed in the story, indicates Black's continued concern over the plight of the poor, first voiced in meetings in the late 1870s. The majority of the narrations, between the 1886 *Kusaba no tsuyu* and the 1893 *Minashigo*, reflect increasing concern about negative impacts of modernity, including urban poverty, unemployment and the abuse of women's rights.

The 'first foreigner on the Japanese boards'

In August 1892 audiences at the Haruki Theatre in Tokyo enthusiastically applauded *kabuki*-style performances by Black in the play *Suzugamori*. He played Banzuin Chōbei, the leader of a band of downtrodden *machiyakko*, who fights a group of samurai suppressing local townspeople.[23] The performances by storytellers (*kōdan shibai*) were designed to promote popular *rakugoka*. The English-language *Japan Weekly Mail*, announcing 'the appearance of, probably, the first foreigner on the Japanese boards', described Black's acting as 'a clever and conscientious rendering of a difficult part':

> The unique spectacle of an Englishman essaying such a role drew large audiences, who showed their feelings in ways thoroughly characteristic of the people. Black had evidently made a study of Danjūrō in the part, and every successful imitation of that popular actor evoked a spontaneous burst of applause; on the other hand, any marked lapse from the stereotyped rendering caused the house to shake from end to end with irrepressible mirth (*Japan Weekly Mail* 1892).

The *Chūō shinbun* stated on 20 August 1892 that the performances were 'unexpectedly well received' (Kurata 1984:156). The former *Yomiuri shinbun* journalist Yamamoto Shōgetsu also described Black's performance in a collection of memoirs:

> Black appeared after lifting aside the curtain on the *kago* [palanquin], and suddenly stood up with a gesture that looked as if he might be about to shake someone's hand. When he spoke his lines with that characteristically familiar foreigner's manner of speech, the theatre erupted in applause. It was an accomplished Black-style performance (Yamamoto 1936:96–7).

Black's *kabuki* performances illustrate the extent of the impact of the reform debate upon the art. Participation in such plays afforded *rakugoka* opportunities to perfect certain stereotypical gestures and facial expressions, which, once perfected, helped them compensate for their lack of props (Ōta 1998:208).

Black's 1892 Banzuin Chōbei performances were not his first *kabuki* role. He had already appeared in 1890 in the female roles[24] of Omiwa, in *Imoseyama* (*Mt Imo and Mt Se*),[25] and Osato in *Senbon zakura* (*The thousand cherry trees*).[26] Both tales involve thwarted love and mistaken identity. In 1891 Black played Kumagai in *Heike Monogatari*, Roshishin in *Suikoden*, and Omura in *Ibaraki Dōji, Sōzaburo no Imōto Omura* (*Asahi shinbun* 1891; also in Shogei 1977:4). In April that year he threatened to quit the San'yūha if he could not play one of the major roles in *Chūshingura*: either of Yuranosuke, leader of the 47 samurai retainers, or Kampei or his wife Okaru.[27] No foreigner had previously accomplished such feats, and none has since done so.

His most famous role as Banzuin Chōbei was also set apart by his being a foreigner. Word that Black would play the part reached the public via the *Tōkyō asahi*, which on 5 August 1892 reported that 'the renowned English-born Black' was memorising dialogue for the role of Banzuin Chōbei, 'that trueborn citizen of Edo' (Kurata 1984:154). Black told the *Yomiuri shinbun* that he took the role at the suggestion of his mentor, Shōrin Hakuen, who also had a role in the play. Black at first protested to Hakuen that he could not act, but was persuaded to give it a try (Nyorai 1896c:1). In another account, Black recalled that the idea for the performance came from a comment made to fellow *rakugoka* San'yūtei Hakuchi after seeing it performed by Ichikawa Danjūrō IX (1839–1903). Black expressed admiration for Danjūrō and joked to Hakuchi that he would like to try the role, adding that a Chōbei with different colored eyes and hair to the usual 'might be interesting'. According to this version, his wish later came true, when San'yūtei Hakuchi and San'yūtei Hakukaku urged him to take on the role. The result was that, 'in any event, when it came to the performance, the fact that my Chōbei was different was much talked about and drew a full house' (Nishūbashi 1905:299).

Performing in Japan as a foreigner required inventiveness and empathy. Being unable to read Japanese, Black transposed his lines into roman letters and memorised them. His surprised colleagues praised him for his fluent rendition during their first practice session.

> When it came to actually reading it in rehearsal, everyone gathered on the second floor of a tea house and the script writer was there and at last I did it. While all the others were using their script and dictionaries and looking at each others' faces, I had already memorized it so that I didn't bring my script, and everyone thought it odd and said they were sure I must have been given a script (Nyorai 1896c:1).

Black's training for the part under the actor Ichikawa Shinzō impressed the Tokyo *Asahi shinbun*, which on 5 August 1892 praised his 'fine declamation, foot stamping, stance and forceful gaze' (Kurata 1984:154). This style, known as *aragoto*, had been associated with the Ichikawa family line since it was pioneered by Ichikawa Danjūrō I (1660–1704) (Leiter 1979:18). Word of the performances also reached the expatriate community via the *Japan Weekly Mail*.

Mr Black, a son of the author of Young Japan, and already favorably known as one of the hanashika or story-tellers of Tokyo, made his debut a few days ago as Banzuin Chōbei, in a scene taken from the 'Story of the Otokodate of Yedo'...Hakuen, the noted hanashika, a stout-built man apparently on the wrong side of fifty, as the maiden Yaegami Hime in the drama of 'Nijushiko' was a ridiculous spectacle, but after the first shock of surprise, the audience listened to him with sympathetic attention. Black's acting, however, was far removed from any suspicion of caricature; it was a clever and conscientious rendering of a difficult part and has been deservedly praised by the play-going public (*Japan. Weekly Mail* 1892).

The *Chūō shinbun* also praised Black's performance, adding that 'a Westerner donning Japanese garb and taking to the stage is unprecedented' (Kurata 1984:156). The publicity thus generated attracted the attention of the one actor whom Black most admired, and with whom the role of Banzuin Chōbei was synonymous, Ichigawa Danjūrō IX.

On the fourth or fifth performance, people from the household of [Ichigawa] Danjūrō [IX] came to see the play and suggested I come next morning to learn from him because some of the gestures and lines were wrong. So I went to the Tsukiji home of Danjūrō and he was very pleased. He took me in hand and very kindly taught me this, that and the other, and I immediately carried out what he had taught (Nishūbashi 1905:299).

Black's co-operation with Danjūrō was a meeting of reformist minds. As early as the second decade of the Meiji period, in response to calls for reform in kabuki, Danjūrō had begun exploring more realistic acting techniques to reflect psychological states with greater verisimilitude. Danjūrō's initiative reflected a political and diplomatic agenda, which in 1886, at the urging of the oligarchs Itō Hirobumi and Inoue Kaoru, culminated in the formation of the Society for the Reform of Drama (Leiter 1979:187). Raising the status of kabuki, by making it acceptable to the upper class and to foreigners, was an element in their campaign for a modern institutional infrastructure (Karatani 1993:55). Danjūrō was one of three leading players who, in 1887, contributed to this campaign by performing in the first presentation of kabuki to the emperor (Leiter 1979:187). Foreigners in the audience, together with newly installed electric lighting and its performance in the grounds of the residence of Foreign Minister Inoue Kaoru, all helped boost the status of the art (Shively 1971:90). And so did the participation of the foreign-born Black in kabuki.

Black's awareness of change emerges from narrations and his 1886 English primer. The primer states that, on the European stage, 'everything is more real than in Japanese plays'. The question, 'Whom do I consider the best actor in Tokio?', draws the response that 'Danjūrō is certainly the cleverest'. The conversation concludes with the lament that 'actors are very much despised

Studio portrait of Henry Black posing in formal *hakama*. The insignia on his outer coat consists of the initials HJB. Date unknown. Photo from 'The story teller in Japan', *East Asia Magazine* (1902:218). Reproduced with permission of Mrs Harold S Williams.

in Japan' (Black 1887:lesson 14). Black mentioned reform of *kabuki* in his 1891 murder mystery, *Eikoku Rondon gekijō no miyage*. Praising the newspaper editor and former Finance Ministry bureaucrat Fukuchi Genichirō for his promotion of theatre reform, Black told audiences that 'one of the issues is whether it is better to reform by adopting the Western style, or whether the Japanese theatre is better reformed while retaining its unique aspects entirely' (Burakku 1891:12).

Reinforcing Black's credentials as a moderniser on the stage were his Japanese-language renditions of Shakespeare, which the Australian Harold S Williams recalled him performing 'in his fine speaking voice, inherited from his father' (George 1987).[28] Early performances of Shakespeare by foreigners were an important means by which intellectuals and the general public could experience the playwright's works. In the early Meiji years *kabuki* emerged as the form initially entrusted with absorbing Western influence, including Shakespeare (Minamitani 1990:181). The appearance of Shakespeare in Japanese translation and in *kabuki*-like adaptations on stage, from the 1880s, may well have inspired Black to include the bard in his repertoire from this early stage. Shakespeare's 'realistic personages, who spoke a language alive with individualistic character and philosophy', ultimately influenced Tsubouchi Shōyō and other initiators of the *ge'nbun itchi* movement in 'laying the conceptual basis' (Minamitani 1990:181)[29] for modern Japanese literature.

A question of identity

The key cultural components of Black's hybrid identity were in place with his elevation to *shin'uchi* status in 1891, but restrictions that applied to the movement of foreigners outside the treaty ports and certain parts of Tokyo soon limited his range. As a Briton, Black needed permission to travel elsewhere.

On 6 August 1891 the *Tōkyō nichinichi shinbun* reported that police had denied Black a request to travel to Shizuoka Prefecture to perform. This confirms they were prepared to apply the law (Kurata 1984:114). Another obstacle was the government's issue on 15 August 1890 of Police Order No. 15 requiring special permission for *yose* performances by foreigners (Morioka & Sasaki 1990:251–2). It is not apparent whether the regulation was aimed at Black or not, but it placed *yose* within the government purview with regard to foreign cultural influence. This attempt to restrict foreign influence in the popular arts represented a further step in the ascendancy of those who favoured a Japanese path to modernity by the mid-1890s.[30]

With Black's status as a British citizen hindering his career opportunities, a novel solution presented itself. In April 1893 the 33-year-old Black entered a marriage of convenience with Ishii Aka, the 18-year-old daughter of Ishii Mine, a sweet shop operator in Tokyo's Kyōbashi Ward.[31] The move facilitated Black's legal adoption into the Ishii family and gave him access to Japanese citizenship. Henry Black became Japanese citizen Ishii Burakku. Virtually no subsequent reports about Black mention Aka.[32] It was not until 1899 that the treaty port system, which prompted the marriage, completely disappeared.

Black's sexual preference lay elsewhere. A police report on Black compiled as part of paperwork prior to the marriage noted that Black was living in Tsukiji in 'virtually a husband and wife relationship' with a 23-year-old Japanese male, Takamatsu Motokichi, but that there were 'no other indications of untoward behaviour' (Asaoka 1992:11–12).[33] While there is evidence that forms of male–male sexuality tolerated during the Edo period were marginalised as the Meiji period progressed, due to the influence of Western psychoanalysis and legal codes (Pflugfelder 1999:147–8), Black's liaison with Motokichi suggests that homosexuality was still officially tolerated in the 1890s.

Evidence indicates that Black was with Motokichi at least from 1891, when they co-operated over compilation of a beauty, health and cosmetics book, *Danjo seibi keshōhō* (*Beauty and makeup methods for men and women*).[34] The book's cover states that it was 'edited' by Black and 'translated' by Motokichi. Priced at 35 sen, it had three sections: 'Skin', 'Hair' and 'Mouth'. The first of these urged readers to emulate foreigners and take personal hygiene and cosmetics seriously. An advertisement in *Yamato shinbun*, in May 1891, stated that the book was available through Takamatsu Motokichi of the company Eidendō at the same Tsukiji address as Henry Black.[35]

Black's use of the name Motokichi in his crime mystery *Shachū no dokubari*, also published in 1891, was possibly a tribute to Takamatsu. The central character is the artist Kanō Motokichi, who finds true love by marrying his beautiful life model Onobu. Black promoted Eidendō in another narration in the same year. In *Eikoku Rondon gekijō miyage* (*Story from a London theatre*), when the nobleman John Smith (Jon Sumisu) disguises himself by dyeing his hair, Black urges listeners to obtain such products through Eidendō (Burakku 1891:116).

Despite Japanese citizenship, Black never completely escaped his European origins. His change of citizenship came at a time when government and intellectuals were redefining the meaning of the nation predicated on race, language, religion, a community of interest and geography. As much as Black could claim affinity with Japan, reports ensured that ethnicity remained a sticking point. The Tokyo *Asahi shinbun* typified this on 30 June 1891 when it described him as 'the *rakugoka* and Englishman Black' (*rakugoka eijin* Burakku). Even when the *Chūō shinbun* reported his marriage to Aka, it referred to him as the 'Englishman Black'.

Nevertheless, numerous reports reflect admiration for Black's mastery of *rakugo*, and appreciation of his hybrid identity as a European willing to commit to Japan. The 30 June 1891 edition of the *Tōkyō asahi*, for example, commended Black as a 'clever fellow' (*kiyōna otoko*) (Kurata 1984:108). On 8 August 1891 the *Hinode shinbun* announced his performances in Kyoto, describing him as 'not only well versed in Japanese affairs, but also no different in his command of the language than a Japanese, and possessed of a fine speaking voice' (Kurata 1984:114). On 7 October 1891 the *Ōsaka asahi* lauded Black as 'a species of Englishman raised in Edo' (*eikoku dane Edo sodachi* Burakku) (Kurata 1984:126). By the 1890s this invocation of Edo reflected nostalgia for Edo culture (Gluck 1998:272; 1985:24), as much as reliance by *rakugo* on Edo for inspiration. Again, on 10 August 1893, the *Tōkyō nichinichi shinbun* praised 'the imported Japanese Ishii Black' (*hakurai no nihonjin* Ishii Burakku) and commended his appearance dressed in a *haori*[36] as 'every bit the perfect Japanese' (Kurata 1984:187).[37] On 21 January 1894 the *Fusō shinbun*, announcing performances in Nagoya, noted that Japan had so appealed to Black that he had taken Japanese citizenship and a Japanese name by marrying Ishii Aka. It stated that he had affiliated with the San'yūha, and was in Nagoya as a 'citizen of Tokyo' (Kurata 1984:199). By 2 July 1896 the *Ōsaka mainichi shinbun* signalled its recognition of the then 37-year-old Black by referring to him as 'that amiable fellow among *rakugoka*, Ishii Black' (*rakugoka chū no aikyō mono* Ishii Burakku) (Kurata 1985:87). More than any legal procedure, such descriptions assisted in the 'naturalisation' of Black over time.

Black's homosexual lifestyle ensured that he did not have offspring, but he did acquire a de facto family. Although the date is not clear, Black formally adopted a Japanese boy named Seikichi, whose parents were known to Black. Both had died within a short space of time, leaving the boy without any means of support.[38] On adoption, the boy took Black's Japanese surname, becoming Ishii Seikichi. He later took the stage names of Shōkyokusai Tensa and Hosuko. He married a French woman, Julie V Pequignot (1885–1949), who was an accomplished singer of *gidayū* and used the stage name 'Rosa' (Morioka & Sasaki 1986:183–4). Like Black, Rosa was a foreign-born performer of a traditional art form, an embodiment of the eclectic spirit of the Meiji period. Black also fostered a boy called Gunji, the illegitimate son of a Buddhist priest. He encouraged Gunji to learn the violin as a member of a Western-style band, which he maintained. Gunji had a falling out with Black (circa 1914) after getting a woman in their household pregnant while Black was absent on tour. He returned to find that Gunji had also misspent money meant for maintaining the household, and pawned a cloth impression of *kabuki* makeup (*kumadori kaogata*) worn by Danjūrō, several valued antiques and calligraphy. Gunji left the household and worked as a violinist accompanying silent films in Hokkaido, but any ill-will was forgotten when he was well received on visiting Black some years later.[39]

End of an era

On 21 August 1908 colleagues found Black backstage in agony at a theatre in Nishinomiya after overdosing on arsenic, in what newspapers described as an unsuccessful suicide attempt. According to the press his career was in decline. In its report, the *Ōsaka mainichi shinbun* praised the 'London-born' Black for devotion to Edo, commended his dedication to *kabuki* and *rakugo*, and noted his decision to abandon his British heritage to take Japanese citizenship. It listed his other achievements as the gaining of *shin'uchi* status under the San'yūha banner, his taking of a Japanese family name upon marriage, and his presentation of detective and other serialised stories. But the paper said Black's popularity, which had 'attained great heights', had not lasted long, and that he had been performing hypnotism for the past seven or eight years. It also noted that Black was experiencing financial difficulties, and had combined with his adopted son to create a troupe specialising in Western conjuring tricks. It added that Black was depressed over a tumour-like lump in his throat, and may have feared he had cancer. 'Whatever the case, it is a sad state of affairs', the paper concluded (Kurata 1987:175–6). The *Asahi shinbun* reported Black had dissolved his large household and relocated to a smaller house in Tokyo. It claimed his mother and General Tōgō Heihachirō had given him financial support (Morioka & Sasaki 1983:150). Tōgō's interest may have stemmed from an unsuccessful offer by Black, during the Russo–Japanese War, to volunteer for military service. Tōgo may also have known Black's father, John. The *Yamato shinbun* claimed that Black's motive for the suicide attempt was 'said to have been a general weariness of life rather than any specific reason' (Morioka & Sasaki 1983:149–50; see also Shogei 1977:5).

The problems cited in the papers also relate to the perennial difficulties that Black experienced in reconciling his identity as an entertainer with the novelty of his foreign origins, and to changing tastes. By 1907 Black had dropped to ninth (*Higashi Maegashira Yonmaime*) on a list of rankings for *rakugo* performers.[40] To make matters worse, the conditions that had sustained interest in his presentations of European themes, as examples of modernity, no longer existed. This state of affairs had worsened since the dawn of the 20th century and was largely beyond Black's control. Thus, although he remained affiliated with the San'yūha until at least 1917 (Morioka & Sasaki 1983:150),[41] there is evidence that he worked as a cinema narrator (*benshi*)[42] in the era of silent motion pictures, which were shown in Japan from 1896.[43]

Black did not comment publicly on the arsenic overdose. But family-related factors, not reported by the press, may have contributed to depression. On 6 August, almost two weeks prior to the Nishinomiya incident, Black's younger brother, John, had married in England.[44] John was to return to Kobe soon afterwards to begin work as an insurance agent and surveyor. John's marriage and imminent return may have brought home to Black the gulf between his own itinerant and homosexual lifestyle and the monogamously heterosexual norm, upon which John had embarked. The difference would have exacerbated Black's concern over family disapproval of his stage career, waning popularity on the stage and financial insecurity.

By the summer of 1920, Black was with Seikichi and Rosa 'in retirement, a little forgotten by the world in a comfortable home in Meguro', Tokyo (*Miyako shinbun* 1920:1). The innovative Black incorporated Rosa and Seikichi in performances, together with musicians playing Western-style music.[45] Black continued to perform in *yose*, and visited China in 1916 and 1917 with Rosa and Seikichi to perform for Japanese communities in Shanghai and Hong Kong (*Miyako shinbun* 1920:1).

Around this time the writer and artist Okamoto Ippei encountered Black visiting a bathhouse near his home. Ippei described Black as rotund, leading a Pekinese dog, and needing a walking stick. He regarded Black's demeanour as a statement of quiet confidence in being a *geinin*. Black took off his *yukata*[46] to reveal no underwear, and entered the bathroom 'scratching the flea bites on his backside and patting his fat body with its flabby midriff resembling that of a celluloid kewpie doll' (Okamoto 1929:13). Black entered the bath 'with all the caution of a warship entering Tateyama Bay'. Once in, he whistled a local tune evoking Fukagawa, a district nostalgically linked to the old *shitamachi* region of Edo. He then emerged to have his back scrubbed by an attendant. Ippei's references to Black as 'this discarded elderly, foreign entertainer' (*kono sutareta ijin no rō geinin*) and to the tune associated with Fukagawa reinforce the impression that Black had become an irrelevance who inspired thoughts of a bygone era (Okamoto 1929).

The Great Kanto Earthquake of 1 September 1923 destroyed much of the world Black knew and had loved. Already, in the preceding year, his mother had died on 7 October in nearby Shirogane Sankōchō. But his sister, Pauline, out of spite, had not informed him (Morioka & Sasaki 1983:151).[47] Then much of Tokyo and Yokohama, including many of the *yose* where Black had performed, were laid waste. The aging actor stubbornly refused to budge from his room during and immediately after the quake, despite the pleadings of family members. Fortunately the house escaped serious damage.[48] Just over two weeks after the earthquake, however, Black died in his home on 19 September 1923. He was 64. A doctor who signed the death certificate gave the cause of death as 'senile decay'. Without consulting with the household, Pauline had the body taken away for burial in the Foreigners' Cemetery in Yokohama, in a grave shared with their parents.[49] An inscription on their grave ignores his accomplishments as an entertainer, stating merely: 'Also Henry James, their eldest son, died 1923, aged 66'.[50]

Conclusion

By ignoring his friends' advice and becoming a *yose geinin*, Black actively participated in the debate about Japan's choice of paths to modernity. His acquisition of citizenship, as well as his narrations and *kabuki* performances, were made possible by a new generation[51] of Japanese prepared to accept a foreigner in the country's oral and stage arts. Black's career peaked while *rakugo* flourished as an accessible medium of entertainment and information for people who migrated to the cities and towns following the social dislocation unleashed by the post-1868 government. Black seized the opportunity. He adapted material from European sources as serialised representations of modernity, containing the key elements of suspense and humour. His statements, style of presentation, and choice of subject matter in narrations reflected his perception of his role as a medium for the transmission of ideas from the West.

In the 1880s and 1890s the rapid social and political changes, the presence of foreigners and the influx of new ideas, mainly from Europe, stimulated a receptivity in audiences for the adaptations of European detective and sensation fiction that Black provided. While his rise to fame and subsequent obscurity reflected changes in definitions of modernity throughout his lifetime, his career also shows that the debate over reform was not solely the preserve of government ideologues. That debate, begun in the 1870s by the adherents of the Freedom and People's Rights Movement, had a trickle-down effect, with elements of the pro-democracy message filtering through to the common people via *yose* and *sokkibon* well into the 1890s.

Black's encounters with pro-democracy activists gave him an intimate knowledge of the people and philosophies motivating the formation of the new government in 1868. Equipped with empathy for Japan, he used his understanding of European culture and his status as a foreigner to become a successful *rakugoka*. Black's entry to *rakugo*, together with his later taking of Japanese citizenship to evade government restrictions on foreigners on the *yose* stage, ensured the continued presence of a foreign-born voice in the debate over modernity. And this occurred in a period of acknowledged backlash against Western influence. Black's case illustrates the complexity of the arguments brought to the debate, at least among *yose* audiences and *sokkibon* readers. His narrations are an indication that even the indigenous path to modernity was an unavoidably hybrid one that incorporated Western elements.

Hybrids, such as Black, suffer from an inability to fit into set categories. Newspaper reports invariably treat his European origins as integral to his identity. Black himself continued to trade on that identity in his stories. Nevertheless, his many acts of identification with Japan contributed to an affinity that Japanese felt towards him when the tide turned against foreigners during difficult negotiations over the unequal treaties. Although this did not redeem Black in the eyes of family members, others of the foreign community perceived him differently. Harold Williams and Francis McCullagh, for example, wrote in admiration. But positive representations of Black by expatriate colleagues and Japanese never completely abandoned the notion that he was an eccentric. The dismissal of Black as a mere eccentric is a failure to appreciate the importance of hybridity during the 1880s and 1890s, when many Japanese themselves aspired to the kind of hybridity that Black portrayed in his narrations. The hybrid nature of Black's identity and his enthusiastic participation in the reform debate epitomised the eclectic spirit of the Meiji era.

The contrast between Black's popularity in the 1880s and 1890s, and retrospective interpretations of him as an eccentric on the margins of the historical narrative, indicate that perspectives altered after the 1890s. The absence of Black, and of the popular arts, from much historical narrative indicates a subsequent failure to acknowledge the complexities of Meiji cultural history. There are a number of reasons for this. One appears to be the fact that the popular appeal of Black's adaptations lasted only until the late 1890s. Another is the prominence accorded Black's mentor San'yūtei Enchō in accounts of Meiji *rakugo*. Similarly, social historians, documenting the role of foreigners in Meiji Japan, have displayed a propensity for restricting their focus to certain classifications of foreigners, such as the *yatoi*, whose activities have left a lasting impression upon the narrative of the period. Yet another reason appears to be the prominence accorded the so-called mainstream arts of *kabuki* and *nō*, and mainstream literature in cultural histories of the Meiji period. Official reinvention of *kabuki* as a hallmark of a civilised country contributed to the marginalisation of *rakugo*, the one oral art that had displayed links with the opposition Freedom and People's Rights Movement. At the same time, the incorporation of the vernacular into mainstream literature has bequeathed to subsequent generations a narrative of the country's modern literary history, which fails to appreciate the role of *rakugo* in facilitating the changes.

Henry Black poses major complications to conventional histories of the Meiji period. Black's life suggests a need for historians to question more deeply the reasons why certain foreigners have been privileged, and others marginalised, in narratives related to Meiji Japan. Since Black was Australian-born and at least initially held British citizenship, he defies the conventional wisdom that a *rakugoka*, an exponent of the uniquely Japanese narrative art, should have been born Japanese. For Black, the stage was a neutral zone, where sexual and ethnic identity diminished in significance alongside other members of the *geinin* class (Nishiyama 1997:210). The participation of the Australian-born Kairakutei Black at the creative heart of Japan's narrative art, at a time when many assumed that the government had eliminated foreigners from positions of influence through a decrease in *yatoi* numbers, shows that many ordinary Japanese welcomed foreign influence. Black's example shows that a more comprehensive understanding of the Meiji period can only be gained from broadening the narrative range to include the popular culture of the ordinary people.

Notes

1. A copy of Henry Black's birth certificate is available from the Births, Deaths and Marriages Registration Office in Adelaide.
2. For these and other details on expatriate life in Yokohama at this time, see Williams (1958a:51–2).
3. A literal translation of *oyatoi gaikokujin* as 'honourable foreign menial or hireling' suggests the derogatory origin of the term. The derogatory aspect later lost much of its force but the expression suggested the underlying distaste for foreign tutelage (see Jones 1985:248).
4. The large number of foreigners in Japan during the Meiji period has prompted historians to assess it as perhaps unprecedented in the history of cultural borrowing. Jones estimates that *yatoi* alone may have numbered 4,000 'in all areas of government', with the largest groups being British, French, American and German (see Jones 1985:225).
5. Saigō Takamori (1827–77) led the movement to overthrow the *bakufu*. He served as head of a caretaker government while the Iwakura Mission was overseas, but resigned after mission members refused to support his proposal for a military expedition to Korea. Disappointed, Saigō returned to Kagoshima, from where he led an army of disaffected former samurai against the central government. The army was defeated and Saigō committed suicide on 24 September 1877.

    Itagaki Taisuke (1837–1919) was a former samurai who supported Saigō Takamori in attempts to get rid of the *bakufu*. Itagaki joined the new government but, like Saigō, resigned over its refusal to become embroiled in Korea. Itagaki was a founding member of the Aikoku Kōtō (Public Party of Patriots) and a leader of the Freedom and People's Rights Movement.

    Itō Shōjirō (1857–1929) was a former samurai from the Tosa domain who also urged the *bakufu* to hand power to the emperor. He was appointed to a government position after 1868, but resigned over the government's refusal to sanction a military expedition to Korea. Gotō joined Itagaki in forming the Aikoku Kōtō and again joined him in 1881 to form the Jiyūtō (Liberal Party).

    Etō Shinpei (1834–74) was a former samurai from Saga Prefecture who, following his appointment as Minister of Justice in 1872, accomplished a number of legal reforms, including the drafting of the penal code. He resigned from government service in 1873 out of dissatisfaction over the government's refusal to mount a military expedition to Korea. Etō returned to Saga, where he led an unsuccessful samurai rebellion in 1874 against the government.
6. For reports of the July performance that appeared in the 13 July 1876 edition of *Yūbin hōchi shinbun* and 8 July 1876 edition of *Yomiuri shinbun*, see Kurata Yoshihiro (1980b:157). Morioka and Sasaki (1983:136) mention the Seizōin Hall performance. 'In its report of the performance, the *Yūbin hōchi shinbun* stated that Black would appear with Yanagawa Ichōsai to perform conjuring tricks (*tejina*)'. They cite *Tokyo hanauta*, 25 October 1876, in Kurata Yoshihiro (1980a:85).
7. Given Henry Black's Scottish ancestry and the timing of the performance, it is not surprising that he should have chosen the stories of the Scottish prince, Charles Stuart, and Joan of Arc. His father's Freemasonry traced links to the

Stuarts from when the Knights Templar had fled France for sanctuary in Scotland. Throughout the 14th and 15th centuries, Scotland and France were united by treaty in opposition to England. Scottish soldiers occupied upper ranks in French armies, while Scottish families also supplied courtiers, emissaries and ambassadors to French courts.

8 *Tōkyō akebono shinbun*, 28 May 1880 (Kurata 1981:96).
9 Numa was owner–editor of the *Mainichi shinbun*.
10 The house was probably at the Yamato-cho, Kanda address cited in the 1883 and 1884 editions of the *Japan Directory* (Japan Gazette 1883; 1884).
11 A copy of this letter was supplied to me by Asaoka Kunio. It is a handwritten transcription of Black's original letter dated 23 July 1885. It was transcribed by the then Assistant Vice Consul JC Hale. Black's original letter was transcribed into the consulate's official documentation, with a notation on the opposite page stating that the case was a result of a 'complaint by the Japanese government'.
12 Morioka and Sasaki (1990) note that:

> A *yose* performer is proud of being called a *geinin*, artiste of the common people, although the expression *geinin*—because of its association with 'low class'—has been included in the list of 'discriminatory vocabulary' which should be avoided in public. The list has been compiled by mass-media associations since 1973.

13 For a discussion of the origin and significance of *sokkibon*, see Miller (1997).
14 The journalist, socialist and labour activist Arahata (1887–1981) recorded how his father often took him to a *yose* at Isezaki in Tokyo to hear *rakugoka*, including Black.
15 For a fuller description see Novograd (1974).
16 The word *kyōdō* implies *moral* guidance.
17 Morioka and Sasaki (1983:141) cite a report in the 17 September 1890 edition of *Asahi shinbun*.
18 These included *Matsu no misao bijin no ikiume* (*A beauty buried alive*) in 1886 and *Kōshōbi* (*The yellow rose*) in 1887, which Morioka and Sasaki (1983:152) note are 'said to be based on French novels', *Meijin kurabe: nishiki no maigoromo* (*Master artists: the brocade dancing robe*), published in 1893 and acknowledged as an adaptation of Victorien Sarodu's *La Tosca*, and *Meijin Chōji* (*Master cabinetmaker Chōji*), published in 1895 as an adaptation of Guy de Maupassant's *Parricide* (see also Nakagomi 1998:281).
19 The article attributed the comment to the *Japan Herald*. Extract in Harold S Williams Collection, National Library of Australia.
20 *Kairaku* means pleasure in its hedonistic sense, while *tei* is a suffix accorded the names of professional *rakugoka*. *Burakku* is the Japanese rendering of the surname 'Black'.
21 This was a contemporary euphemism for a non-Japanese, usually a Caucasian.
22 Morioka and Sasaki describe *Nagare no akatsuki* as 'a colorful, but complicated story of an aristocrat taking refuge in London from the French Revolution, his ugly wife, their twin sons (one of whom is thrown into the Thames, but is fortunately

rescued by a fisherman), embezzlement, blackmail, and execution'. They praise Black's 'vivid' description of the French Revolution, adding that his depiction of the carnage has all the hallmarks of a *kōdan* narration.

23 The real Banzuin Chōbei lived from 1622 to 1657. His adventures gave rise, after his death at the hands of the samurai Mizuno Jūrōzaemon, to legends that are still portrayed in *kabuki*.

24 Morioka and Sasaki (1983:142) cite reports of these performances as appearing in the 17 September 1890 edition of *Asahi shinbun*.

25 *Imoseyama* dates from 1771. The tale relates to Fujiwara Kamatari's defeat of Soga no Iruka in the seventh century. The character of Omiwa is the daughter of a sake shop proprietress. Omiwa is in love with her neighbour Motome, whom she believes is a maker of ceremonial headgear. Motome is really Tankai, the brother of the emperor's concubine. In one scene, a love triangle leads to a confrontation between Omiwa and Princess Tachibana. The scene is 'superficially comic', but 'drenched in pathos' (Leiter 1979:217–19).

26 Also called *Yoshitsune senbon zakura* (*Yoshitsune and the thousand cherry trees*). *Senbon zakura* relates to the legendary general Yoshitsune. Osato appears in a scene set in a sushi shop. Osato is in love with Yasuke, whom she believes is the shop's apprentice, but Yasuke is really Koremori, a married novice priest on the run (Leiter 1979:708–11).

27 Morioka and Sasaki (1983:144) cite *Asahi shinbun*, 11 March 1891.

28 Gilbert George (1987) mentioned that Mrs Williams had told him that her husband knew Henry Black and 'went to Shinkai-ichi to hear him give a Japanese rendition of Shakespeare in his fine speaking voice, inherited from his father'. Given Williams's age at the time he received the letter, it is likely the performance he witnessed was early in the 20th century.

29 Tsubouchi was in the audience at *Hamlet*, one of the earliest recorded unadapted performances of Shakespeare, on 1 June 1891, at the Gaiety Theatre, the main entertainment venue for foreign residents in Yokohama.

30 For a discussion of the debate over modernity at this stage, see Waswo (1996:94).

31 Reported in *Chūō shinbun*, 24 May 1893 (Kurata 1984:177–8).

32 The Tokyo Metropolitan Government archive of public documents contains a record of the marriage, but no detail about Aka. There are no known subsequent references to her in any newspapers apart from unsubstantiated and unreliable reports in the English language media that she may have died soon after the marriage. The researcher Asaoka Kunio has attempted to trace Aka via searches of family registers, but to no avail. Henry Black's descendants by adoption also know nothing about her.

33 The report for the Home Ministry deals with Black's occupation, age and moral standing (*hinkō*).

34 *Eijin Burakku* (*The Englishman Black*), compiled by Takamatsu Motokichi, 85 pages, published 12 May 1891, *Danjo seibi keshōhō*. The cover page includes the following English-language notation: 'Beauty, how to increase and preserve the beauty of the complexion, hair and teeth', compiled by HJ Black and M Takamatsu.

The address of Black and Takamatsu is given as Irifune-chō 8 chōme 1 banchi in Tokyo. An English subtitle on the cover is *Beauty, how to increase and preserve the beauty of the complexion, hair and teeth*. The book was rediscovered in 1989 by researcher Asaoka Kunio at the National Diet Library in Tokyo (see Asaoka 1988:13).

35   An advertisement for the book appeared in the *Yamato shinbun* on 23 May 1891 (Asaoka 1988:13).
36   A hoari is a short garment worn over a kimono.
37   *Hakurai* means 'brought in by ship'. It was applied to the sort of imported goods one might buy at a department store.
38   Personal interview with one of Seikichi's grandsons, Sudō Mitsuo, Tokyo, 3 May 1991.
39   The information about Gunji comes from personal interviews with his sons Kanō Hisashi and Kanō Ichirō on 8 October 1991.
40   See citation '*Rakugoka mitate*' in Shogei (1977:3).
41   Black's name appeared on its list of members in that year.
42   *Benshi* were sometimes known as *katsuben*. Both words were an abbreviation of *katsudō shashin benshi* (narrator of moving pictures) (see Katsura 1976:18).
43   Sudō Mitsuo, personal interview, Shizuoka, 3 May 1991. Black's great-grandson by adoption, Sudō Mitsuo, has explained that his grandfather, Seikichi, worked as a *benshi*, having trained under one of the country's more famous *benshi*, Tokugawa Musei. Mr Sudō has suggested that it might have been Black who introduced Seikichi to Tokugawa Musei, but this is only conjecture.
44   The marriage was reported in the English-language *Japan Chronicle* (1908). Extract in Harold S Williams Collection, National Library of Australia.
45   Personal interview with daughter of Rosa and Seikichi (Black's granddaughter by adoption), Ishii Kiyoko, Shizuoka, 3 May 1991. Mrs Ishii told of seeing a performance involving her parents in which a moving image of a flying dove was projected onto a screen following the appearance of a real dove on stage. She thought Black had been involved in devising the performance.
46   A yakuta is an informal summer kimono.
47   Morioka and Sasaki (1983) cite Akabane (1956:166) and Kanai (1967:10ff).
48   Personal interview with Ishii Kiyoko, 3 May 1991.
49   Personal interview with Ishii Kiyoko, 3 May 1991.
50   The incorrect age on the gravestone could be based on an old Japanese tradition which assumed that a child was one at the time of its birth. The error might have been compounded when whoever did the calculation did not account for the fact that he was born in December and died in September, a few months short of his birthday.
51   See Pyle (1969) for an account of identity and attitudes toward Westernisation during this period.

2 Harold S Williams and his Japan

Keiko Tamura

In November 1919, a 21-year-old Australian medical student, Harold Stannet Williams, arrived in Yokohama from Melbourne. He had started to learn Japanese a few years before and was sent to Japan by his father to improve his language skills. In Japan he visited cultural and historical sites, as well as hospitals in Tokyo. The temples and gardens impressed him, while the level of medicine practised at the hospitals did not. After his short 'summer' holiday, he had planned to return to Australia to resume his study, but, on an impulse, he applied for a job at a Scottish trading firm and was offered a position. This completely changed his life. From then on he lived in Japan, mostly in Kobe, for over 60 years until his death in 1987.

During his long residence in Japan, Williams developed a keen interest in historical interactions between Westerners and locals and collected many monographs and manuscripts on this topic. He devoted many hours to researching and writing articles on this subject. Over many years, he built up a collection of books and manuscripts around the main theme of the Westerners' roles and contributions to Japan after the country had opened up to the outside world in the mid-19th century.[1] His collection is now housed in the National Library of Australia as the Harold S Williams Collection. This rich source of information has in recent years attracted a high level of interest from researchers all over the world.

Williams wrote numerous pieces in English, which were published in Japan between the 1950s and 1970s as newspaper columns, magazine articles and later in book form. The cross-cultural encounters that took place when Japan opened its doors after 200 years of isolation fascinated the general public and academic researchers. His readable accounts of those encounters were popular in his day. Regrettably, most of his accounts and his remarkable life remained forgotten until recent times. Hence, this chapter focuses on Williams's experience as a Westerner living in Japan and on his responses to its culture. In spite of his long residency in the country and his dedication to research, which was closely related to Japan, this chapter reveals that he maintained some distance from the local culture and people. As a result, he retained his identity as an outsider—unlike today's Japan experts who immerse themselves in the local culture and customs. This chapter explores the interplay between his long-term residency and his identity, as well as using his story to demonstrate how Westerners lived in Japan through a period of drastic changes in its history and society, including its tumultuous involvement in the Pacific War.

An elusive individual

Research into Harold Williams himself is unexpectedly difficult. He wrote numerous articles and several books, which all include a short autobiography. His manuscript collection at the National Library contains some files with biographical information, such as one with all the certificates he ever received in his life: from his high school days in Melbourne to a certificate for safe driving, which he received at the age of 79 from a local police station in Kobe. Through the numerous private photograph albums in the collection, we can observe a young man in a business suit in 1919 gradually aging to an old gentleman in his eighties.

In spite of the numerous certificates and photographs, Williams's personality remains very elusive. No private letters or journals were included in the collection. In his articles, he narrated historical stories skilfully, but he did not tell his own story in his own voice. I eventually realised that it was a deliberate decision on his part to exclude most of his personal feelings from his writings and his files. He may have believed that how he felt was unimportant for historical writing and his collection. Consequently, he hardly wrote anything about his own experience of being a foreigner in Japan. This essay attempts to address this shortfall by casting much needed light on Harold Williams's fascinating life and experiences in Japan between 1919 and 1987.

Discovering Japan

Williams was born in 1898 in Hawthorn, Melbourne, as the second son of a pharmacist, William Williams, and his wife, Helene. Harold's elder brother, William, was one year older and studied pharmacy to follow his father into the family business. Harold also had two younger sisters, Grace and Laurice.

Harold was a bright student. He attended Trinity Grammar School and then entered Melbourne High School, which had a reputation as a highly elite academic school. After graduating from Melbourne High School, he worked for a year for the Commonwealth Laboratory of Australia as a junior analyst. Around that time tragedy struck the family. Harold's elder brother, William, who had volunteered for the Australian Imperial Force at the beginning of the First World War, was killed in Armentières, France, in February 1917, while serving in the 10th Field Company of Engineers. He was one of the first in his unit to be killed. William's death was mourned greatly by his parents. In 1917, soon after his brother's death, Harold entered the University of Melbourne to study medicine. The family expectation of Harold may have been quite high, as the only remaining son, especially as he was to become a medical doctor, a step up socially from that of a pharmacist.

Harold was a diligent student with a flare for languages. While he was studying medicine, his father suggested he should learn Japanese to 'take his mind away' from his study. Apart from providing a certain 'recreational activity', the father believed that Japanese language study would be useful for his son. His motive for encouraging Harold was interesting. He predicted that Australia would inevitably have a closer relationship with Japan, not because he felt that the friendly relationship, which then existed with Japan, would continue, but because he strongly believed that 'Japan would eventually become a menace' (Williams 1989).

Harold's father engaged a Japanese tutor, named Moshi Inagaki, who lived in the neighbourhood and was working in a laundry at that time. Inagaki later taught Japanese at the University of Melbourne. Inagaki was born in 1880, in Shizuoka, and arrived in Australia in the early 1900s. His wife, Rose, an Australian woman, supported him through her work as a schoolteacher.[2] It was unusual for a young Australian to learn Japanese at that time and Harold was taught privately, as there was no other way to learn Japanese in Melbourne. Harold liked studying the language and Inagaki spent all day on Sundays teaching him. As Harold was absorbing the language so quickly and eagerly, Inagaki suggested that he should be sent to Japan to improve his language skill. His father agreed and Harold travelled to Japan in November 1919 for a summer holiday.

While Harold was touring Japan, he saw an advertisement for a clerk's position at Findlay Richardson & Co, a Scottish trading company that exported silk from Japan and acted as an insurance agent for trading and transporting firms. Different accounts exist of how he obtained the position at this foreign firm. Williams wrote that he applied for a job out of curiosity to explore a trading company in Japan but had not believed that he would be offered the position. His wife said, however, that he was asked to apply for a position when a company representative noticed his sharp brain and language skills (Williams 1989). Whatever the circumstances, he obtained a position as a clerk and decided to stay in Japan instead of returning to Melbourne to resume his medical studies. Initially he intended only to defer his studies but, in effect, he did not return to Melbourne until 1925, and never resumed his medical studies at the university.

Williams never explained the reason why he decided to stay in Japan instead of returning to Melbourne. Even after many years, his parents never approved of the fact that Harold had abandoned his studies (Williams 1989).[3] It is possible that the tragic death of his elder brother, William, was an important factor in his decision to remain in Japan. The parents' grief must have been enormous

Findlay Richardson & Co Ltd. Front row from left: Yonehara, HS Williams, H Bell, A Ormiston, HC McNaughton, Chinese comprador, W McLean, Mabel Ailion, George Russell. Photo courtesy of the Manuscripts Collection, National Library of Australia.

and their expectation of Harold great. He may have wanted to move away from this grave atmosphere and pressure at home, and the offer of work in the Kobe branch office of Findlay Richardson & Co provided a promising alternative. It was the beginning of his long engagement with Japan.

The father's encouragement of Harold's Japanese language study, because 'Japan would eventually become a menace', displayed one stereotypical perception of Japan that existed early in the 20th century among the strongly ambivalent feelings Australians held towards Japan. Australian public interest in Japanese arts and crafts had been relatively high towards the end of the 19th century. At the same time, Australians became more aware of Japanese military power when Japan won the Sino–Japanese War (1894–95), and particularly after Japan defeated Russia at Tsushima in the Russo–Japanese War (1904–05). Under the Anglo–Japanese Alliance of 1902, Australia became an ally of Japan. Yet there was a strong uneasiness about Japan's rapid military development after 1905.

In the First World War, however, Australia and Japan were allied against Germany. It is well known that a Japanese cruiser, *Ibuki*, escorted the Australian convoy in the Indian Ocean heading to Gallipoli. Also, a mortar, which was forged in Osaka and used at Gallipoli, is exhibited in the Australian War Memorial in Canberra. In this way, Japan was a loyal ally to Britain and Australia during the First World War. At the same time, from an Australian point of view, Japan became a more probable threat after the war, as it expanded its territory southwards by gaining former German colonies north of the equator in the Pacific region.

Foreign residents in Kobe

Kobe was opened as a treaty port to the outside world in 1868. It was destined to thrive as a trade and transportation hub.[4] Closer to the British trade centres of Hong Kong and Shanghai than Yokohama, Kobe developed rapidly as an international port. Many British traders moved to Kobe from China, accompanied by their Chinese *compradors*, who acted as interpreters. Kobe also benefited from the wars that Japan fought against China and Russia, which stimulated domestic industry and international trade. The First World War provided further opportunities for expansion of its port facilities. Moreover, in the Great Kanto Earthquake of 1923, Tokyo, Yokohama and the surrounding areas suffered large-scale damage. As a consequence, many trading firms shifted their offices and operations to Kobe. In addition, the military and colonial expansion of Japan into China in the 1930s brought more business to Kobe, as large consignments were processed through the port.

A thriving community of Westerners had existed in Kobe ever since the port's opening to foreigners in 1868. The foreign concession (*kyoryūchi*) was established close to the harbour, where many new Western-style houses were built. In these buildings, business was usually handled on the ground floor, and the upstairs allocated to residential quarters. Initially foreigners were required to live and conduct business within the concession, but the delay in constructing the concession district meant that they had no choice but to live outside, adjacent to the concession. They were also not permitted to travel freely in Japan. In exchange for restricted movement and business activities, the Western residents were granted free leases, self-government and their own judiciary inside the compound. The concession system was eventually abolished in 1899.

On Williams's arrival in Kobe in 1919, the firm's business activities were still concentrated within the concession, but many Western residents had moved out of the area because of significant population increases. In 1869, a year after Kobe was opened as a port, 185 Westerners lived in the area. In 1893 the total population of Westerners had increased to 651, of which 389 were men and the rest women and children. Thus the adult male population comprised 60% of the Western population, and the number of single men who moved to Kobe to seek employment was large. The Western population reached 980 in 1897 (Chūka Kaikan 2000:49). In 1930 the population of Westerners and Indians was approximately 3,800. According to the *Chronicle directory* for 1941–42, the population of Westerners was 8,000, although this figure may be too large, as many of them left Japan between 1940 and 1941 through fear of prosecution as enemy spies and because of the increasing difficulties they faced in trade and business activities (*Chronicle directory* 1940:97). The main residential area for Westerners shifted to the northern part of the city, Kitano-chō, on the foothills of the Rokkō Mountains, and gradually expanded westwards.[5]

Westerners quickly established ethnic clubs where people from the same language and cultural background could associate. In Kobe the first club, the German Club, held its inaugural meeting on 4 February 1868, only one month after the port opened. The International Club was established in 1869 for non-German expatriates, and it eventually developed into the Kobe Club. This club maintained strong British associations until the beginning of the Pacific War. Other ethnic communities established their clubs and by 1941, beside the Kobe Club, seven such clubs were listed in the *Chronicle directory*.[6]

Harold Williams in Kobe

Williams integrated well into the expatriate community. His accommodation in Kobe was arranged at a lodging house run by Mrs James, wife of the Inland Sea pilot, Captain James. Captain and Mrs James had seven children and the younger ones, about the same age as Williams, were still living at home. Williams became good friends with them, and met others through sporting activities. He was quick to join the Kobe Regatta and Athletic Club, where young people gathered and played many different types of sports, such as hockey, rugby and swimming.[7] Matches were organised with other foreign clubs in Yokohama, or with Japanese university sporting clubs in Tokyo. Club membership was offered only to men, but women were invited to observe sporting events and competitions from the clubhouse. The club hall was also hired out for parties, concerts and performances of amateur groups. Thus the clubhouse served as a centre of social activity for the younger population of the foreign community. Williams was also a keen hiker, and he spent one New Year's Eve hiking across the snowy mountains from Kobe to the Japan Sea with his friends.

At the prompting of his employers, Williams joined the Kobe Club, which operated in a very similar style to a London gentleman's club. The clubhouse was an impressive Victorian-style brick building and stood near the harbour and the old concession area. Its membership was restricted to 'respectable members' of the business community, thus unwritten rules of 'no shopkeepers, no Eurasians, no mariners' were initially set for membership, although this was later revised. Women were also excluded, not only from membership but also from the club premises, and kept at bay by a loyal Japanese doorman who was affectionately addressed as 'Boy-san'. Typically, for instance, when a wife had been left waiting for her husband over a cold dinner, the loyal 'Boy-san' would take her distressed telephone call, say her husband had just left the club for home, then quickly order a rickshaw and inform the member that he needed to go home as rapidly as possible (Williams 1975:28). The Western business community met in the Kobe Club at lunchtime. Business information and gossip were exchanged at the bar, whose counter was reputedly the longest in Japan. Here deals were struck and seating positions were informally decided by the status and seniority of the member: old and established businessmen were assigned one end, and junior clerks, including Williams, congregated at the other.

When Findlay Richardson & Co was liquidated in 1925, Williams visited Australia for six months to see his family. Soon he found employment at another firm in Kobe, Cooper Findlay & Co, which also traded in silk. He joined the company as a manager, and eventually became a director. By 1934 he was the representative director of Cooper Findlay & Co. In this way, by his early thirties, he achieved considerable success in his business career.

In 1934 Williams returned to Australia for a holiday. During this trip, he met Jean, his New Zealander wife-to-be, on a boat from Australia to New Zealand. They were married in Auckland only five weeks after their first meeting, and their honeymoon trip was the return voyage to Kobe. The efficiency with which Williams organised his proposal and marriage was impressive. Harold and Jean were attracted to each other while they were on the boat, but they had to part and go their separate ways when the boat arrived in New Zealand. Jean returned to her family and Harold went to meet his business clients. Then Jean received a marriage proposal in a telegram from Harold, complete with 'reply paid' arrangements from her business-like suitor. This choice of a partner cemented his place in the foreign, as distinct from the Japanese, community.

Williams arrived back in Kobe with his new bride and they settled in a Japanese-style house in Kitano-chō, where two live-in servants looked after them. Jean said that Harold had given her a glowing account of the people and the country before their arrival, and she became very interested in Japan. But initially she was not impressed with Kobe. She said:

I was prepared to like it [Japan], but I wasn't prepared when I saw Kobe. I thought it was the most dismal town. All the roofs were grey tiles and it looked grey, everything looked grey...the shops, the streets were I thought very old, about a hundred years before. I wasn't pleased (Williams 1989).[8]

For Jean, a newcomer from the New World, Kobe and Japan looked dauntingly ancient, but she soon developed a keen interest in Japanese art and culture and started to visit temples in Kyoto and Nara at weekends. Jean was understandably curious about how her husband had led his single life in Kobe before her arrival. To her relief, she did not hear any scandals relating to her husband, either because he had been circumspect regarding women or had taken steps to protect his reputation in the community.

The Pacific War

With the dramatic increase in nationalism and militarism in the latter half of the 1930s, it became more difficult for foreigners to live and run businesses in Japan, particularly for those who had British or American backgrounds. Australians were treated like the British. Japanese police suspected those who were involved in trade of being spies, while members of the foreign community, anticipating Japanese war aims, made plans to depart. At the end of 1940, Jean, who was pregnant with their second child, left for Australia with their two-year-old daughter. In July 1941 the Japanese government froze American and British residents' assets in response to similar measures passed by American, British and Australian governments against Japanese citizens. Williams left Kobe in August 1941 on a Dutch cargo vessel, via Java, with a minimum of luggage.

Soon after his arrival in Australia, Williams joined the Australian Army and, despite his age, he was appointed to the rank of lieutenant in intelligence. He was attached to Local Headquarters in Melbourne for most of the war and was later sent on various missions. His strengths were his language skills and cultural knowledge of Japan, which had been nurtured during his long residence in the country. In addition, he proved himself a brilliant investigator and analyst. Because the Japanese captured thousands of Australian servicemen in the early stages of the war, his work concentrated on Australian prisoners of war (POWs). One of his assignments involved collecting information on the servicemen and civilians captured by the Japanese in Rabaul in January 1942. Initially the information was based largely on anecdotal accounts provided by evacuated Australians, but in May 1942, over Port Moresby, a Japanese plane dropped two mailbags containing many letters from Australian prisoners. Williams examined the correspondence in detail before the letters were forwarded to the families. After this incident, however, there was no direct communication with most of the captured Australians. Even though sporadic information filtered through to Australia, families had to wait till the end of the war to learn the fate of their loved ones.

Williams was involved in diverse POW-related issues. In 1943 he went to the Middle East, on an Australian hospital ship, to meet the first group of Australians released from POW camps in Italy. He was sent to India on a similar assignment to meet POWs from Burma, and he worked to set up a POW reception camp in Colombo. He was asked to investigate the Cowra outbreak of 5 August 1944 when about 1,000 Japanese POWs broke out of the Cowra internment camp. During this incident, four Australian soldiers and 234 Japanese POWs died, and 108 were injured. Williams was flown to Cowra the day of the outbreak. As well as collecting information, he attended the burial ceremony of the Japanese POWs, and organised aerial photographs of the camp to assist the investigation.

Williams was part of the ensuing court of inquiry that sat in Cowra for nine days between 7 and 15 August 1944 (NAA ACT A3688/48). During its deliberations, many Australian and Japanese witnesses were summoned to testify to what exactly had happened during and after the breakout. The transcript of the inquiry shows that Williams concentrated his investigation on the weapons that the Japanese POWs possessed at the time of breakout. These included table knives, bread knives, baseball bats and pieces of firewood, which were used as weapons when they charged towards the camp fence during the escape. This line of inquiry suggests that Williams wished to establish that the breakout was a premeditated incident, and hence the actions of the Australian Army were justified even though a large number of deaths and injuries resulted. Williams ordered the knives and other implements to be assembled and photographed for the record, and the desired verdict was handed down.[9]

Williams was particularly worried about how the news of the Cowra breakout would be received in Japan. If the Japanese government was dissatisfied with the conclusions of the inquiry, there could be retaliations against Australian POWs under Japanese control. To his relief this did not occur, even though the report was sent to Japan through the International Red Cross. It is not clear why there was no response from Japan. It could be that an administrative error caused the report to be misdirected to another section, or it could be that a sense of shame about the Japanese POWs prevented the government from responding officially.[10]

Harold Williams in post-war Japan

Williams's work relating to POWs continued after the armistice. He was sent to Japan in September 1945 to work in the 2nd Australian War Crimes

Section, attached to the Legal Section, General Headquarters, Supreme Commander for the Allied Powers, in Tokyo. In just over three months between September and December 1945, Williams carried out an extraordinary number of investigations of POWs, including those captured at Rabaul, and made major contributions towards solving mysteries that troubled the Australian government and agonised Australian families during the war. En route, during a three-week stay in Manila, he interviewed many Australian POWs who had been repatriated from Japan and were waiting return to Australia.[11] He arrived in Tokyo on 27 September, almost exactly four years after his hurried departure from Kobe in 1941. His assignments included investigating the fate of Australian servicemen in Ambon, the fate of Royal Australian Air Force airmen missing from Rabaul, and various other issues regarding Australian POWs. Immediately he swung into action. The day after his return he made a personal visit to the Tokyo Furyo Joohookyoku (Prisoner of War Information Bureau) to meet the Bureau Chief, Lieutenant General Tamura. The upshot was a dramatic revelation: the passenger list of the *Montevideo Maru* revealed that it was transporting Australian prisoners out of Rabaul, en route to Hainan Island, when it was sunk by an American submarine off the Philippines.

Personnel in the Second Australian War Crimes Section. Back row: unknown, Captain Munro, Major Campbell, Major HS Williams. Front row: Sergeant Webster, Lieutenant-Colonel DLB Goslett, unknown. Photo courtesy of the Manuscripts Collection, National Library of Australia.

Below is a court transcript in which Williams vividly described what happened at the Prisoner of War Information Bureau.

Q: How did you find this list?

A: I attended the bureau on, I think, it was the 28th of September for the first time, and I stated the nature of my visit; and as the officials replied that they had no information concerning those men I asked that they should produce their files covering about that period and place. A number of files were produced, possibly five or six Japanese files, each about nine inches long and six inches wide and about six inches thick. Japanese official files are very bulky.

We were sitting at a table discussing the problem, and a number of us were turning over these files. My attention was directed to one file because there was a document about a half-inch thick that was in that file. I noted that that document was written in kana and contained a great number of names written in kana, which I recognised to be the names of English personnel. In that way my attention was directed to the list.[12]

As Williams stated, the initial response from the officials of the bureau had been that no information was available about the fate of the Australian POWs from Rabaul. It was true that an enormous number of military documents were destroyed prior to the surrender, both at army and navy departments and their headquarters.[13] The bureau also received similar instructions from the Japanese Army Ministry, and destroyed some documents before the arrival of the Allied forces. Its officials, however, had obviously not realised that the files that they had put on the table included the passenger list of the *Montevideo Maru*. Williams's language skills, knowledge of bureaucratic procedures and record keeping, and his insistence on examining all available documents, achieved this break-through. He already had the list of missing personnel from Rabaul, and it was possible to decipher some of the transliterated names in Japanese back into English. Besides translating the list, Williams made enquiries of the navy, of Osaka Kisen Kaisha, the merchant shipping company that owned the *Montevideo Maru*, of the International Red Cross, the Japanese Red Cross and other relevant organisations in order to clarify the fate of the ship and its passengers.

Williams continued his involvement in war crime investigations until his discharge in 1949, displaying initiative and a capacity for independent action. In one two-month period, he stated that the number of his visits to the Prisoner of War Information Bureau exceeded 25. His familiarity with Japan and its language made this possible, whereas other allied investigating officers often relied on interpreters (AWM83 251:766).[14] Williams acknowledged these personality traits and said, many years later, that the Director of the Directorate of Prisoners of War in Australia referred to him as 'a rank individualist' (NLA Williams 1975). His independent characteristics were also remarked on in

Japanese records. On 16 October 1945 Williams attended a meeting between Major General Archer L Larch, the United States Provost Marshal General, and Lieutenant General Tamura as an observer. At the end of the minutes of the meeting produced by the bureau, an urgent point was made to other sections of the Japanese government, including the army and the navy, that they should become more aware of the importance of the POW issues to the Allies. It warned that disregarding the importance of such issues would have grave consequences for the Japanese government, and that serious attention was lacking at present. As an example of the lack of awareness among the Japanese, an Australian officer's visit to the Army Ministry and its implications are cited in the following minutes (translated from the Japanese by the author):

> Point 4: Necessity to heighten awareness on prisoner of war issues.
>
> An Australian major visited a certain section of a certain department in the Army Ministry with the direction from his government to investigate prisoner of war issues. (Later, it became clear that the issues he was investigating involved grave matters, which might have fatal outcomes for Japan.) He requested to see a colonel who was in charge of the section. Since the colonel was away, a major met him on his behalf. However, the reception the major gave to the Australian officer was extremely cold and unfriendly, which caused unpleasant feelings. The Australian officer was not willing to visit the Army Ministry after this encounter, and its personnel had made an extremely bad impression on him.
>
> The officer, who was mentioned above, did not have an impressive presence and he turned up on his own without an appointment. This circumstance might have produced an impression on the Japanese side that his visit was of no importance. We suspect, however, that the pre-existing notion that prisoner of war issues should not be important was still strongly imbedded among the military personnel, and this led to the Australian officer being treated in that manner (Utsumi & Nagai 1999:357–8).

The description of the Australian major fits Williams perfectly. His height was five feet five inches and he was balding. He certainly did not match the image of tall and imposing Allied officers. In addition, he tended to turn up on his own at the ministry without making an appointment. Yet the bureau realised how capable and how sharp Williams was in his investigations even at this early stage of his involvement.

Williams was also fascinatingly objective and detached as an investigator. His statement as a witness at the trial of Lieutenant General Tamura, before the war crimes tribunal, revealed this aspect clearly. During the proceedings Tamura's defence lawyer asked Williams about his feelings during the investigation into the sinking of the *Montevideo Maru*. In the ensuing exchange Williams offered a rare insight into his views about the investigation:

> Q: Major, you are pretty bitter about this whole thing, aren't you?

A: By 'this whole thing,' sir, if you refer to the ill treatment of prisoners of war and to the needless mental anguish that a thousand and fifty-three families needlessly went through over a period of two and a half, three and a half years—yes, to that extent I am bitter.

Q: Now, what action if any did you take against the persons who withheld this information in the first place?

A: I did not take any action. My mission to Japan was to ascertain facts. I reported the facts. I took no action beyond that.

When the defence lawyer asked further if Williams wanted to do anything towards the person who caused the anguish, Williams again stressed his point.

Q: Did you recommend that action be taken against him or any of the predecessors of the accused Tamura for their part in the dereliction of duty in reporting on the Montevideo?

A: I made no recommendations concerning this matter. I reported facts. That was my assignment.

It is revealing that Williams insisted that his mission was solely concerned with finding facts and reporting them, rather than contemplating the implications. For Williams, investigating facts through documents and interviews was completely separate from reflecting on their meaning. Williams felt 'bitter' about the ill treatment of the POWs and the anguish many families had to endure, not knowing if their loved ones were alive or not. However, he stated clearly that his emotional side would not affect the direction or nature of the investigation. In other words, his investigation was motivated by a rational need to find the facts. Certainly his self-controlled attitudes towards investigation were expected from a professional. Crucially, too, this definite separation between fact-finding and contemplation was characteristic of Williams's later research and writing, when it became a strength as well as a weakness in his work as a historian in the post-war period.

Williams and his historical research

In 1949 Williams secured his discharge from the army in Tokyo, and returned to Kobe with his family to resume his business career. Originally he planned to resurrect his company of the pre-war period, but Ernest Williams James, a British expatriate and proprietor of A Cameron & Co, asked Williams to join him in his company. They had been friends for years since Williams had lived in lodgings run by James's mother. Thus he joined the company as managing director, but their partnership came to an end when James died in 1952. Williams was appointed sole executor of his estate. James was an immensely wealthy businessman and his assets included the James Estate, an exclusive residential development for Westerners, with over 50 Western-style houses in Shioya, 20 kilometres west of Kobe (Williams 1984). Eventually Williams, as executor, had no choice but to sell James's private mansion and the estate to a wealthy Japanese businessman in order to pay inheritance taxes to the Japanese government.

In 1962 Williams became the sole proprietor of A Cameron & Co. By this stage he had established his social and financial standing in the community, and wanted to contain his business activities so as to devote more time to his historical research and writing. The firm became an agent for cobalt import to Japan, and he described the business as 'manageable' for a full-time researcher and part-time businessman. Nonetheless, he continued his business involvement well into his seventies and maintained his disciplined daily schedule. In an interview with the *Mainichi* shinbun (1971), he said that he worked in his office for six hours, in his library for eight hours, in his garden for eight hours, spent two hours over meals and tried to sleep eight hours a day. Thus he needed 32 hours in a day.

Williams launched his historical research career in 1953 by contributing articles for a series, 'The shade of the past', in the *Mainichi* shinbun. In these he wrote about episodic encounters of Westerners with Japan and its people. The stories he chose to write related closely to the history of the concession and the experiences of foreigners in late 19th century Japan. During that period new Western goods were introduced into Japan, and Westerners lived within the designated area of the foreign concession. The series continued for over 20 years until 1976 and, in total, 66 articles appeared in the newspaper. Many of those articles were later included in four commercially published books (Williams 1958a; 1959; 1963; Williams & Williams 1996). The last one, written by Jean Williams and illustrated by Harold Williams, was published after his death. He also contributed numerous articles to English language magazines in the Kobe–Osaka area. In addition, he was commissioned to write three privately published books on the histories of local foreign organisations; the Kobe Club (Williams 1975), the Kobe Regatta and Athletic Club (Williams 1970), and a trading company, Holme Ringer & Co (Williams 1968).

In his books and articles, Williams recounted historical episodes relating to the foreign concession and its residents in the 19th century. For example, 'The first British Consul' was about Consul Hodgson, who arrived in Nagasaki in 1859 to open the first British consulate in Japan. Williams told the story of Hodgson's experiences in Nagasaki based on his study of Hodgson's letters (Williams 1958a:17–26). As the dust jacket of one of his books indicates, a sense of 'you were there' was achieved skilfully through his writing. Most of the time his research utilised primary sources, such as personal letters, and the dates were double-checked with newspapers and other sources of that period. He managed to present readable tales on unusual topics, such as the Carew case, the poisoning with arsenic of an Englishman in Yokohama by his wife, which was based on close study of the court transcript (Williams 1959:184–99). Williams also paid special attention to Australian involvement with Japan. Thus he wrote about John Reddie Black, who was the proprietor and editor of the first newspaper ever published in Japan, and his son, Henry Black, who became the first 'foreign' *rakugoka* (comic story teller) under the Japanese name Ishii Burakku (Williams 1958a; 1975). Another subject selected was the Australian coach company Cobb & Co, which provided the coach service from Yokohama to Tokyo in the mid-19th century (Williams 1963:122–31).

In preparing his articles, Williams carried out comprehensive archival research within Japan and collected extensive published material on the topic of Westerners in Japan. For Williams, holidays were always combined with archival research in libraries and visits to second-hand bookshops, both inside and outside Japan. Through those visits he became familiar with the archives and libraries in Japan, and concerned with the way historical material was handled there. This influenced his decision later, when he needed to choose an appropriate depository for his collection of books and manuscripts. Neither time nor money was spared as he visited all the possible depositories in Japan, Asia and England to search for relevant research material. His wife, Jean, also played an important role as an enthusiastic research assistant throughout her husband's research career and illustrated his many books with her ink drawings. As he and his wife did not have access to photocopiers or scanners at that time, documents needed to be hand-copied initially, then typed up, while illustrations and images had to be professionally photographed. The extravagance and depth of his monograph and manuscript collection contrasted starkly with the frugality that he exercised in his research management. While the collection boasted an extensive assembly of photographs and expensive rare books, his research notes were typed on the backs of used sheets of paper, such as business letters, old invoices and even his child's school reports. Dividers in the research files were never purchased stationery, but were made out of used envelopes, which were cut open. As a wealthy businessman, he could afford almost anything, but he exercised restraint in practice.

As his 70th birthday was approaching, he started to initiate the search for an appropriate institution, either within or outside Japan, to which he could donate his monographs and manuscript collection as a whole. For him, the most important consideration was that the collection as a whole would be housed in perpetuity. Since he had personally experienced various natural and human disasters in Japan over many years, such as flood, earthquakes, fires and war, he started to look for an institution outside Japan. Furthermore, he felt he could not totally trust Japanese institutions for safekeeping and maintenance of his precious collection. Syd Crawcaur, then Professor of Japanese Studies at the Australian National University, was instrumental in initiating the contact between the National Library of Australia and Williams.[15] Agreement was eventually reached in the early 1970s, and the collection was shipped to Canberra from Kobe in instalments between the late 1970s and the early 1980s. Williams's good health and longevity were very fortunate factors for the collection, because he spent many hours cataloguing, organising and indexing it after he retired from active research and writing. He was highly motivated to put the collection in order because he was painfully aware of the importance of collection management. From his extensive archival research he knew that, without proper cataloguing and indexing, all the information he collected might end up as a pile of old sheets of paper. The information needed to be retrievable in order for the collection to be utilised to its full potential.

Harold Williams died at his home in Kobe on 15 January 1987 at the age of 88. He was buried in the Shuhoogahara Foreigners' Cemetery on the spot he had chosen a few years earlier. As he had seen many expatriates die in Japan without sorting out their affairs, he was very well prepared for his passing. He even had a manuscript ready for the last episode of his 'Shades of the past' series in the *Mainichi* shinbun, which was to be published after his death. Entitled 'A shade of the past', it was published a month after his death and the essay starts as follows: 'This is the last article in the series Shades of the past. It must of necessity be the last, because recently I died, and so I am now, myself, a shade of the past' (*Mainichi shinbun* 1987).

This particular article summarised Williams's philosophy towards his research and ultimately his mission in life. He aimed to provide accurate information on the history of foreign residents in Japan. He wrote in the article:

> I am…determined to tell the history of the past with strict regard to the truth, so far as it was in my power to do so, and without thought as to whether the result might be pleasing to Japanese readers or acceptable to foreigners.

Here he was touching on what was of vital importance to him, not just for his research and writing, but also throughout his life: finding out facts. This characteristic was clearly evident in the latter half of his life, which involved two careers, first as an army officer investigating the whereabouts of POWs and war crimes, and, second, as a researcher writing about the history of

Westerners in Japan. Even though these two careers were so different, what Williams pursued in both was fundamentally the same.

He put facts above all else and disregarded how they might be received by Japanese or Westerners. Fact-finding became his self-assigned mission. He described his own attitude towards war crime investigation when he wrote, 'My attention and enthusiasm was focussed upon a search for facts, with some unwillingness to accept as facts anything which I had not personally verified' (NLA Williams 1975). Exactly the same attitude was revealed throughout his work on Westerners in Japan.

Harold Williams and his Japan

Harold Williams lived in Japan for over 60 years, and died there. He spoke and understood the language reasonably well. He dedicated a large part of his life to researching and writing about Japan. He loved Japan in his own way, as his long residency and his dedication to his research demonstrated. Apparently, however, Japan did not enchant him. It remained a subject he was interested in, but it did not absorb him. He did not fit with the images of typical Japan specialists who tried to immerse themselves within the local culture professionally and privately. He married a New Zealander and maintained a Western style of living. He did not learn any Japanese art or sports. He met Japanese on social occasions, but did not seem to have close friendships with Japanese people. In this sense, Williams himself remained a foreigner in Japan. There were always 'us' and 'them' for Williams, and this divide was clearly marked. He knew Japan and its people very well from his long association with them, but he never wanted to become one of them. Japan was fascinating for Williams but it remained an object of research and investigation.

The articles Williams wrote and the books he published have been long forgotten, and his research is rarely referred to. As the titles of his books indicate, he wrote the *tales* that, he believed, should not disappear and should be recorded accurately. His commitment to historical facts, based on meticulous research, is evident in his writing. Subsequently, the tales that Williams wrote still have some attraction as interesting reading about a past that has mostly been forgotten. Unfortunately, however, they lack relevance to present-day people and society. His own view was not expressed directly, except through subtle humour and irony. Throughout his writing Williams remained an invisible narrator. depicting historical incidents as objectively as possible. That was what he aimed at, and successfully achieved.

Williams visited London in 1973 to do library research. He wrote to Alan Fleming, who was the Director-General of the National Library at that time, and told him his impressions. In his old age and after living in Japan for more than 50 years, he found London more peaceful than Tokyo. His detachment from Japan is clear in the following excerpt from his letter.

> It was a great pleasure to arrive back in London and experience again the orderliness, the beauty, and the general commonsense which seems to prevail throughout much of the U.K. Nobody seemed to throw stones at dogs or tease animals. For us especially, after living in Japan it was good to meet dogs which did not bark at everyone and everything, to see pigeons that did not expect to be shooed away, to cross roads knowing that in most cases there was not an impatient speed maniac at the wheel, to find that on the highest buildings there was no security netting to prevent our committing suicide, and most of all to be able to walk in hundreds of fine parks and look at hundreds of thousands of magnificent trees. And when elderly saleswomen called me 'Love' or 'Darling' or 'Dear', I was vain enough to imagine there was far more sincerity there than in the conventional 'Mai-do-arigato' (Thank you very much for shopping in our shop) to which I was accustomed in Japan. We enjoyed the UK immensely and I regained there some of my lost sanity (NLA Williams 1973).

His comments in this letter are very revealing. Despite long residency in Japan, his yardsticks of normality and desirable behaviour have remained thoroughly British. London, and by extension the West, represent order, beauty, commonsense and, implicitly, sincerity. Japan, by inference, is their antithesis, with added suggestions of inconsiderateness, rashness, insensitivity and conventional, empty gestures. Emotionally, as well as mentally, Williams remained detached, in some respects apparently alienated, from his host country of almost 60 years. There is, however, no evidence to suggest that this biased the nature or the objectivity of his research and collections. But unlike Henry Black, he never tried to translate himself into Japanese life and society; his self-chosen role and later subject was the foreigner.

Informing these attitudes is a definite ambivalence, which seems an offshoot of prevailing Australian perceptions of Japan current at the time he left Melbourne.

A strong fascination with Japanese culture was counterbalanced by an awareness that Japan, as a nation, was becoming a military threat to Australia. Furthermore, though Japanese artists and craftsmen could produce beautiful and exotic artefacts, Japanese immigrants to Australia were not always welcomed. This uneasiness was heightened by wartime experience, and Williams felt its full brunt through investigating POW issues and war crimes. He obtained direct knowledge of the tragedies and atrocities that occurred and of the attitudes of the Japanese military and bureaucratic personnel.

He resided in Japan for more than 60 years and researched topics that were closely related to Japan. However, that did not convert Williams into a Japan sympathiser or Japan enthusiast, who keenly hoped to be accepted in the local community. What had driven Williams was the quest for facts and books, and Japan provided the opportunities for his venture. He sought knowledge, as well as an understanding of the past and individual motivation. He knew Japan well and appreciated the differences between himself and the Japanese, but he remained an expatriate until the end.

Notes

I carried out the major part of this research as a Harold White Fellow at the National Library of Australia in 2002. I would like to thank the National Library for the opportunity and support during my fellowship. I would also like to thank DCS Sissons, Syd Crawcaur, Hank Nelson and Peter Williams for their insights into Williams's life.

1. Williams generally used the term 'foreigners' to indicate Westerners in his writings. The use of this term closely relates to a Japanese term, *gaijin*, which literally means 'foreigners' or 'outsiders', but the term was generally used to identify Caucasian people from Europe, America and Australia. In recent years, a term, *gaikokujin*, which incorporates all the non-Japanese whether they are Asian or European, is more widely used.
2. Inagaki also taught Japanese in a radio language course around 1929 (Punshon 1987). Inagaki was interned during the Pacific War and Rose tried to secure his release from the internment camp unsuccessfully (Zainu'ddin 1985).
3. Jean Williams stated that her parents-in-law were not happy that Harold stayed in Japan instead of completing his medical study.
4. Five ports were opened for international trade under the Ansei Commercial Treaty of 1858. They were Yokohama, Hakodate, Niigata, Kobe and Nagasaki.
5. Several restored Western style houses remain in Kitano-chō and the area is a major tourist attraction in Kobe at present.
6. They were German, Indian, Jewish, Dutch, Persian, Scottish and English.
7. For information about the Kobe Regatta and Athletic Club, see Williams (1970).
8. Jean Williams also wrote about her life in Kobe in *West meets East* (Williams & Williams 1996).
9. A photograph of those weapons can be found in the Australian War Memorial photographic database (www.awm.gov.au/database/collection.asp), negative number 073486.
10. In September 1945, when Williams arrived in Tokyo as a liaison officer for the Prisoner of War Office, he directly asked Lieutenant General Tamura, the current chief of the Prisoner of War Information Bureau, about the Cowra breakout and the reaction of the bureau. Williams did not think that Tamura had been informed of the breakout by his predecessors.
11. Williams interviewed Australian nurses captured in Rabaul and interned in the Yokohama area. He also interviewed KG Parkyns of the Royal Australian Air Force, who was interned in a propaganda camp, the Bunka Camp, in Tokyo (AWM54 779/1/1).
12. I would like to thank DCS Sissons for alerting me to Williams's statement in Tamura's court transcript.
13. For information regarding the destruction of official records, see Hara (1997).
14. It is difficult to assess Williams's language competency objectively. After living

in Japan for many years and working with Japanese employees in his trading companies, it is most probable that he had a high level of proficiency in spoken Japanese. When he was asked about his Japanese literacy by the defence lawyer at the Tamura trial, his answer was: 'I do not read and write Japanese in the sense that I think you use those words. I have a knowledge of the written Japanese' (AWM83 251). Frank Wilson, Williams's colleague of the 2nd Australian War Crimes Section, recounted that during the war crime investigation, Williams could conduct their investigation directly in Japanese without using interpreters (AWM MSS1641:39). I would like to thank DCS Sissons for sharing this information with me.

15 Williams had known Syd Crawcaur since the 1950s, when Crawcaur was carrying out research in Japan (personal communication with Syd Crawcaur).

3   Frank A Nankivell's Japan: from means to marker

Ron Stewart

From 25 April to 31 May 1938, the Smithsonian Institution in Washington, DC, held a one-man show of the prints of Australian-born artist Frank A Nankivell. It was official recognition of his life-long devotion to the art of printmaking. For Nankivell, who had aspired to be a creator of fine art since his youth in Melbourne in the 1880s, this was a crowning achievement in a long and successful career as a professional artist.

A press release announcing the exhibition stressed Nankivell's stature and craftsmanship: 'Mr. Nankivell's fame among printmakers is almost legendary' (WPA 1938). Nankivell had been an important figure in the American printmaking revival of the 1920s and 1930s. This short press release twice mentions his Japanese experience. Its overview of his life covers his birth in Australia as the son of an East India Company explorer, his education and first published works, his departure overseas to become an artist and his arrival, almost penniless, in Japan. It notes that he worked as a lithographer and cartoonist in Japan, before recounting his move to the United States to work, first, in San Francisco and then in New York, where he was eventually based. After this brief overview, the press release states that his interest in printmaking began with his time in Japan, where 'he made a thorough study of the art and technique of Japanese wood-block color prints'. Further, it notes his mastery of a number of graphic art media, his etching and aquatint work with the famed Arthur B Davies, and his involvement with the United States Federal Arts Project.

When Nankivell departed for Japan in the early 1890s, he had little interest in the country or its people. His stop there was intended only as a step towards his real goal of becoming a fine artist in the United States or Europe. However, his Japanese experience became a defining period in his life and career. It was mentioned with varying details in almost every exhibition catalogue and bibliographic entry about him.[1] Despite his short stay in Japan of just over two years, he devoted almost one quarter of his autobiography to his journey to and time in Japan. His choice of title for the autobiography, 'A bowl of rice and other grains' (Nankivell 1945–47), also underscores the significance for him of his Asian experience.

Nankivell's encounters with Japan, direct and indirect, were important to him in a number of ways, not only because Japan was where he embarked on his career as a professional artist, but also because Japanese became markers of otherness, helping reaffirm his own Anglo identity as a member of the British Empire, as an Australian and later as an American. His experience was a marker of identity as a traveller and adventurer, a passage into bohemian circles and a badge of authority in art and printmaking. Drawing mostly on his autobiography, it is these meanings of Japan and Japanese to Nankivell that I will examine in this chapter. First, a background account of this largely forgotten artist's Australian years and visit to Japan is appropriate, followed by a brief sketch of his career in the United States.[2]

Australian beginnings

Francis Arthur Nankivell was born in the gold rush town of Maldon, Victoria, on 16 November 1869 (Registrar of Births, Deaths & Marriages 1992:3377) to two English immigrants, mining engineer John and amateur landscape painter and piano teacher Anne. Nankivell had his first encounters with Asia through the Chinese goldmining community at a time when there was animosity towards Chinese.[3] He was about five years old when his father, unsuccessful at gold prospecting, moved the family to Melbourne. After attending Mr Templeton's State School, he was certified in 1881 as a 'child being sufficiently educated'.[4] In 1883 he attended Wesley College.[5] Although a good student,[6] his interests lay in drawing and sports rather than in study. His grades declined and he was eventually taken out of school. He found employment making perspective drawings as an apprentice to a leading Melbourne architect. However, his father insisted he continue studying under a tutor in the evenings to pass the highly competitive examinations to become a Victorian Railways engineering student (Nankivell 1945–47:22–3). He began work with the railways on 8 August 1886 (Thornton 1988:282) and produced survey maps and drafted railway line plans, and attended university classes. Importantly, it was here that he learned the lithographic techniques that served him well in Japan (Nankivell 1945–47:24–5).

Nankivell wanted to become an artist and took his first serious steps to achieve that aim while working at Victorian Railways. He began evening art classes at the Public Library of Melbourne. He lasted no more than a few weeks under a 'tight' and 'old-fashioned' painter named McCubbin.[7] Nankivell then rented his own studio and spent all his spare time there. He worked on caricatures for publication and on a few commissioned portraits in the hope of earning enough money to travel overseas. Despite the establishment of the National Gallery School in Victoria in 1870, he, like many other Australian artists at the time, felt Australia was in its pioneering stages and that he needed to travel to Europe or the United States to develop his talent (Nankivell 1945–47:25–6). He shared the views of Australian artist Mortimer Mempes, who moved to England in 1879, that Australia was a place 'where the chances of gaining any real artistic training were few and far between' (Menpes 1904:57). Many artists still felt the same way ten years later when Nankivell was thinking about departing and a number of National Gallery School students left for Paris and London. These included artists respected by Nankivell, such as John Longstaff, who departed in 1887[8] and *Bulletin* cartoonist Phil May, who had encouraged Nankivell but left to study art in Italy and Paris on funds raised by friends in 1888 (Mahood 1973:189; Nankivell 1945–47:212, 228). In 1892 Nankivell took leave from his Victorian Railways job with no intention of returning (Nankivell 1945–47:26). But his first destination was neither Europe nor the United States: it was Japan.

Time in Japan

Unlike other artists who visited Japan in the late 19th century, such as Mortimer Mempes or the United States artists Theodore Wores and Robert Blum, Nankivell was not drawn to Japan by a fascination with its arts or aesthetics. Nor was he inspired to any great extent to capture picturesque Japan in his artwork, as those artists or British artist Frank Brangwyn, whose landscapes were later compared to Nankivell's, had been (Morrow 1947:v).[9] Although Nankivell became interested in Japanese printmaking during his time in Japan, his initial motivation for going there was purely to make enough money to study art and begin an artistic career in the United States.[10]

> The amount that I had saved was not sufficient to take me to the United States, so I consulted shipping companies on their various routes and passenger rates. Before this I had made the acquaintance of officers of a tramp ship trading between Australia and Japan. They persuaded me to embark with them, assuring me that there was a prospect of my earning sufficient money to carry me on to America by contacting an importer and being appointed to select Japanese products for him on commission basis, the goods to be shipped on sight drafts (Nankivell 1945–47:26).

Nankivell appears to have been little affected by increasing interest in things oriental, from chinoiserie to japonaiserie, or by the deeper aesthetic impact in arts of Japonisme that had reached Australia by this time, but it would hardly have escaped his notice.[11]

Nankivell left for Japan from Sydney with his wife[12] soon after their marriage on 28 January 1892.[13] Travelling second class aboard the *Taiyuan* of the China Steam Navigation Company, they arrived in Yokohama via Thursday

Island, Darwin, Hong Kong[14] and Kobe. On Thursday Island Nankivell had his first encounter with Japanese, a negative one. In Hong Kong, in preparation for their Japan stay, he bought a Japanese phrase book. However, he threw this away in disgust in Kobe Harbour after a Japanese boatman, unable to understand Nankivell's Japanese, asked him to speak English. On arrival in Yokohama[15] the Nankivells were disappointed, as it 'did not look very Oriental'. After checking into cheap lodgings, the Club Hotel, they realised they had barely enough funds to survive for more than a few days. The next day, on exploring the town, they came across American EV Thorn's establishment, Box of Curios (Nankivell 1945–47:121–2). An importer and exporter, Thorn had turned to printing and publishing, and in 1889 began the newspaper *Weekly Box of Curios* (Itō 1995:108–11; *Japan Weekly Mail* 1889). Nankivell noticed Thorn's newspaper was not illustrated, even though he had the means, a lithographic press. When Thorn indicated the Box had no artist, Nankivell collected samples of his work from his hotel to show him. According to Nankivell, Thorn was impressed enough to give him a job that began the next day (Nankivell 1945–47:122). According to the company's official history, however, Nankivell was employed more out of pity for his financial situation that for his ability (Box of Curios 1904).

Nankivell continued to work for the Box until his departure from Japan two years later. Using his lithographic experience, he trained a number of Japanese staff as lithographic press operators, and the company was able to expand its commercial printing and publishing work. Soon after his arrival, the company began publishing a humour magazine, the *Illustrated Monthly of the Box of Curios*, featuring Nankivell cartoons on every page.[16] At the Box Nankivell was mostly engaged in producing commercial artwork, cartoons and character sketches of prominent residents and visitors in Yokohama (Nankivell 1945–47:129, 131, 133; Box of Curios 1904).

As Nankivell's wage increased he was able live a life of relative luxury in a large Japanese-style home outside the foreign settlement in Negishi Mura.[17] He was impressed with his 'beautiful house' inside and out. He admired its sliding panels (*shojis*), shutters, spacious servants' quarters and lamp-lit entrance gate. He liked its view overlooking a valley, and his garden's bamboo, winding paths, 'dwarfed pines' and summerhouse. He used a glass-enclosed structure in his garden, built for strolling minstrel performances, as a studio. He was able to rent the house cheaply, as locals thought it was haunted. He hired a cook, who lived with his family in the servants' quarters and whose wife and daughter were also paid to wait on the Nankivells and clean. A dustman (*gomia*) swept the doorway every morning and kept the entrance oil lamp lighted. Nankivell had his personal *ricksha* with driver, Yoshi, at call for himself and his wife

'God save the Queen', *Illustrated Monthly Box of Curios* (1892, May). Courtesy of the Yokohama Archives of History, Blum Collection.

at any time day or night. The rent and servants' wages, totalling a mere 32 yen per month, was well within his means. The Nankivells's idyllic life in the house was disturbed only occasionally by breezes from nearby fields, where human excreta was used as fertiliser, by typhoons and by earthquakes (Nankivell 1945–47:125–9).

Nankivell was active among the foreign settlement community, feeling comfortable and secure as a member of the dominant group. In Yokohama, the British made up roughly 40% of the residents. English was the main language and Nankivell was answerable to British rather than Japanese law (Nankivell 1945–47:122; Hoare 1994). For entertainment he enjoyed evenings at 'the club' and joined in performances at the theatre and at a visiting circus (Nankivell 1945–47:127, 162–4). His remaining artworks in the *Illustrated Monthly of the Box of Curios* (May 1892) are mostly of happenings at the Nippon Racing Club and hint that he also enjoyed horse races. Through his work he met a number of notables, such as long-term resident Dr James C Hepburn, the Orientalist Sir Edwin Arnold and his Japanese wife, English theatre critic and dandy Clement Scott, and American artist Robert Blum. Nankivell's closest friend was Japanese-born bookstore clerk and amateur painter George Gibbs, who lived outside the treaty port with his Japanese 'common-law' wife and 'spoke better Japanese than English' (Nankivell 1945–47:134, 147).

Nankivell's activities were not restricted to the foreign community. Gibbs was his guide to a broader Japanese experience, explaining the 'artistic side of Japanese rituals and manners', which contrasted favourably with the crude materialism Nankivell had encountered in Yoshiwara.[18] Gibbs introduced Nankivell to roadside teahouses and high-class geisha houses. Nankivell was enchanted by the geishas' beautiful kimonos, and felt that their tea ceremony, with its 'solemnity and graceful rhythmical moves', was 'beyond description'. He judged their games, in which the loser was totally disrobed, as good, harmless fun. But Nankivell, who later becomes well known for his images of women,[19] gave a damning assessment of their figures (Nankivell 1945–47:148–51).

> [T]he loser sometimes would blatantly stand or dance in a state of complete nudity. The average man is not inspired by this; there is no grace in their form. They lack the beauty of a well proportioned American Girl...In nudity, her paint and powder graduates into her yellow skin. Above the waist, she has all the subtle features of a girlish figure. Below the waist, she is shortlegged, and her limbs are distorted. This is the case with all Japs, resulting from the sitting, bent-legged posture of years. As an artist I could find neither beauty nor grace underneath the kimono (Nankivell 1945–47:149).

Nankivell gained personal pleasure from other aspects of traditional Japanese culture. He journeyed to the hot springs of Miyanoshita, and the Cherry Festival held in Tokyo was one of the highlights of his time in Japan. He took in the attractions of the theatre district, watching portions of Japanese plays days in length, as well as jujitsu and sumo bouts. Here he at times sketched, drawing some 'over-fat specimens' wrestling (Nankivell 1945–47:151–2, 158, 160).

Nankivell's position at the Box of Curios allowed him to have contact and build relationships with Japanese. He represented the Box of Curios at an invitational banquet for foreign newspapermen at the Nobles Club in Tokyo.[20] Here he was entertained by performances by actors and geishas, listened to speeches, and ate and drank sake with his Japanese hosts. On a less extravagant daily level he was in charge of a number of Japanese staff at the Box. They included three lithographic printers he had trained and a Japanese artist's assistant, Yoshida Bunkichi. Yoshida traced and touched-up Nankivell's commercial designs, following his instructions 'deftly'. Nankivell became close to Yoshida, on occasion inviting him to his home. According to Nankivell, he found it necessary to learn Japanese, as none of the staff under him could speak English. He felt spoken Japanese to be simple and learned to converse freely in a fairly short time. The dialect that he picked up from Yoshida was 'higher-class' Japanese. Even so, he still required the help of the company bookkeeper Nakanishi, who 'spoke English fluently', to act as interpreter between Nankivell and other Japanese (Nankivell 1945–47:131–2, 136–140).

An unexpected consequence of Nankivell's direct encounters with the Japanese is that he became a medium for the transfer of artistic practices both to and from Japan. Nankivell appears to be one of the earliest bearers of photolithographic and multicolour lithographic techniques into Japan.[21] Nankivell also brought wood-block printing techniques from Japan to the United States. Yoshida sparked his interest.

> Yoshida, my assistant, presented me with a Japanese water color print, a masterpiece in drawing and technique. My curiosity again reached a high pitch. Not comprehending his attempt at explaining the process, I accepted an invitation to a print factory (Nankivell 1945–47:161).

In his autobiography, Nankivell describes his visit to a print factory (*hanmoto*) and the printing process he learned. Later in the United States he experimented for a number of years with this technology, demonstrating the process and exhibiting his work (Morrow 1947:i, 222; Notman 1907). Another important exchange while in Japan, although unfortunately not mentioned in his autobiography, was with a teenager, Kitazawa Yasuji. He approached Nankivell at the Box in the hope of learning Western caricature techniques. Later known as Kitazawa Rakuten, he came to play a large role in the development of modern cartoons and comics in Japan.[22] Rakuten became famous in the late Meiji period with the eye-catching, multicolour, lithographed cartoon humour magazine *Tokyo Puck*, which he created in 1905. His initial exposure to this printing technology was most likely from Nankivell or from Nankivell-trained lithographers at the Box, where Rakuten made his debut as a cartoonist after Nankivell's departure (Kitazawa 1936). Rakuten, in all of his reminiscences of Meiji period cartooning, credits Nankivell not only with teaching him caricature, but, also, almost ten years later, with suggesting to him the name *Tokyo Puck* (Kitazawa 1928; 1936; 1952).[23]

After a comfortable stay of just over two years, Nankivell decided to leave Japan in order to pursue his original goal of becoming a fine artist: 'I had been told that five years' residence in Yokohama, with its easy life, was fatal to further ambition and that a permanent abode would result, but not for me.' In about May 1894, the Nankivells, their one-year-old son and a young Japanese nursemaid left for San Francisco.[24] Back at the Box of Curios, Nankivell was confident that he left behind a fully operational lithographic department and a Yoshida capable of working alone on lettering and commercial art (Nankivell 1945–47:164–6).

American career

In San Francisco, Nankivell quickly found his place in the art community but had difficulty breaking into the local newspaper industry. This led him to begin a humour magazine called *Chic* with a journalist in a similar predicament, Bob Davis. The Sino–Japanese war and Anglo–Japanese Treaty were among the major events they covered. The magazine was a financial failure and lasted only nine months, but won praise for its journalism and for Nankivell's drawings (Boeringer 1895; Nankivell 1945–47:167–94; *Oakland Daily Evening Tribune* 1894; *Overland Monthly and Out West* 1894).

After two years in San Francisco Nankivell decided New York was the place to further his career. With a loan from a wealthy patron of his artwork, James D Phelan, and armed with his reputation from *Chic*, he moved to the east coast. He soon found work with the influential New York humour magazine *Puck*, then boasting a circulation of over 90,000. Nankivell stayed with the magazine, drawing social and political cartoons until around 1910 (Marschall 1980a: 707; Nankivell 1945–47:199, 206, 241–3). He then continued to do some commercial work, cartooning, illustration and even animation, but from this time on he was able to devote most of his energy to fine art.

Nankivell's work initially focused on oils, painting portraits, landscapes and seascapes, and later some cubist work. In 1912 he became involved with a group of artists rebelling against the academies, The Society of American Painters and Sculptors, and through them assisted with the creation of the famous 1913 Armory Show (Nankivell 1945–47:245–51). This was a hugely popular exhibition regarded as having introduced the American public to modern art. The nine works exhibited by Nankivell included two Japanese-style woodblock prints (Brown 1988:298). By the 1920s Nankivell was focusing on printmaking, working mostly in drypoint, etching, aquatint and mezzotint. He became an acknowledged master of printmaking and printed for other artists including leading American modernist Arthur B Davies. Nankivell made the United States his home and became, according to William Moore (1980:19), 'the first Australian artist to become established in New York'.

Nankivell only returned to Australia once when, during a brief visit in 1897–98, he called on relatives and contributed to the *Bulletin* (Nankivell 1945–47:217–19).[25] Nevertheless, he maintained links with Australia. He met with Louis Esson while in San Francisco. In 1903 he spent time with *Bulletin* artist Frank Mahony, with whom he attended the funeral of Phil May (Nankivell 1945–47:201, 226, 229). In 1922, an old Melbourne acquaintance, Randolph Bedford, stayed with Nankivell in New York. Former members of Bedford's bohemian Ishmael Club, *Bulletin* artists and etchers Norman Lindsay and

Will Dyson also visited Nankivell there in 1929–30 (McMullin 1984:19–22; Butler nd). In 1937 an exhibition of Nankivell's prints was held in Sydney (*Bulletin* 1937).

By the time of Nankivell's death in 1959 at the age of 89[26], he had compiled an impressive list of achievements as cartoonist, poster designer, animator, painter and printmaker. His work was held in over 40 American institutions, including the prestigious Metropolitan Museum of Art. While he is little remembered today in Australia, Japan or the United States, his work continues to appear in exhibitions. In 1992 a number of his prints were exhibited in the National Gallery of Australia ('Australian printmakers in America 1900–1950' 1992), and in 1999 at the New York Public Library ('Order and disorder: architectural transactions in print and photographs' 1999). In 1999 one of his cartoons was exhibited in Ginza, Japan ('Yume [dream] the year 2000 they dreamed of' 1999). In 2001 his oil painting of Washington Square was the centrepiece of a New York exhibition ('Homage to the Square: picturing Washington Square, 1890–1965' 2001).

Constructing a Japanese other

In his autobiography, Nankivell constructs his self-identity as white, Australian, a proud member of the British Empire, an American, an adventurer and an artist/craftsman. Japan plays a role in all of these areas, at times as a negative and inferior 'other' to his autobiographical self, at other times as a source of valuable knowledge and technique. His autobiography, moreover, was mostly written during the Second World War, some 50 years after his experience in Japan. Negative war sentiment undoubtedly contributed to his often critical image of the Japanese and Japan. Demonstrably he embellished and supplemented his slightly faded memory of Japan with subsequent encounters, anecdotes of acquaintances and snippets of information picked up over the years. Fear, the rhetoric of empire and of friends, contributed to these negative pronouncements; however, they by no means constitute a systematic attack and his picture is complicated by contradictory hints of more sympathetic reactions to, and positive experience of, Japan and its arts.

Nankivell left Australia when fears of China had changed to growing anxiety about Japan, and 'British Race Patriotism' was supported enthusiastically (Meaney 1999:15–18). His father had earlier presented a negative portrayal of China in his 1875–77 Straits Settlement journal, much as his son would subsequently respond to aspects of Japan. For Nankivell's father, the Chinese on the Malay Peninsula were opium-eating and foolish, thieves and murderers; wealthy Chinese were arrogant and cruel to their coolies (Nankivell 1945–47:44, 50, 57–8, 62, 64). For Nankivell, it was the Japanese who were problematic, from his first encounter on Thursday Island with Japanese who were 'as slick as thieves as you would ever find' to their trickery and treachery in his experience in Japan (Nankivell 1945–47:26, 29). Though unlike his father's more immediate account, Nankivell was able to bolster his case against the Japanese with negative portrayals gleaned from the Pacific War and earlier.

Nankivell, like his father, also sought to justify British colonisation. For his father, order on the Malay Peninsula was thanks to colonisation. Chinese breaking out into open rebellion were overpowered by 'well disciplined Malay police with the assistance of a few British soldiers' (Nankivell 1945–47:44). Nankivell contrasted what he saw in Canton with British order in Hong Kong. In Canton he visited a prison, saw evidence of torture and beheadings, and thought the judges' decisions fickle. He concluded that 'there was no justice in Canton'. However, in Hong Kong, 'for all residents of the British Island, justice was equal regardless of race or rank' (Nankivell 1945–47:104–5).

In Japan, Nankivell was aghast at hearing many Japanese, 'even from lower and working classes', referring to their country as *Dai Nippon*, or Great Japan. He scoffed at Japanese considering themselves to be, or in the process of becoming, the Great Britain of the Pacific (Nankivell 1945–47:35, 117), and showed his pride in the British Empire in a cartoon, intended to celebrate the monarch's birthday, headed 'God save the Queen'. In the cartoon, which appeared in the *Illustrated Monthly of the Box of Curios* in May 1892, a bust of the Queen overlooks a group of young women in flowing white robes, each representing a Crown colony, dancing around a maypole. One of these women wears a headpiece labelled 'Yokohama'.[27]

In addition, Nankivell resided in Japan at a time when the foreign community feared losing its extraterritoriality and the special privileges that went with it through treaty revisions (Hoare 1994:100–104). The threat of impending revisions, which eventually happened in July 1894 with the Anglo–Japanese Treaty, is another possible reason for Nankivell's departure from Japan. Certainly in San Francisco he and his partner Bob Davis, in their magazine *Chic*, lashed out at England for allowing its subjects to come under Japanese law. Describing the Japanese as a backward people who had 'acquired a most violent hatred for the Caucasian race', they asked, 'What chance will a white man have in a Japanese court, conducted by a race of people who wear clothes only when they are photographed and who believe it is good form to play football with a Chinaman's head' (Nankivell 1945–47:115–16). Nankivell drew a cartoon to accompany the article, which showed John Bull reading 'a copy of his lunacy', the treaty (Nankivell 1945-47:116). Nankivell and Davis were no doubt fired up by accounts of Japanese atrocities in the Sino-Japanese War, which appeared in interviews for *Chic* by war correspondents Frederic Villiers, Julian Ralph and James Creelman (Nankivell 1945-47:115-17).[28] Anti-Japanese feeling in San Francisco encouraged this type of reportage. By the time of Nankivell's arrival there, calls for Japanese exclusion were forthright. A headline for the 4 May 1891 issue of the *San Francisco Bulletin* read, 'Undesirables; Another Phase in the Immigration from Asia; Japanese Taking the Place of Chinese; Importation of Contract Laborers and Women'.

Finally, Nankivell's attacks on Japan and Japanese in his autobiography are in some cases direct references to later Japanese expansion and the Pacific War. For instance, after quoting an 1894 James Creelman story of Japanese affront, Nankivell asserts, 'Japan will always remain the old Japan and must be wiped off the face of the Pacific and driven into the confines of its island until China can develop its power' (Nankivell 1945-47:117). After describing the Japanese puppet state in Manchuria and Chinese resistance, he wrote, 'The future of China and the Pacific depends upon China, the United States and Australia' (Nankivell 1945-47:120). Nankivell replicates in his autobiography the Japan-as-enemy, China-as-friend structure of American wartime propaganda.[29] Obviously proud of his father's adventures in the Straits Settlement in the 1870s, he quotes his journal from 70 years earlier, with the justification that it 'give[s] an insight into conditions existing in Siam until the Peninsula was invaded and conquered by the Japanese' (Nankivell 1945-47:99). Similarly, his descriptions of points along the way on his 1892 voyage to Japan reflect wartime experience rather than what entered his mind at the time. The Great Barrier Reef is depicted as protecting 'North East Australia against the Japanese menace' (Nankivell 1945-47:27). He describes the Philippines as being 'coveted by Dai Nippon', while the lack of a common language has saved 'the white man' in the Pacific, as otherwise 'the yellow and brown could have dominated the Pacific' (Nankivell 1945-47:35).

Amongst Nankivell's friends and acquaintances were some noted supporters of imperialism and white supremacy, though how complicit he was in their discourses is difficult to establish. His first and 'best' patron was James D Phelan, who, as Mayor of San Francisco and later as a United States senator, was a leader in the fight for Japanese exclusion.[30] His friend Randolph Bedford, while in the United States promoting Australian industry in 1922, was vocal in praising the white Australia policy and American imperialism, damning the Anglo-Japanese Treaty and warning of the Japanese threat.[31] Nankivell maintained a connection with the staunchly pro-white Australia policy *Bulletin* and its artists, like Norman Lindsay, who created ferocious cartoons that attacked Chinese and Japanese. Lindsay also thought that Chinese and Japanese art was trivial, and that people sympathetic to Japanese were 'Japanomanics' (Lindsay 1976:118, 221). Yet Nankivell need not have shared these views. They had much else in common, such as the fact that Phelan, Bedford and Lindsay had, like Nankivell, all been members of bohemian clubs around the turn of the century and shared his interest in art, while Nankivell, unlike Lindsay, enthusiastically embraced Japanese art.

Nevertheless, Nankivell did draw freely on negative, second-hand accounts of Japanese and Japan. In his initial meeting with them on Thursday Island, he described the Japanese quarter as 'uninviting for the white-man; it was filthy, a breeding ground of pestilence'. His evidence of Japanese untrustworthiness to accompany this was a four-page story of two Japanese pearls thieves, a story told to him by Randolph Bedford while staying with Nankivell. 'Knowing I had lived in Japan, he was particularly expressive in his opinion of Japs in general; they were the number one enemy of Australians' (Nankivell 1945–47:29–34). Similarly, in relating the Chinese desire to 'drive back those Japs', he retells a story told to him by a prominent Chinese in San Francisco. And his evidence of Japanese brutality is based on evidence of James Creelman and Frederic Villiers (Nankivell 1945–47:108, 113–17, 179–81). Even examples of negative Japanese traits from his time in Japan were not from his direct experience. For example, his assertion of poor treatment of women in Japan, in particular the sale of young girls into prostitution, is backed up by a tale by 'a Jap who had a thorough knowledge of the innermost workings of Yoshiwara' (Nankivell 1945–47:138–40). His evidence of Japanese duplicity in business, namely that many Australian business houses received Japanese goods not matching initial samples and that Japanese infringed copyright in labelling canned goods, also appears to be anecdotal (Nankivell 1945–47:156).

In contrast, most of Nankivell's charges against Japanese and Japan based on his experience appear to be much milder. Japanese were noisy and superstitious, they got drunk easily, served too little food, lacked respect for women and were not as polite or clean as they seemed. Japanese also placed little importance on sports, their women had poor figures, and their Buddhist and Shinto priests were greedy for money (Nankivell 1945–47:125, 138–9, 143, 149, 152–5, 158).

A recurring characteristic of his autobiography is to attribute negative traits to the group rather than individuals. Apart from his assistant to whom he gives a full name, he depicts most Japanese as a group or as unnamed individuals who more easily become representatives of the group. However, white Europeans, Americans and Australians he describes are more often given names, acting as individuals rather than as a racial or national type. When Nankivell and his wife were tricked out of their pearls in Japan by their female missionary companion (Nankivell 1945–47:125), all whites and/or all women are not branded as devious. Nor do the Dutch become thieves when the takings of a lottery organised by the Box of Curios were embezzled by a Dutchman (Nankivell 1945–47:157–8).

Not all of Nankivell's account of his time in Japan falls into typical Victorian-era male travelogues (Sterry 2003:179). Typically, he adds a smattering of local words to impress the reader and claim a degree of Japanese mastery. He makes fun of his Japanese co-workers' attempts at English, and creates a caricature of Japanese by exaggerating their use of honorifics in his translations. However, he escapes in part the claims to linguistic mastery of many chauvinistic male travellers in the age of colonialism by admitting he relied on interpreters (Nankivell 1945–47:131, 137, 139). He also appears to escape Victorian values in part. He is not judgmental of the games of geisha or mixed bathing, and laughs at the prudery of two missionary women who, unaware of mixed bathing customs, screamed and rushed out of a bath when a Japanese male proceeded to disrobe and enter after politely asking permission (Nankivell 1945–47:148–52). Possibly the experience of a different system of values had expanded Nankivell's thinking and judgments (Clark 1999:20, 39), or these allowances may reflect an erotic or bohemian sensibility.

In short, his response to Japanese and Japan is at times elusive, and he enjoyed relationships of trust with selected Japanese. He was close with his assistant Yoshida Bunkichi, whom he found competent and reliable, barring his drinking of the lithography-use alcohol. Nankivell invited him as a guest to his home, and was also grateful to him for introducing him to Japanese prints (Nankivell 1945–47:131–3, 138, 164). He was impressed by the reliability and hard work of his rickshaw man, Yoshi (Nankivell 1945–47:127). Nankivell and his wife trusted their son's young Japanese nursemaid enough after two years in Japan to take her to San Francisco with them and leave him in her charge (Nankivell 1945–47:166–7). Also, Nankivell's contact with his student Kitazawa Rakuten was maintained well beyond his departure from Japan.

In addition to this, depictions of Japanese in Nankivell's cartoons are also reasonably free of hostility to Japanese. In the *Illustrated Monthly of the Box of Curios* in May 1892, his depiction of Japanese working for the foreign community is surprisingly free of stereotypical facial features and that backwardness in dress or action common in cartoons of the time. At *Puck* in New York, Nankivell mostly produced social satire, but on occasion was charged with drawing front-cover political cartoons. Two of these can be read as being sympathetic to Japan and Japanese. One was drawn during the Russo–Japanese war, headed 'Unconditional surrender: when Your Majesties?' (*Puck* 1905). It depicts the Emperor Meiji and Czar Nicholas II of Russia, equal in stature and dressed in military uniforms. They are kneeling before the goddess of peace with hands clasped over swords driven into the ground and their somber faces look downward. The other cartoon is titled, 'As to Japanese exclusion: perhaps, if they came in kimonos, the *real* undesirables might be kept out' (*Puck* 1907). It shows an immigration official stopping a ragged group of immigrants of various nationalities arriving in the United States. They are all dressed in kimonos and *geta* (wooden sandals), carrying daggers, bombs and guns. The cartoon hints that calls for Japanese exclusion peaking at the time on the west coast were simplistic and did not address the problem of real undesirables entering the country.[32]

'Mr Bibliocrank', a poster for *The Literary Collector*, 1904, by Frank A Nankivell. A technically hybrid work printed from a woodblock key plate and colours added by etched zinc plates. The print also shows the fan-shaped signature often used by Nankivell. Print Collection, Miriam and Ira D Wallach Division of Arts, Prints and Photographs, New York Library, Astor, Lennox and Tilden Foundations.

Japan as marker of adventure and art authority

Nankivell's Japan experience was important for his self-projection as an adventurer and traveller. This self-image can be seen in his emphasis on his father's more adventurous occupational pursuits over the mundane. Nankivell's father, a Victorian Railways 'labourer/blocker' from 1877 (Thornton 1988:282), modestly wrote his occupation as 'engine fitter' in Wesley College's entry book, and simply as 'railways' on Nankivell's marriage registration. However, for Nankivell he was something much more impressive, a gold prospector,

'As to Japanese exclusion' by Frank A Nankivell, *Puck* (13 March 1907). Collection of Ron Stewart.

mining expert and explorer. His father had been contracted to manage a gold mine and explore for other prospects on the Malay Peninsula from 1875 to 1877. The figure of his tanned father's return, 'the only white man at that time known to have lived in the jungle for so long a period', remained etched in Nankivell's mind (Nankivell 1945–47:4). He proudly included 52 pages of his father's Straits Settlement travel dairy in his autobiography. The emphasis bore fruit. In a number of artist biographies, Nankivell was referred to as the son of an explorer (see Strickland 1970:170; WPA 1938).

Travel, too, was crucial to his self-imaging and here again his experience of the Orient received an emphasis disproportionate to the time spent there. With his well-paid job at *Puck,* Nankivell was able to travel extensively and did so.[33] He was proud of his resulting adventures and felt that his stories of travel inspired his *Chic* publishing partner, and later *Munsey's Magazine* literary editor, Bob Davis, to take up world travel (Nankivell 1945–47:202). He also became a member of the exclusive Circumnavigators Club, open only to those who had made a circuit of the globe longitudinally.[34] Yet it was his trip to Japan, his arrival when he was almost broke and his residence there that became most often repeated in catalogue and artist biography entries, and given the most space in his autobiography.

Nankivell was respected for his artwork and was a well-liked character in art circles[35] (S 1900:67; Sessions 1896), but what helped set him apart was his Orient connection. In particular, his experience of Japan enhanced his bohemian image[36] and aided his entry into art circles. Despite strong anti-Asian immigration currents on the west coast of the United States, things

Oriental and the local Chinese community were popular subjects among the art community.[37] Local artist Theodore Wores travelled to Japan twice and made a name for himself specialising in Oriental subjects. Both Wores and Nankivell were members of the San Francisco Bohemian Club. Nankivell's patron there, James D Phelan, paid a record price for the painting *Interior of a joss house* by another club member (Hjalmarson 1999:164–7).

In New York Nankivell's Orient connection was also important. While working at *Puck* he often initialled his cartoons 'FAN', set within a Japanese-style fan, a visual pun and allusion to his Orient experience. He could use or satirise Japanese accoutrements as he wished, as when he poked fun at the oriental interests of bohemian artists of the time in a full-page illustration for the poem *A ballade of bohemianism* in *Puck* (1906). In it he depicted a kimono-clad model in a room cluttered with, among other things, a broken oriental vase and Chinese characters on paper tacked to the wall. Yet he shared an interest in Japanese prints with such important American modernist artists as Whistler, Maurice Prendergast, Robert Henri and Arthur B Davies,[38] while with Davies, a fellow collector of woodblock prints, he formed a close friendship and working relationship (Perlman 1999:111, 127, 299, 332–4).

Nankivell's Japanese experience conferred on him authority in printmaking and art. In the United States he reapplied the printmaking techniques learned in Japan, improvising in theme and working practices. A 1907 *New York Times* article noted his study of Japanese art and work in woodblocks, adding: 'It had occurred to him that American pictures in Japanese art form might be very attractive. He has spent much time working out the idea…' (Notman 1907). Judging by the titles of his woodblock prints exhibited at the 1913 Armory Show, *Fowls* and *Football player*[39], he eventually achieved this goal. Nankivell also demonstrated Japanese woodblock printmaking techniques at his studio in Greenwich, Connecticut, in the early 1900s. In New York, also, he made his own *baren,* an essential tool in the process, using the more readily available palm leaf (*bast*) packing of Havana cigars rather than bamboo leaf (Nankivell 1945–47:161, 222). His knowledge of Japanese printmaking also enabled him to produce technically hybrid works of art, going beyond merely reproducing a Western version of Japanese aesthetics, Japonisme. American graphic arts historian and critic Frank Weitenkampf singled out a 1903 Nankivell poster, *Bibliocrank*, a woodblock print coloured by two etched zinc plates, as a genuine attempt to create something 'out of the ordinary'.[40]

At a glance the influence of Japonisme can be discerned in many of Nankivell's colour cartoons and posters in his use of flat colours and thick, black brush outlines. People also detected an oriental or Japanese flavour in his paintings and prints. However, this could be just as much a result of the spread

Nankivell in his New York studio with printing press and printing plate, ca 1938. Image is courtesy of the 1913 Armory Show, 50th anniversary exhibition records, 1962–63, in the Archives of American Art, Smithsonian Institution.

of Japonisme as it was his Japanese experience (the same qualities can be seen in the cartoons of fellow *Puck* staff cartoonist Rose O'Neil). Nankivell was acutely aware of Japonisme-influenced design trends, like art nouveau, and of poster artists such as Toulouse-Lautrec and Dudley Hardy. Nevertheless, to many his

Japanese experience made these qualities in his artwork more authentic and authoritative. BF Morrow, in his foreword to Nankivell's autobiography, makes this connection: 'Being stranded there proved to be the proverbial ill wind, for in many of his later woodcuts and etchings we find a charming oriental influence'.[41] Art critic James Huneker, on viewing Nankivell's paintings, made the connection more eloquently in 1910:

> The skill and sincerity were apparent, and a sort of Japanese quality not precisely inherent in the pattern of the picture; rather an influence, remote yet unmistakeably present. Our astonishment was aroused when Mr. Nankivell informed us that he had once lived in Japan and was a devoted student of Japanese art, astonished, not because of the exotic strain in the 'Berry Pickers,' rather because it was so delicate as hardly to be distinguishable. Nankivell has absorbed what is excellent in the art of Japan; the avoidance of symmetrical monotonous patterns, the way of seeing nature as a decorative pattern, and the thin, gay, tender colors (Morrow 1947:v).

Nankivell begins his account of his visit to a *hanmoto* or print factory, 'I have something to tell that will be of interest to artists' (Nankivell 1945–47:161). He writes this knowing of the interest in Japanese prints in the art world, and knowing of the rareness of his experience.[42] This experience gave him not only a direct link to Japanese art and printing processes, but also a breadth of experience in printmaking forms unattainable to most printmakers. For this reason it contributed to his authority on the art of printmaking in general, and was noted in artist biographies, such as the press release for his Smithsonian exhibition.

Japan first appealed to Nankivell as a financial means to beginning a career elsewhere, but proved to be the start of his professional art career and an important event in defining himself throughout his life. He constructed Japanese as a negative other, complex and varying with the times, and relying heavily on secondary accounts. However, the positive aspects of his direct contact with Japan and Japanese contradict this image. It also runs counter to the positive use during his career of his Japan experience, which marked him out as an adventurer and a bohemian, and conferred on him additional authority, aesthetically and technologically, in art.

Notes

Acknowledgment: I am greatly indebted in putting together this research to Frank A Nankivell's granddaughters—from his first marriage to Julia Holister and from his second marriage to Jody Herriot—for materials including his unpublished autobiography. I have also been given generous help from Kenneth W Park of Wesley College, Nankivell genealogical researchers Brent Hussey and Anne Williams, and Senior Curator from the Australian National Gallery, Roger Butler. I am also grateful for help from staff at the Museum of Modern Art and Metropolitan Museum of Art, New York Public Library, University of Virginia Library, the Australian National Library, Saitama Municipal Cartoon Art Museum and the Yokohama Archives of History. Some long-distance newsapaper and magazine archival reasearch for this chapter was made possble by the online archives of the *New York Times*, newspaperarchives.com and the University of Michigan's digital library, 'Making of America'.

1. For example, one quarter of the artist biography for the exhibition 'Color etchings' (Ferargil Galleries 1929) said:

    Paris was his first objective, but the wherewithal had to be considered. Gambling as to destination, the Orient won; so with a meager sum a one way passage was purchased to China. The pocket book grew leaner until, when Yokohama was reached, the possession of a single yen bill made the Far East a compulsory habitat...

2. This background expands on and corrects information in an earlier paper published in Japanese (Stewart 2003).

3. Nankivell lamented being too young to participate in the raids by other boys on Chinese camps using rope to put down makeshift housing on their occupants' heads (Nankivell 1945–47:3).

4. Nankivell's schooling before he attended Wesley College is recorded in the college's entry book 'Certificate of a child being sufficiently educated', No 48762, Victoria Education Department, 7 August 1881 (Park 1998).

5. According to Nankivell's autobiography, he entered Wesley College in his 16th year (Nankivell 1945–47:.22). However, the entry book of Wesley College indicates that he enrolled in 1883, at the age of 13.

6. His name appeared on the school's 1883 honours list for 'Bible', 'Arts', 'History, Geography & English' and 'Languages'. Nankivell's earliest instruction in drawing was from an Italian neighbour and Victorian Railways engineer, Luigi Datari, during his first year at Wesley (Nankivell 1945–47:23).

7. Nankivell's mention of another student, John Longstaff, who did manage to succeed under this teacher, leaves little doubt that his teacher was none other than Frederick McCubbin and the classes those of the National Gallery of Victoria's school where McCubbin worked from 1886 to 1917.

8. Other artists who left Australia to study include Josephine Muntz and Charles Condor in 1890, and Rupert Bunny in 1894.

9. Nankivell did draw some pictures of Japanese subjects and planned to reproduce one in his autobiography. However, the lack of artwork left behind by him with

Japanese subject matter is one of the reasons why Nankivell is largely forgotten in Japan. In contrast, French cartoonist and artist Georges Bigot's numerous images of the late 19th century Japanese still sell books today; for example, Shimizu Isao's *Bigō Nihon sobyō-shu* (1984) has been reprinted 29 times.

10 Nankivell does not make it clear in his autobiography why he finally chose the United States over Europe. The reasons may have been financial, linguistic and/or the result of his association with EV Thorn.

11 The interest in things Japanese in Australia, which peaked around 1888 not long before Nankivell's departure, has been described by Broinowski (1996:16–17), Meaney (1999:43–7) and Walker (1999).

12 Unfortunately, very little is known of Ada Nankivell's Japan experience. Her family still possesses a hand-coloured photograph of her posing in a kimono before what is probably her and Frank's Negishi residence.

13 According to the records of the New South Wales Registry of Births, Deaths and Marriages (record 3586, extract courtesy of Anne Williams), Nankivell's marriage to Ada J King, daughter of a Sydney tobacconist, took place in Glebe on 28 January 1892. Nankivell's autobiography makes it clear that he and his wife left for Japan after their marriage (Nankivell 1945–47:27). Confusingly, the year of arrival in Japan given in the foreword to Nankivell's autobiography by his friend Dr BF Morrow is 1890 (Morrow 1947:i), and most secondary sources give 1891 as the date of his arrival (Butler nd; Marschall 1980b; S 1900; Strickland 1970:170). The entry for Nankivell in *Who's who in America* (1912–13), which would have been checked by Nankivell himself, gives the year of his departure from the Victorian Railways, his marriage and his arrival in Japan as 1891.

14 The duration of the Nankivells's stay in Hong Kong is unknown. Nankivell had to sell one of three pearls they acquired on Thursday Island to meet expenses there (Nankivell 1945–47:125). According to an early account of his trip, Nankivell worked in Hong Kong doing commercial artwork (S 1900:66)

15 Their arrival can be placed sometime between their wedding on 28 January and the first edition of the *Illustrated Monthly of the Box of Curios* in April 1892.

16 A copy of the May edition of this monthly is held in the Blum Collection of the Yokohama Archives of History. There appear to be no remaining copies of the *Weekly Box of Curios* newspaper from this period in Japan. The British Library has probably the oldest existing issue, 28 December 1895. This issue appears to carry Nankivell's artwork on the front page title banner.

17 Their residence was at 3584 Negishi Mura (*Japan Gazette* 1894:211).

18 Nankivell (1945–47:141–6) gives reasonably lengthy descriptions of both the government-controlled district of Yoshiwara in Tokyo, and the highest-priced brothel of the 'Yokohama Yoshiwara' number nine, which worked to attract foreign customers.

19 For example, he is described in the *Encyclopaedia Britannica* (1911), as 'FA Nankivell, whose pretty athletic girls are prone to attitudinizing'.

20 This would have been the *Kazokukai-kan*, the famous Joseph Conder-designed *Rokumeikan* bought by the *Kazokukai* in 1890.

21 For an overview of changing printing technology in the Meiji period, see Clark (2000:200–5).
22 On Kitazawa Rakuten as the father of modern Japanese cartooning, see Ōmiya-shi (1991). For an overview of the changes from Edo-style and *ponchi-e* to *manga*, or modern comic art, during the period of Kitazawa Rakuten's activity, see Nyūsupaaku (2003) and Miyamoto (1995).
23 For more on Nankivell in Japanese manga history, see Stewart (2003). I hope to publish a separate paper in English on Nankivell's cartooning and place in Japanese comic art history.
24 The editorial in the *Weekly Box of Curios* edition of 19 May bids Nankivell farewell (Morrow 1947:iii).
25 His caricatures can be found in the *Bulletin* between 25 December 1897 and 19 February 1898. His photograph appeared in the 22 January issue, captioned 'Frank Nankivell, the Victorian Artist'.
26 Nankivell's obituary was printed in the *New York Times* on 8 July 1959.
27 The editor, American EV Thorn, comments in his introductory notes on Nankivell's cheek in representing Yokohama as a British colony. The cartoon could also be read as being a show of friendly British rivalry against growing American imperialism.
28 See Creelman (1894) for examples of his reportage on Japanese atrocities during the war.
29 For a good example of this, see the 1941 *Time* article 'How to tell your friends from the Japs' on how to differentiate Japanese from Chinese (Johnson 1988:9).
30 For an example of Phelan's views on the Japanese, see the article 'Tokio…' (*Woodland Daily Democrat* 1920).
31 Bedford's views were reported in American newspapers during his visit (see *Coshocton Tribune* 1922:1; Daily News 1922:13).
32 Nankivell tended to be restrained in his cartoons and admired the work of Phil May because it was free of viciousness (Nankivell 1945–47:228). However, it must be also noted that Nankivell would not have had complete freedom, as it was usual practice at *Puck* for all cartoons to pass muster at the 'conclave'. This was a regular gathering of staff artists and editors, where events and topics for treatment were decided and where all cartoons had to be given approval before publication (West 1988:241).
33 His son Francis John Nankivell recalled that he had travelled around the world twice with his father while still very young (personal correspondence with Julia Hollister daughter of Francis, 18 June 2001).
34 Nankivell had his membership to this club listed in his *Who's who in America* entries, and he drew cover illustrations for its club magazine, *The Log of the Circumnavigators Club*, in 1912 and 1913.
35 'If you are thrown in among writers and artists here, the first question put to you is, "have you met Nankivell yet?"' (Sessions 1896).

36 Both Nankivell and his artwork were labelled 'bohemian' by some commentators of the time. For example, 'Bohemian sketches by Frank A Nankivell' (*Oakland Daily Evening Tribune* 1894). Nankivell was included in Pierre Boeringer's article on bohemian artists, 'Some San Francisco illustrators—curbstone Bohemia' (Boeringer 1895).

37 As Edward Said (1985) illustrates in his book *Orientalism*, fear and fascination often go hand in hand. For examples of interest in oriental images in San Francisco, see the Chinese images in Boeringer (1895). Also see Hjalmarson (1999) on oriental subject matter and turn-of-the-century San Francisco artists.

38 Nankivell attended Whistler's funeral while in England in 1903, and his etching *Whistler's funeral*, based on a sketch he produced at the time, is part of the permanemt collection of the Metropolitan Museum of Art, New York.

39 For a full list of his Armory Show works see Brown (1988:298).

40 This work is described in Weitenkampf (1924:284), and on the New York Public Library's collection index card for its copy of this Nankivell print.

41 Morrow repeated this connection in his article about Nankivell's printmaking in *Prints* (Morrow 1931). *New York Times* critic Otis Notman (1907) also implied that this was the reason for the authenticity of Nankivell's prints, which were 'exactly like' Japanese prints.

42 Ironically, Nankivell was one of the mediums for the transfer of technological skills and work practices into Japan, which helped bring about the decline and eventual demise of Edo-style *hanmoto* print shops.

4 Peter Russo and Japan: a controversial relationship

Prue Torney

In 1972 the journalist and broadcaster Peter Russo was one of several experts invited to give advice to a government standing committee on Japan–Australia relations. Russo had studied and taught in Japan from 1931–41, written extensively on Japanese history and culture for over three decades and earned a reputation as one of Australia's leading authorities on Japanese affairs. By any measure he was well qualified to contribute. Yet he declined the invitation, remarking sardonically that his earlier efforts at improving Australians' understanding of Japan had not been particularly welcome at the time. In fact, he recalled, he had been regarded as a Japanese 'spy', planning the destruction of the British Empire. These were the years roughly spanning 1935–45, when Russo's loyalties to Australia came into question largely as a result of his Japanese associations. He was acutely aware that the respect he had earned was still tainted with the suspicion that he had been an apologist for Japan from the mid-1930s until well after the outbreak of the Pacific War. At this stage of his life, he had little inclination to assist Australian projects based on a renewed interest in Japan (NLA MS 8202/6/12, Sim 1972; Russo 1972).[1]

Russo's response to the standing committee was a telling moment in the story of his relationship with Japan. He began his working life in Tokyo, reached a position of considerable status there and was regarded as a Japan expert after his return to Australia in 1941. While his expertise was widely acknowledged, his personal sense of accomplishment became clouded with bitterness, owing partly to his treatment by Australian officialdom before and during the war. This chapter traces the development of Russo's relationship with Japan, paying particular attention to the 1930s and Second World War periods. After considering his background and the circumstances in which he was introduced to Japan, the chapter examines his official work in promoting Japan's cultural relations with Australia from 1935–41, the increasing security concerns about him, his controversial return to Australia in 1941, his wartime role as commentator on Asian affairs, and his responses in the early post-war period to the virulent anti-Japanese sentiment prevailing in Australia.[2]

Growing up in Australia

There was little in Russo's background to suggest that his life's work would centre on Asia or Japan in particular. He was born in Ballarat, Victoria, on 26

June 1908, one of four children of Italian parents who had emigrated from the Aeolian Islands, near Sicily. Raised in a devout Roman Catholic household, Russo was educated at Catholic schools in Ballarat and Melbourne. He had limited exposure to Asian culture before adulthood. Most of what he learned as a boy was acquired by observing Ballarat's Chinese inhabitants, veterans of the gold rushes who had stayed on in the town, opening laundries, greengroceries and cafes. The young Russo took a close interest in their activities, and it is possible that his lifelong obsession with Chinese calligraphy dated from this time. One day his mother handed him a laundry ticket and asked him to collect the family's washing from one of the Chinese laundries. He went away and copied the Chinese characters onto another piece of paper and duly presented the forged ticked at the laundry. The attendant produced the parcel, and Russo left the shop, delighted with his achievement (Hetherington 1960:27). These were the years of the First World War and a difficult time for Australians from an immigrant background. Russo's awareness of his own ethnicity probably heightened his interest in other minority groups such as the Chinese.

For the most part, however, Russo shared the same preconceptions about Asian people as most Australians of his generation. He did not begin to discard them until he went to Japan in 1931. The only real continuity between his schooldays and his later interest in Asia was his aptitude for languages, which he first demonstrated as a teenager. After completing his secondary education, he enrolled in dentistry at the University of Melbourne but abandoned it after two years and transferred to an arts degree, specialising in languages. Although Russo's academic performance was undistinguished and he did not complete his degree, his linguistic ability made him an ideal candidate for the university's Mollison Travelling Scholarship. He set his sights on winning the lucrative award. The terms of the scholarship enabled the winner to spend a period in the country of the language in which the examination was set for that year. One year it was held in French, the next in Italian, and every third year in Japanese or another Oriental language. Russo first sat the scholarship in 1929 in Italian, and lost by a narrow margin. The following year, after an intensive course of study in Japanese, he sat the exam again and was successful (*Herald* 1930:5; *Courier* 1930:4). There was a strong element of serendipity in Russo's introduction to Japan, especially when it is considered that he first sat the scholarship in Italian, his family's native language. A period of study in Italy would have been a natural option for Russo, and it is worth speculating that his life might have followed a different course had he won the award on his first attempt.

Nevertheless, Russo embraced the unexpected opportunity to encounter the region that had first aroused his curiosity as a small boy. He sailed for Japan in April 1931 aboard the *Atsuta Maru*. He was struck by the fact that his ship did not land in an Asian port, except in a geographical sense, until he reached Nagasaki, despite having docked in Batavia, Singapore, Manila, Hong Kong and Shanghai. It was not until later, however, that he started to think about colonialism in terms that were not influenced by the interpretations of old Asia hands. He arrived in Tokyo only months before the Manchurian Incident of September 1931, which set Japan on the course leading to the Pacific War. His first reaction to Tokyo—by then a modern cosmopolitan city rebuilt from ruins after the Great Kanto Earthquake of 1923—was a desire to return immediately to Australia. But despite his initial culture shock he made an early decision to mingle with ordinary Japanese and immerse himself in Japanese culture. He enrolled in an extension course at Tokyo University, and from the beginning he endeavoured to live a Japanese lifestyle. He did not do this, as an early biographer, John Hetherington, observed, 'with any idea of chastening his soul or of making an act of condescension to the Japanese surrounding him'. It was simply the quickest route to success in his chosen studies (Hetherington 1960:29–30). As we shall see, however, Russo's rejection of the traditional lifestyle of Westerners in Tokyo, as well as his tendency towards irreverence and provocative behaviour, did not endear him to British Embassy officials and contributed to suspicion about his loyalties (NAA: SP1714/1, N45868, Barnwell).

A cultural envoy

Russo's immersion in Japanese culture may have been shaped partly by pragmatism, but nonetheless it impressed the Japanese. Within a year of his arrival in Japan, after sitting a tough examination in commercial law and several languages, he was appointed adviser to a trade mission to Europe organised by the Japanese Chamber of Commerce (*Sun News-Pictorial* 1932:7). The mission lasted about 12 months and returned to Japan in October 1932 to find a country reeling from the report of the Lytton Commission, which had investigated the causes of the Manchurian Incident and concluded, in effect, that Japan had been the aggressor. Russo resumed his studies and, having formed a genuine liking for Japan, began to make arrangements to extend his stay after the expiry of his scholarship. He was offered a lectureship in modern languages at the Tokyo University of Commerce (now Hitotsubashi University) and was appointed to the position in April 1934 (NLA MS 8202/6/11/8; Hetherington 1960:30–1). This was the second major demonstration by the Japanese of their esteem for Russo, and a significant step in his career.

In the same year, Sir John Latham, the Minister for External Affairs in Australia's Lyons government, visited Japan in the course of a goodwill tour of the Far East. This part of the tour was particularly important for commercial and diplomatic reasons. Commercially, Japan wanted to redress its adverse balance of trade with Australia, while Australia desired to maintain its level of exports to Japan and to conciliate Japanese business circles. In terms of diplomacy, Australia believed that Britain's censure of Japan over its actions in Manchuria was too severe. None of these motives, however, were overt during the visit, which was promoted purely as an expression of goodwill (Megaw 1973:247–63). Writing to an acquaintance at the University of Melbourne from what he called the 'pulse of Japanese student life', Russo reported that Latham's frankness had first surprised and then pleased the Japanese people. For weeks after Latham's visit, the various university clubs had discussed Pacific relations, the importance of a thorough understanding between Japan and Australia, and the need for closer cultural ties between the two countries (NLA MS 1009/58/62). Russo clearly welcomed the opportunity presented by the Latham visit to provide a first-hand assessment of Japan's attitudes to its relations with Australia and the West generally. He had a highly developed sense of being a witness to history and a compulsion to interpret the developments to his compatriots.

Russo's next chance to interpret Japanese policy to Australians came in 1935 when he was invited to give a series of lectures in Australia and New Zealand on behalf of the Kokusai Bunka Shinkokai (KBS) (Society for International Cultural Relations). Established in 1934 with the purpose of encouraging interest in and study of Japanese culture, KBS activities included writing and publication, the establishment of chairs in Japanese language and culture at overseas universities, and student exchanges. Since the re-opening of Japan to foreign contact in the 1860s, Japan's emphasis in cultural relations had been on the importation of Western culture rather than on the promotion of Japanese culture abroad. After the First World War, and especially after Japan's withdrawal from the League of Nations in 1933, the importance of cultural promotion abroad had been recognised. The KBS had been formed with the primary aim of fostering international understanding of Japan (*KBS Quarterly* 1935:ii–v).

Russo always insisted publicly that the KBS had no political goals and no affiliations with Japan's pre-war militarist regime (Russo 1948a). This was naïve, at best, because the newly founded society had close links to the Japanese government and openly publicised them. Its president was Prince Fumimaro Konoe, who, later, as prime minister, oversaw the policies that brought Japan to the start of the Pacific War. Its advisers included the then prime minister, Okada Keisuke, and foreign minister, Hirota Koki. The society's journal, established in 1935 and published quarterly, acknowledged these official connections, observing in the first issue that the KBS had been assisted financially and morally by the parliament, government, businessmen, scholars, and representatives of the arts and literary world; that it had received 'a gracious donation' from the imperial household; and that it was 'co-operating with government bureaus, in particular, the Foreign Office, Ministry of Education and Ministry of Railways as is customary in Japan for any new movement of national importance'. The listing of benefactors and associations undermined the journal's further claim that the KBS's independence was 'strictly preserved' (*KBS Quarterly* 1935:3–4).

Whatever Russo's precise motives were for his continuing refusal to acknowledge the society's political agenda, he was flattered to be asked to represent the KBS in Australia in 1935. He was also asked to act as personal adviser and speech writer to Japanese diplomat Katsuji Debuchi on a forthcoming goodwill tour of Australia and New Zealand. The tour was to reciprocate Sir John Latham's visit to Japan of the previous year, and happened to coincide with Russo's home leave. Russo accepted both assignments, though not without some misgivings. He doubted that the lecture tour would have any effect on Australian perceptions of Japan, and he was concerned that the considerable work involved would encroach on valuable time with his family, whom he had not seen for five years (NLA MS 8202/6/11 *KBS Bulletin*:3).

Despite these reservations, Russo threw himself into the role of cultural envoy. From the moment he arrived in Australia he emphasised, in speech after speech, the need for mutual understanding between Japan and Australia, and, in particular, for Australians to abandon their traditional fears of invasion from the north. Japan had no sinister designs on Australia, he repeatedly told the press, despite resentment of the white Australia policy (see for example SMH 1935:8; *Herald* 1935a:10; 1935b:12). Russo's principal lecture, entitled 'The mind of Japan', was delivered to a large audience at the University of Melbourne on 9 August, followed by an exhibition of Japanese arts and crafts that Russo had brought with him on behalf of the KBS. The lecture focused on the problems associated with cultural generalisations. The West, said Russo, and Australia in particular, had unjustifiably portrayed the Japanese as unscrupulous. The present Japanese government was doing its utmost to build a reputation of integrity and fairness internationally, but while Australia continued its indifference towards Japan there was little hope of harmonious relations between the two countries (*Age* 1935a:8). In addition to his lecture series, Russo worked with the Commonwealth librarian, Kenneth Binns, to organise an exchange of books and craft items. Russo later recalled that there were simply not enough books to meet the demand. Nor were all the works sent by the KBS sympathetic to Japan. The society was well aware that the distribution of books could be interpreted as an attempt to spread pro-Japanese propaganda and had sent a number that were critical of Japan (NLA MS 8202/6/11 *KBS Bulletin*:5).

Russo's primary duty was to disseminate and interpret Japanese culture to the Australian public, a task he performed to the letter. His speeches and interviews were used not only to explain aspects of the culture such as books, clothing, floral arrangement, geisha girls and superstitions, but also to correct assumptions and stereotypes, especially about the status of Japanese women (see for example *Herald* 1935a). Russo frequently chastised Australians for their ignorance of Asian affairs and constantly emphasised his own authority to comment. The sense of moral superiority he displayed on the lecture tour was clearly exhibited in a piece that he published soon afterwards, entitled 'The Australian in Japan'. Prompted by complaints he had received from Australians who claimed they had been treated as 'coolies' while visiting Japan, Russo laid down a few ground rules. 'Don't', he wrote, 'when travelling in this part of the world, use the words "Jap" or "Chinaman". They are exceedingly offensive, although this fact appears to be unknown to many Australians.' A prominent Australian businessman had used the word 'Jap' three times while speaking at a recent luncheon given in his honour. 'Everybody squirmed, and, perhaps, for many the dessert was completely spoiled' (Russo 1936:33). Russo's formal agenda was to educate and to promote goodwill; but his close identification with Japan and heightened sense of his authority compelled him to step beyond those boundaries when he saw evidence of cultural ignorance.

In the course of his KBS lecture tour Russo received confirmation that he was to accompany the Debuchi goodwill mission on its tour of Australia and New Zealand. Katsuji Debuchi was a personable and experienced diplomat with previous postings in Berlin, Peking and Washington, where he served two terms, 1907 to 1920 and 1928 to 1932. The mission stopped briefly in Sydney before a formal beginning in New Zealand in mid-August. The Australian visit commenced in Canberra. The itinerary included Melbourne, Sydney and Brisbane, as well as other places of interest such as the Dandenong Ranges outside Melbourne and Sydney's Blue Mountains. At the time Japan was preoccupied with its trade imbalance with Australia, which was heavily in Australia's favour. But Debuchi studiously avoided discussing trade issues and stressed repeatedly that the sole purpose of the mission was to return the courtesy of Latham's visit to Japan the previous year and to convey a message of friendship and goodwill from the Japanese people (*Age* 1935b:10; 1935c:21; NLA MS 8202/7/16; NLA MS 8202/6/11 *KBS Bulletin*:3).

Russo's 'advisory' status on the tour was far greater than suggested by his low profile. It was not revealed until much later that he wrote all the speeches that Debuchi delivered to Australian and New Zealand audiences (see for example *Castlemaine Mail* 1942; Russo 1948a). When it is considered that the Australian press dissected the speeches for evidence of Japan's political intentions, Russo's contribution to the mission takes on an even greater significance. The overall importance of the tour in the evolution of Japan–Australian relations, however, was minimal. There is no doubt that Debuchi left a favourable impression in Australia, but the relationship was already strained owing to Japan's adverse balance of trade and was to deteriorate further in 1936 with the Australian government's announcement of a trade diversion policy designed to protect Britain's textile industry from Japanese competition.

On Russo's return to Japan the KBS offered him a permanent position as adviser on Australian matters to the society's secretary general (NLA MS 8202/6/11/1). This appointment reflected the importance that the Japanese attached to fostering relations with Australia. Over the next few years, it led to a series of positive cultural exchanges, including the appointment of a Japanese representative to an educational conference in Australia, the sponsorship of a University of Melbourne debating team, and the appointment of a Japanese lecturer to a position at the University of Queensland. In addition, Russo organised essay competitions on aspects of Japan–Australia relations, sent Japanese literature to Australia and generally worked to maintain a continuity of cultural engagement between the two countries (NLA MS 8202/6/11 *KBS Bulletin*:6–7, Browne, Cunningham). These activities were complemented by his writing on Japan for the Australian press and radio. In late 1937 he started to write regularly for the Melbourne *Herald* and its associated publications. From late 1939 he sent a monthly 'newsletter' to the Australian Broadcasting Commission (ABC), which was also reproduced in the ABC's magazine *ABC Weekly* (Torney-Parlicki 2001:356).

Despite these efforts and Russo's outward sense of achievement, the cultural exchange relationship between Japan and Australia remained unequal. The Australian involvement, as Russo later admitted, was limited to educational and cultural institutions and it decreased over time. By 1940 Australia was making virtually no attempt to reciprocate in kind, and Russo was donating books about Australia, purchased out of his own pocket, to Japanese libraries (NAA: SP1714/1, N45868, Barnwell). The one-sidedness of the arrangement privately concerned him. As the situation in the Pacific deteriorated, he resolved to work even harder to consolidate the small gains he had made as cultural envoy.

Rumours and suspicion

Russo's opportunity came in 1940 when his second period of home leave fell due. The KBS again asked him to fulfil his advisory role in Australia as far as war conditions permitted. He accepted the task, but was uneasy about the reception he might receive at home. The Japan–Australia relationship was now extremely fragile. Australia's announcement of a trade diversion policy in 1936, Japan's invasion of China in 1937, the outbreak of the Second World War and the concern—shortly to be realised—that Japan would join her Axis partners, Germany and Italy, had helped to erode the cordial relations that had prevailed in the mid-1930s. Aware that his words alone would fail to convince a wary Australian public, Russo took steps to obtain personal messages of goodwill from Japanese leaders to the Australian people, most notably from Prince Fumimaro Konoe, a personal friend and the KBS president (NLA MS 8202/6/11 *KBS Bulletin*:6–7; NAA: A461/8, 748/1/569 Konoye).[3] On arrival in Australia, Russo released Prince Konoe's message to the press and followed it up with speeches stressing the need for mutual understanding between the two countries. In particular, he urged the immediate appointment of an Australian representative in Japan with a distinctively Australian outlook (see for example *Courier-Mail* 1940a:3; 1940b:4; *Argus* 1940b:1).

Following the announcement on 18 August that Sir John Latham had been appointed as the first Australian minister to Japan, Russo endorsed the decision, publicly declaring it the first real effort Australia had made to preserve peace in the Pacific (NLA MS 1009/65/83; *Courier* 1940:3). Although Russo was in tune with officialdom on this issue, in other respects his actions served to fuel the rumours and suspicion about his loyalty that had increased over the past few years. He had become aware that he was under suspicion in Australia, but was offended to learn from Japanese friends that Australian and British officials were making inquiries about him in Tokyo (NAA: SP1714/1, N45868, Caiger 1940). He knew that rumours had been circulating since his acceptance of an Italian decoration in May 1940. The Italian chargé d'affaires in Tokyo, acting on behalf of the King of Italy, had conferred the Order of the Knight of the Crown of Italy on Russo for his work in promoting Italian cultural relations with Japan and Australia. As well as teaching Italian at the University of Commerce (which had been added to his duties when a lectureship in Italian was instituted in 1937), he had contributed to local Italian publications and had acted as interpreter for Italian economic missions that had visited Japan in recent years. Russo believed that the timing of the award was unfortunate given the political climate but felt that it would be churlish to refuse (*Argus* 1940a:3).[4]

In fact, security concerns about Russo were based on the belief that he was attempting to loosen the ties between Australia and Britain by stressing Australia's independent interests in the Pacific region. An intelligence report compiled shortly after his arrival in Australia in 1940 concluded that he was in the country on behalf of the Japanese Foreign Office, and that his mission was to suggest in the course of interviews and commentaries that Australia's policy on the Far East should differ from that of Great Britain. Russo, the report asserted, was 'pro-Japanese and thoroughly untrustworthy' (NAA: SP1714/1, N45868, Scott 5.8.1940). A later report by the same officer recommended action to prevent Russo from spreading propaganda that tended to separate Australia from the British Empire 'under the cloak of patriotism' (NAA: SP1714/1, N45868, Scott 21.8.1940). Russo himself made no attempt to disguise his view that Australia's regional policies should be formulated to serve Australian rather than British interests, but he resented the attentions of military intelligence, especially in light of the work he had done to promote Japan–Australia relations. He pointed out to one officer that he had been personally responsible for nearly all cultural contact between the two countries and had received little help from Australia. He considered it a poor return for his efforts to learn that his compatriots were investigating him (NAA: SP1714/1, N45868, Caiger 1940).

Russo had cause to feel hurt by his treatment after five years of solid attempts to educate Australians about Japan. As a KBS representative, he had taken practical steps to increase Australians' appreciation of Japanese culture and to advance understanding between the two countries. Yet his protestations seem a little naïve in light of the general international climate and the tenuous state of Japan–Australia relations from 1936 onwards. Arguably his activities had only a marginal influence on a relationship that was heading inexorably towards conflict. Nor was he helped by his irreverent demeanour and his contempt for the traditions of Tokyo's British community. His speeches and interviews in Australia in 1940 did nothing to lessen the suspicions surrounding him. Given his awareness of the changed climate, he might have been more circumspect when commenting on Japan's aggression. Instead, he exhorted Australians to understand Japan's motives and to forget their prejudices. Japan and Australia would always be neighbours, he said, and it was in both their interests to work out a policy of harmony. Australians in particular should stop regarding anything foreign with anxiety and suspicion. His own efforts over the last decade had only served to impress on him Australians' lack of interest in Asia. Australian teachers made little or no attempt to inculcate a knowledge of Japan's history and culture in their students, and this had implications for an understanding of world politics (*Sun* 1940:2; *Daily Telegraph* 1940:2; *Argus*, 27 July 1940c:5).

Russo's outspoken sentiments were vehemently condemned by some members of the public. The writer of one letter to a Melbourne newspaper remarked sarcastically that a speech made by Russo at the Constitutional Club could not have been bettered by a Japanese ambassador (Morris 1940:2). Another described as 'repulsive' Russo's idea of fraternising with a race responsible for the 'rape' of Korea and Manchuria and now the 'attempted rape' of China (Nettlefold 1940:2). Other writers used Russo's ethnicity to buttress their hostility (for example, NAA: A6119/79, 1256).

Inevitably, the animosity towards him compounded Russo's increasing concerns about his future. It was now becoming dangerous to be a foreigner in Japan. Although Russo's academic post gave him some immunity, his subsidiary work—especially his writing for Australian press and radio – placed him in peril. Over the previous two years his rooms had been repeatedly searched by Japan's military police, the *Kempei Tai* (Hetherington 1960:32–3). For months his Japanese friends had advised him to leave for his own safety, but he was deeply reluctant to walk away from his hard-earned status in Japan and start afresh elsewhere. After almost a decade he had developed a strong attachment to the country and had told at least one acquaintance that he felt his life's work was in Japan (NAA, SP1714/1, N45868, Barnwell). The Japanese consul-general, Masatoshi Akiyama, encouraged Russo to return to Japan, pointing out that there was a great need for an understanding of Japan's policy aims, and that Russo would be of more service by speaking from Japan about conditions as he witnessed them (NAA: C443/P1, J20).

Russo took Akiyama's advice and returned to Japan shortly before Christmas 1940. Significant changes had occurred in his absence. Shortages of food, petrol, drugs and accommodation were making life difficult, but the most noticeable transformation was in public attitudes, which seemed to Russo to signal the end of an era. The surface attitudes of ordinary Japanese towards British, Australians and Americans appeared the same: courteous, sympathetic and occasionally apologetic. However, long-term foreign residents were aware that this warmth could disappear overnight if deemed not to be in the country's interest (NAA: SP1714/1, N45868, Russo 1.1.1941). In February, Russo reported the results of a magazine poll, which showed that the majority of Japanese thought war with the United States could be avoided. Nevertheless, he said, the air was charged with the 'clammy lull', which precedes earthquakes and typhoons, and foreigners kept leaving in droves (NAA: SP1714/1, N45868, Russo 1.2.1941).

Russo's wartime journalism in Australia

Russo's ABC commentaries produced in the first months of 1941 offered rare glimpses of life in Japan in the period leading up to the outbreak of the Pacific War. But almost as he wrote them, he was preparing to leave for Australia. There are indications that he was making tentative plans from the time of his return to Japan, but the catalyst for his decision to leave was a telegram he received from Australian newspaper chief Sir Keith Murdoch, offering him a position as special writer on Asian affairs for the Melbourne *Herald*. Russo seized on Murdoch's invitation, grateful for the opportunity it provided for him to leave Japan legitimately, without loss of 'face' (NLA MS 8202/1/1; NAA: SP1714/1, N45868, Caiger 1941). Yet he was far from overjoyed about leaving. He had delayed his departure as long as possible, and now it was with great regret, he later recalled, that he packed his possessions and boarded ship at Yokohama (Russo 1948b:3).

On his arrival in Australia in mid-April 1941, Russo immediately attempted to extenuate Japan's actions rather than condemn them unequivocally. He told the press that it was useless to analyse Japan's current policy on the basis of reason or logic because Japan had become desperate, and any miscalculation from now on could 'set the ball rolling' (*Argus* 1941:4). This failure to denounce Japan's militarism compounded the suspicion that had dogged Russo over the previous year. The surveillance of his movements by intelligence officers now became relentless. The months preceding the Pacific War and the early stages of the war itself were a period of deep unhappiness for Russo. As his friend and colleague John Hetherington (1960) wrote, anonymous letter-writers and telephone callers:

> accused [Russo] of having returned to Australia on a traitor's mission; he learned from these faceless and nameless enemies that he had come home to assist in selling his native land to the Japanese, even that the Japanese had chosen him to be their Australian *gauleiter*.

Russo could withstand such threats and accusations when they were directed against him; indeed, he must have recognised, at least to some degree, the part he had played in provoking them. But zealous patriots also targeted his family, stoning his mother's house in Ballarat. This assault on his elderly mother, to whom Russo was very close and who was unwell at the time, was the source of much distress for him (Hetherington 1960:34).

Russo's Japanese connections came under the spotlight in March 1942 when he appeared as a character witness for his former University of Melbourne instructor in Japanese, Moshi (Mowsey) Inagaki, during Inagaki's appeal against his internment at Tatura. The Australian government had considered refusing Japanese internees any right of appeal, but realised that discrimination between Japanese and European internees could disadvantage British subjects in Japan and be politically embarrassing for Australia after the war. It also hoped to use the cross-examinations to gain valuable intelligence information (Bevege 1993:134).[5] This was undoubtedly one of the aims in Inagaki's case. The section of the transcript of his appeal that deals with Russo's testimony is clearly more preoccupied with Russo than with Inagaki. Russo was asked a series of fairly predictable questions about Inagaki before being closely questioned about the role and influence of the KBS, his own involvement with the organisation, the activities of Japanese institutions and associations in Australia, and the nature of Italian and Japanese fascism (NAA: MP529/3).

Despite the intense security interest in Russo, his expertise was in high demand throughout the war. From late 1941, when Australia's long-standing fear of invasion appeared certain to become a reality, there was an insatiable hunger for any information that could increase understanding of the enemy, and Russo's knowledge was keenly sought. One of his wartime contributions was a small book he wrote on the Japanese language. The book drew on his experience in compilation and grammar reviewing that he had acquired during the years he worked with Harold Palmer, a linguistic adviser to the Japanese Education Ministry, but it was no conventional dictionary. As Russo explained in the preface, readers would find words and expression that were omitted from traditional tourist literature, including 'hands up!' and 'surrender'. Such innovations, he wrote, would need no explanation 'to those of our armed forces who know how the Japanese enemy has frequently used a smattering of English in an effort to create confusion from which he might profit' (Russo 1943). There was little in this book to support the concerns of those who doubted Russo's loyalties.

It was through his regular column in the *Herald*, however, that Russo made his main contribution as a Japan expert. From mid-1941 to late 1945, he produced a continuous stream of articles on aspects of Japan's history, politics and culture. Although military issues dominated his column, his attention to diverse cultural topics such as Japanese women, language, comic strips, students, geishas and fortune-telling helped to build up a multi-faceted picture of the adversary facing the Allies. Notwithstanding his earlier attempts to rationalise Japan's aggression, Russo's wartime journalism contained little to suggest that he was anything other than a patriotic Australian with a genuine abhorrence of Japan's militarism. He had a tendency at times to resort to the same cultural stereotypes employed routinely by other sections of the press. He certainly shared the public's outrage at Japanese atrocities against Allied troops

(Torney-Parlicki 2000:54, 66, 72–3). However, he remained closely identified with Japan and at the end of the war he openly and publicly distinguished between those he saw as Japan's real war criminals and those whom he claimed had merely acquiesced in, or were too weak to challenge, their policies.

In September 1945, when Australian prisoners of war emerged from three and a half years of captivity to reveal the horrific details of their maltreatment, Russo joined the clamour for Emperor Hirohito to take responsibility for Japan's war crimes. In the aftermath of surrender there had been much criticism in Australia of General MacArthur's lenient approach to Japan, but for Russo mere talk of retribution was not enough. He stressed that punishment could only be effective if it targeted the one area in which the Japanese people were vulnerable: emperor worship. Their reverence for the emperor was such that 'any crime, any perfidy' could be justified in his name. Physical punishment would have little effect, since Japan's own legal code and police methods were more brutal than any Westerner could imagine. While it was clear that Hirohito would not be tried as a war criminal, he should be 'prodded' into admitting guilt for Japan's war crimes (Russo 1945a:4).

By contrast, Russo's first article for the Melbourne *Argus*, where he commenced employment in December 1945 after a disagreement with Murdoch, expressed a view that few Australians would have shared. The article offered a lengthy defence of his friend, former prime minister Prince Konoe, whose first cabinet (1937–39) had overseen the outbreak of the Sino–Japanese war, and whose second cabinet (1940–41) had determined the foreign policies that introduced Japan into the Second World War. Konoe had been indicted as a war criminal, and on 16 December 1945, the day before he was due to surrender to Occupation authorities, he ended his life by taking poison. For Russo, the very form of atonement chosen by the prince epitomised his difference from the war criminals. As a member of Japan's nobility, he argued, Konoe was 'not obliged to resort to [the militarists'] vulgar stomach-cutting…to vindicate his honour'. During his time in office he became identified with slogans and polices that seemed to link him intimately to the criminals. In one particularly provocative speech in 1937 (written by an adviser), he had boasted that China would capitulate within six months. But despite 'alleged' documentary evidence of his complicity in Japan's war crimes, Russo did not doubt that 'the prince's guilt derived from the feudal pattern to which he was born, and not from personal ambition or grandiose design'. In short, he was a man 'who belonged to a guilty system and who was too weak to dissociate himself from it' (Russo 1945b:4). Russo could not have ended his wartime journalism on a more provocative note.

Russo's post-war work

In the immediate post-war period, Russo monitored Australian press commentary on Japan and found it left much to be desired. He spent the years 1946–47 chiefly in Hong Kong and Shanghai as China correspondent for the *Argus*, before returning to Melbourne to write a regular column on international affairs. From 1950 the column was entitled 'Behind the news', and for the most part that is where Russo took his readers. But for Russo, the news industry itself and its practitioners were centrally important in shaping Australians' understanding of international issues and he regularly criticised their performance, particularly where it related to Japan. He had plenty of opportunities to do so, especially in the late 1940s when it became clear that Japan would not be punished for wartime actions as severely as most Australians wanted. Both politicians and the press complained loudly and bitterly that Australia's security interests were being overridden by American attempts to cast Japan as an ally of the West in the struggle against communism. Misinterpretation and cultural stereotyping had been constant features of Australian commentary on Japan, but they increased during this period to a level that Russo found intolerable (Torney-Parlicki 2000:109–10, 144–7).

He occasionally vented his disgust in his *Argus* column, but his most concerted attack on the Australian press was made during the course of his Arthur Norman Smith Memorial Lecture in Journalism in 1948. In this lecture, which he entitled 'Honourable information' (an allusion to the type of information he saw as lacking in Australian commentary on Japan), Russo complained about the tendency for certain Australian war correspondents, who had reported from Asian battle theatres during the war, to assume the role of interpreters after the war without adequate training or experience. He argued that the consequences of their lack of linguistic and other expertise were to be found in the columns of ill-informed comment about Japan that had filled Australian newspapers since Japan's surrender three years earlier, and singled out examples of such writing to support his case (Russo 1948a). There were traces of smugness, elitism and even malice here, all of which were characteristic of Russo, particularly where Japan was concerned. Nevertheless, the lecture offered a salutary reminder that the complexities of post-war international relations called for informed commentators who had studied the history, and preferably also the language, of the countries about which they wrote. The alternative, Russo maintained, was 'ominous': 'Either we move towards this free exchange of trained reliable interpretation, or we move in the other direction—towards the shallow and uninformed interpretation which sustains rabble-rousers, provokes international dissension, and reaches its climax in war' (Russo 1948a).

Over the following decades, Russo established himself as one of Australia's leading newspaper and radio commentators on international relations, but the controversy and political surveillance that dogged him from the 1930s continued unabated. With the onset of Cold War hostilities, his refusal to interpret Asian independence movements in terms of the ideological struggle between the West and communism, and especially his trenchant criticism of American foreign policy in Asia, attracted accusations that he was a communist with the same ease that his earlier commentaries on Japan had helped to earn him the label of fascist. He wrote for the *Argus* until it ceased publication in 1957, and spent a brief period as a columnist for the *Sydney Sunday Mirror* in the early 1960s. Subsequently, the main forums for his views were his regular broadcasts for the ABC and his lectures at the Victorian Council of Adult Education, which commenced in 1963 and continued until shortly before his death in 1985.

Russo maintained close ties with Japan for the rest of his life. He travelled there regularly, corresponded with his many Japanese friends throughout the world and donated a collection of his papers to Japanese archives. That these Japanese associations and friendships were partly responsible for the antipathy that he had attracted since the 1930s only toughened his resolve to preserve them.

Notes

1. On the standing committee generally, see *CPD* (1971a; 1971b; 1971c).
2. For a detailed examination of these issues, see Torney-Parlicki (2005:ch 2–6; 2001).
3. Russo also carried with him messages from Kenji Kodama, president of Japan's Foreign Trade Federation, and Katsuji Debuchi, leader of Japan's goodwill mission to Australia and New Zealand in 1935 (NAA: A461/8, 748/1/569, Hard).
4. See also a letter from Russo to his family, 1 June 1940 (NAA: SP1714/1, N45868, Barnwell).
5. On Japanese internment specifically, see Nagata (1996).

5 Paths of wrath and reconciliation: homophobia, Japan and the life-work of Harold Stewart

Michael Ackland

'Some day we must write the history of our own obscurity' (Barthes 1968:4), remarked Roland Barthes, high priest of semiotics and one of a legion of famous homosexuals mown down by the AIDS epidemic of the 1980s, which also carried away close friends of Harold Stewart. But Stewart (1916–95), unlike Barthes, never contemplated such self-exposure, and he would have recoiled from the Frenchman's related proposition of at last making 'manifest the density of our narcissism' (Barthes 1968:4). Yet both notions must be central to any endeavour to make sense of Stewart's life. For his was an existence steeped in obscurity and, despite his later embrace of Buddhism, profoundly narcissistic. From at least his late adolescence onwards, he felt an outcast from mainstream Australian society. Then, as a student at Sydney's elite Fort Street High School, he discovered his homosexuality and received stinging rebuffs. In 1934 he responded to his betrayer, 'RM', with rare directness:

> How, now have you slipped back, and away from me,
> with your littleness and your no other ambitions
> than to live, work and to marry, enjoy, breed and to die
> where to me these seem such little hills.
> I am sick with your petty insignificance
> (Stewart 1934:32).

Stewart, even at 17, had Himalayan aspirations, though the peaks he had in mind were literary and included producing his own version of *Paradise lost*. With time, his proposed subject matter altered, but not his ambitions or his hostility towards those who failed to comprehend his true worth. 'Childhood', he noted bitterly, 'will be the last slavery to survive' while Australia was dominated by moneyed but uncultured bourgeoisie: 'Each class aspires to the one above and they all believe fanatically in the morality of the vulgar: respectability, cleanliness, repression and mutual hypocrisy (whatever will the neighbours think?)' (NLA MS8973/6/1 notebook). In response, Stewart turned his back on his family and rejected conventional measures of success. Although a brilliant student at school, he dropped out of university and began the halting, decades-long quest for a viable identity and original material that would eventually take him to Japan. There he embraced Pure Land Buddhism, wrote the major works by which he hoped he would be remembered, and spent the last three decades of his life in self-chosen exile from his native land.

Stewart's is at once an idiosyncratic and a potentially representative case in the yet-to-be-written social history of Australia–Japan relations. From his adolescence onwards, he pursued a demanding, self-imposed study program, spending hours in the Sydney Public Library reading, copying down key passages and filling notebooks with embryonic ideas. His quest for artistic excellence and spiritual enlightenment went hand in hand. Nevertheless, his solitary trajectory has many parallels with those of other Westerners, of literary and academic inclination, who have immersed themselves in Japanese culture and experienced a sense of homecoming there denied them in their country of birth. But whereas American and British scholarship has charted the phenomenon among its own nationals—most famously with Lafcadio Hearn—in Australia it has gone largely undocumented. Also, Stewart's case poses starkly the question of the extent to which an individual vision and artistic program, informed by Japanese traditions, can still have a significant impact on an increasingly global and media-saturated community. For, by early in 1943, the Australian was describing to a select few his seminal insight, that the East afforded a new realm awaiting conquest by an English-language poet:

> …these are not mere fertilizing interests & agents but the very medium through which I realize myself…What Greece has been from the Renaissance on, to English poets, Ancient China & the East in general are to me, I am most myself, when effacing my self in those times & places & people. He who loses himself…[Stewart's ellipsis]. You see, the Western Renaissance & Medieval Christian traditions are not only worked out, but actually alien to me: they touch my experience at few points. Whereas the philosophy and art of the East coincide exactly with my way of life (NLA MS3925/2/7 Green).

His subsequent work represents a determined effort to fuse Eastern spiritual traditions with Western literary forms, and to reveal to Anglophone audiences timeless but neglected lore of special application to the modern age.

The search for identity

With hindsight, Stewart's early years read like an apprenticeship for his final sojourn in Kyoto. Common to both periods was an acceptance of relative poverty as the necessary price to be paid for intellectual freedom, while repeatedly he focused on fields of interest that confirmed his superiority to the materialistic Australian norm. His first chosen area of expertise was artistic modernism, which he expounded to the uninitiated at Sydney University in the student magazine *Honi Soit*. Whereas curious Americans had encountered the European avant-garde at the great Armory Show of 1913 in New York,

Australia was literally decades behind, and at least as hostile in its reception of the *Herald* exhibition of modern French and British art in 1939.[1] Stewart, flaunting his rarefied knowledge to local philistines, provided in-depth studies of originals by Cézanne, Gauguin, Van Gogh, Picasso, Braque and Matisse, and championed the iconoclastic art of fellow homosexual William Dobell as 'a hopeful sign that the nationalistic sin of the founderers [*sic*] of Australian art shall be redeemed by their greater grandsons' (Stewart 1941). Then came the Pacific War and the Ern Malley affair, in which he joined fellow poet James McAuley in a literary hoax that poured scorn on surrealist pretensions and demonstrated the pranksters' critical acumen at the expense of rival poetic groupings (see Heyward 1993; Ackland 2001:53–82). After the Second World War, Stewart's reliance on part-time and occasional jobs continued, as his focus shifted to Eastern art and religion. His studied Taoism, Hinduism and related beliefs, going up blind-alleys, 'sloughing old skins every 2 or 3 years' to find, like a Zen master, that '7 years of unlearning [are] necessary before being able to fire an arrow, or write a haiku' (NLA MS3925/2/7 Hope). The passing comparison to 'a Zen master' reveals his abiding sense of apartness and election, evident, too, in key poems in his first collections, *Phoenix wings* (1948) and *Orpheus and other poems* (1956).

This spiritual search culminated in the 1950s in the discovery of the traditionalists and, through them, of the religious opportunities still afforded by Japan. The name 'traditionalists' denotes a small group of thinkers, devoted to explicating the original impulse underlying and, to a greater or lesser degree, still discernible in all the world's faiths. Its two principal exegetes were the French philosopher René Guénon and the American curator and art historian Ananda K Coomaraswamy.[2] From the eminence afforded by encyclopaedic learning, they expounded their versions of this esoteric lore to an elect destined to preserve the true tradition through an age of darkness, while implicitly they damned the unenlightened multitude: a position that corresponded to Stewart's need. During the 1950s he assumed a similar hieratic role to a group of devotees, who met weekly in Melbourne to discuss and act upon the teachings of the traditionalists. In the late 1950s, however, the sway of Guénon and Coomaraswamy was challenged by their Swiss confrère, Frithjof Schuon.

Among the changes of emphasis Schuon introduced, the most important for Stewart's future development was to identify Japanese Pure Land Buddhism, in place of Hinduism, as one of the most authentic expressions of traditionalism currently available and, equally important, as one suited to the Western temperament. Thus Japan, the once hated war foe, appeared in a new guise to Stewart. In 1958 he applied for, and was awarded, the fourth Saionji Memorial Scholarship to carry out research in Japan. His proposed project involved studying with Professor DT Suzuki at Otani Buddhist University in Kyoto, in preparation for:

> ...a work in progress which is to embrace the great periods of Chinese art, literature, philosophy and religion, especially the three great formative influences of Confucianism, Taoism, and Zen Buddhism: thus summing up all that was best in the Chinese way of life. Chinese painting provides the setting, and the poem is being written in rhymed couplets in the form of a series of philosophical dialogues between famous poets, painters, sages and religious leaders (NLA MS8973/13/2).[3]

At the last minute, Stewart declined the scholarship, allegedly for reasons of ill-health, and thereby missed the chance to further this project and to take courses in the Japanese language.[4]

Yet such a sojourn, and the potential for intellectual and spiritual enculturation that it promised, were called for by his art, as he well knew. Rejecting the founding Western traditions of Christianity and Renaissance humanism as 'not only worked out, but actually alien to me', he had asserted that 'the philosophy and art of the East coincide exactly with my way of life' (Stewart 1934), and afforded the possibility of losing himself or, more specifically, casting off his mundane and troubling identity. New themes, together with the assurance of personal effacement, made composition possible and, according to one sympathetic critic, early produced significant poetry. The respected academic and poet AD Hope was a friend of Stewart and apparently acquainted with his views, which are echoed in the opening of Hope's 1949 review of *Phoenix wings*:

> Australia, the most insular and the most isolated of the countries of the 'Far East', has a culture almost entirely uninfluenced by those of its Western Pacific neighbours. And yet it is possible that the art and literature of China and Japan will in time have an effect as profound on our own as those of Greece and Rome have had on the literature of England. It is impossible that they should not have some influence in time (Hope 1948:269).

Stewart, according to Hope, is a precursor of this momentous shift of focus. Far from having produced mere chinoiserie or 'English poetry in Chinese fancy dress', Stewart's is 'English poetry which has enlarged its resources by an intellectual penetration of and an artistic comprehension of another culture'. Hope sums up Stewart's fledgling achievement in words that apply equally to later, far more ambitious works: 'Just so, one feels, Chinese art observes and selects, and just so does English poetry speak. It is a remarkable marriage of two habits of mind, two traditions so remote from each other' (Hope 1948:269). But before the poet could essay this 'marriage' on an epic scale, he had to quell his inner demons as well as encounter the East first-hand.

Stewart, for much of his life, was a supremely divided figure. This took many forms. To his acolytes he presented himself as a fount of Eastern lore, a great poet and a traditionalist of stature. And there was justification for these claims. For years he read extensively in Eastern religion, art and culture, amassing a specialist library of many thousands of volumes and furnishing his retentive memory with their arcane detail. He corresponded, too, with international traditionalist such as Marco Pallis and René Guénon, and tirelessly promoted his creative endeavours to his small circle of admirers. Yet to the world in general he was a nobody, a misfit, a failure in life whose poems ran counter to modernist orthodoxy. Publicly he presented himself as asexual and avuncular, yet he was an active homosexual who never came out. Privately he loathed his name, his accent, his physical appearance, his background. Over the years he set about remaking himself, determined to change and choose his own identity. He assumed a variety of pen-names and personas, cultivating a sophisticated voice and script, denying any debt to his upbringing and claiming that rarely was the outer man less suited to his inner aspirations. Behind his unprepossessing professional life as a 'counter-jumper', or attendant in a backstreet Melbourne bookshop, he sought to bury his past as well as his sexual predilection in still deeper obscurity, projecting himself as a rare aesthete and spiritual quester.

The phoenix as prototype

Stewart's desire for self-transformation and transcendence was encapsulated in his chosen device of the phoenix. A fabled bird of the Orient, it allegedly underwent repeated cycles of death and regeneration, arising from its own ashes in resplendent form. Consequently he spoke of his life in terms of avatars, and his identification with the phoenix remained constant. It provided the title poem to his first published collection,[5] recurred frequently in subsequent works, and re-emerged in a last recasting of his oeuvre in canonical form with the heading 'New phoenix wings' (NLA MS8973/10). The man who spoke jocularly in letters of pluming his old tail feathers also collected inexpensive statuettes of the phoenix and, predictably, became a devotee of the *Ho-o-do*, or Phoenix Hall, of the *Byodo-in*, a famous temple on the outskirts of Kyoto. Not all his 'plumage', however, was intended for public viewing. Among the materials left in Sydney (Riley Collection) when he moved to Japan was the typed manuscript, 'The apocalypse of the young phoenix', marked in Stewart's handwriting 'To be sorted and destroyed'. An encrypted autobiography, it deals with individual purification and empowerment, making frequent use of ideas and motifs drawn from the Eastern classic, *The secret of the golden flower*.[6]

Serried images denoting the adept's triumph dominate the penultimate section of 'Stages on the journey out of the soul':

> O you who have swallowed the internal sun, the solar centre of the universe, are now transformed into a golden lion, radiant with spiritual glow of Wrath and Pride, and all about you the timid air glares with an aura of red valour and the courage to aspire, so that whosoever to your bodily presence approaches nigh feels the Power, though you utter never a word.
>
> Crowned with a halo of infernal flames, Saint of the Devil's Party, arise, ascend, out of this underworld of breathing dead, in divine and revolutionary flight, your apotheosis into reality!
>
> In his exalted flame of ecstasy, the Young Phoenix, now reborn, cries out aloud in exultation on his fate: 'Oh I have grown my father's fiery wings! I have his solar energies for flight!'[7] (Riley Collection:26)

But the would-be 'phoenix' was still far from attaining this heroic self-image. The wrath and pride with which he intermittently glowed had carnal origins, and his courage was confined to correspondence and his like-minded coterie. 'Revolutionary flight' would indeed be needed, although it would be propelled by circumstances that he determinedly condemned to obscurity.

Japan: a place of exotic allure

Stewart's encounters with Japan were problematic as well as tantalising, and far different from his own preferred version of events. Over the years he re-edited details, simplified motivation and integrated his trips of 1961, 1963 and 1966 into a single spiritual trajectory. Already in 1967 Stewart was rewriting the recent past to conform to the adage 'when the time is ripe a teacher will appear', and explaining his successive trips to Japan as motivated solely by religious inquiry. 'In 1961, I was mainly interested in Zen and the Shingen or Tantric forms of Japanese Buddhism—the Pure Land Schools were the only ones in which I had taken *no* interest at all'. But 'on the way back to Australia in the boat, quite spontaneously the *Nembutsu* began repeating itself in my mind'. Puzzled by this unsolicited stirring, he was then frustrated in his efforts to find out more about *Jodo-Shin* by a lack of available material, which necessitated a longer exploratory visit in 1963. Again, however, he claimed his investigations proved indecisive. After months of study with a *Shin* priest:

> the total result was a state of mental confusion and doubt as to which was the right way for me: Honen's *nama-japa* or Shinran's Pure Faith. I left Japan again in uncertainty and frustration, and returned to Australia for two years. During this time the Name still continued to work spontaneously, often very much against my will, gradually producing a clarification of mind, until I felt compelled to make yet a third trip to Japan. This time came absolute certainty:

that Shinran's position was the ultimate one for this day and age, and the end-point of development of Buddhism along this line (NLA MS8973/16/6 Forrer).

In fact, the first two trips came close to being complete disasters, and in the late 1960s Stewart had no idea that his third stay would become permanent. A major problem in 1961 was his immersion in traditionalism. Although it corrected certain misconceptions about Asian civilisations, it also offered a typically Orientalist picture of an unchanging, conceptually homogenous East, leaving Stewart ill-prepared for modern actualities. As he confessed to McAuley in 1963, he had encountered a 'ghastly irremediable mess. Japan is much further West than we are, and at first sight there is simply nothing oriental left after a hundred years of industrialisation' (Norma McAuley Collection, letter 14.8.1963). In the National Treasures of Kyoto and Miyajima, however, he finally discovered approximations of an ideal, pre-Meiji Japan. His second trip was intended to prepare him, in accordance with Schuon's admonition, to become a Pure Land Buddhist priest. Yet at the last moment he refused ordination in Tokyo because he could not bear to have his thick locks shorn off—the one physical feature of which he was inordinately proud.

With his spiritual pretensions in tatters but his narcissism intact, he fled to Kyoto. There he met the love of his life, the handsome Ueshima Masaaki, 22 years his junior, whom he later sponsored to come to Australia. Masaaki's return to Japan in 1966 was a major reason for Stewart's decision to make a

Harold Stewart's desk at home in Japan. Photo courtesy of Gwen Smith.

third trip there, little realising that his proposed stay of several months would extend to nearly 30 years and that he would never return to Australia. Though Stewart had craft enough to reconfigure his trips as orchestrated phases leading to religious enlightenment, Japan's appeal to him, as his intimacy with Masaaki shows, was far more personal and invites us to read his life there not only in terms of the Buddhist paradigm he repeatedly evoked, but in terms of other eminent Westerners who found in the Far East both cultural stimulation and an environment more sympathetic to their homosexuality.

For him, as for many of his contemporaries, Japan was a place of exotic allure in which he could refashion himself according to his own script. There the hated difference of being homosexual was subsumed within a stronger marker of alterity: race. No longer clandestinely different, wherever he went he was now noticeable as a *gaijin* or foreigner, from whom strangeness or aberration was almost expected. Hence, too, the theatrical dimension of his existence, or the sense of having one's actions scrutinised by a potentially critical audience, was now at once foregrounded and relieved of much of its stress:

> If, as according to Said, the Orient is a theatrical stage for the West, it is also at root homosexual. Actors, like gay people, rely on others...to let us know we exist. Our ontology is dependent on that reflection, that narcissism, that confirmation...in Japan, where our bodies and our accents put us on stage wherever we go, it makes all of us...gayer than we would ever guess (Treat 1999:208).

Although perhaps not 'gayer', Stewart certainly found in Kyoto new outlets for his narcissism and, as an asexual Buddhist acolyte, developed his most complete persona.[8] As Treat notes, the lives of these displaced homosexuals are often strictly compartmentalised; desires for passion and knowledge are readily confounded (Treat 1999:ix). And he spoke from the heart of many estranged Westerners, including the Australian poet, when he confessed: 'I live with Japan: a place so different from my own, but also a place where I feel I can be myself in a way impossible at home' (Treat 1999:56).

A selective embrace of Japan

Stewart reduplicated these characteristics, but his embrace of Japan remained selective. Admittedly, so profound was his sense of homecoming that he expressed it occasionally in racial terms: 'my skin has turned yellow and my eyes grown aslant...I have become a totally different person from the one they knew'.[9] Yet although he could claim that 'Japanese cuisine is one of the greatest and most delicious in the world' (ADFA MS G233 1980), friends concur that he had no particular liking for Japanese cooking and avoided seafood and fish dishes, except *sashimi*, which 'if fresh never smells or tastes fishy, so I occasionally eat it' (NLA MS8973/16/6 Smith 1989).

Similarly, metaphoric slant eyes did not translate into linguistic competence. Apart from first-hand experience, much of his knowledge of Japan would always depend on contacts with English–Japanese bilinguals and on English-language publications. Even as a scholarship aspirant in 1958, he had been disinclined to learn more than the basics of the language: 'What I really want is to go off quietly somewhere away from people & do some creative writing; not spend a year listening to lectures I won't understand or in acquiring the language'. This, he added defensively, 'would require not more than say 20 years of practice' (NLA MS8973/16/1). With time his excuses became more elaborate, but his knowledge of Japanese, even after long residency in the country, was restricted to rudimentary phrases and selected ideograms. He thus foreclosed many avenues for original research, and for making his work and ideas known in the Japanese community.

Initially his friendship with Masaaki was an important compensation for the lack of Japanese. They had met allegedly in Kyoto's National Museum and Masaaki shared Stewart's interest in Japan's ancient arts. Creatively, too, Masaaki was strong. He matured into a skilled painter, potter and producer of *haiga*, or woodblock illustrations, and he later worked, both in Japan and overseas, as a garden designer. He was thus well suited to play a crucial role as Stewart's gateway to Japanese life and culture. The poet's letters home from 1966–67, and his travel diaries from this period, give an impression of non-stop sightseeing. Throughout his many trips of discovery Masaaki was on hand as guide and interpreter, sharing his knowledge of local crafts with 'Haruldo' and introducing him to family members and to local sights:

> We arrived in Nakatus, M.'s home town and were whisked off by his brother-in-law in the car to his house in the countryside nearby…Next morning he drove us…to see the famous Yabakei Valley—you many remember M.'s slides of scenes of this—fantastic rock spires and pinnacles…Pink flowering mountain cherry trees out everywhere…Then on to Beppu on the seacoast, famous for its hot springs (NLA MS 8973/1/1 Riley 1967).

Stewart revelled in the beauty of the countryside, the rich past and his friend's boundless energy: 'The Monster climbed all over the rocks and took some marvellous shots' (NLA MS 8973/1/1 Riley 1966). This was life shared to the full, and the reader of Stewart's draft *haibun*, a classical Japanese form of travel diary composed of haiku with contextualising commentary, should always wonder who else was there:

> Though already late in March, that night spent at Matsuyama in a fine old *ryokan* on a promontory overlooking the Inland Sea, was one of the most piercingly

cold I have ever endured. I was awakened some time after midnight by a violent gale, and sitting up with my quilts wrapped around me, looked out between the horizontal panes of glass fitted in the shoji [sliding panel] so that each would frame a picture of the scene outside:

> A cold moon watches through the silvered wrack
> Pines on the headland dance with fans of black
> (NLA MS 8973/5/3).

Masaaki had also worked at the Hotel Shirakuso, which became the physical centre of Stewart's world for much of his long residency in Kyoto. A two-storey wooden pension in the north-east of Kyoto, its clientele consisted of Japanese and Western visitors, especially Americans, as well as a handful of long-term guests. None of them outstayed the Australian, who remained there until its demolition in 1984.[10] Over time Stewart cocooned himself in the Shirakuso, turning its institutional routines to his own advantage. At breakfast he could meet new faces, renew acquaintances, pass the day's program in review and satisfy a need for company in a changing, English-speaking enclave. Here, as a considerate guide and knowledgeable denizen of the city, he appeared to best advantage, while the pension afforded realms of varied intimacy. On closer approach to the poet the degree of control heightened, whether in his own living space or on a fully programmed walking tour of Kyoto. Visitors to his compact room upstairs were impressed with its 'microscopic order' and unexpected plenitude:

> ...in your little room were contained, in immaculate order, almost anything that anybody might want. Indeed your little room was like one of those magic bowls or boxes in fairytales, from which innumerable treasures can always be drawn forth. There were copies of offprints and scrolls and books and music and cinnamon cakes and exquisite china and white antarctic underwear (NLA MS 8973/3/6).

Here, too, compensation was found for the lost Melbourne group in another circle of devotees and admiring friends, who often came to the Shirakuso on his recommendation, while the obliging landlady helped him cope with the practicalities of living in Kyoto, from paying bills to deciphering mail.

Stewart's relationship with Japan was extremely complex. Friends recount that he lived in a Willow-pattern world, or mentally among a set of shifting woodblock scenes, of which the central print was imperial Kyoto and into which he read the iconography of a Buddhist paradise. Certainly he was steeped in the city's past, or those parts of it available in authoritative English sources like Ponsonby-Fane's *Kyoto, the old capital of Japan* or in scholarly articles published in *The transactions of the Oriental society of Japan*. But he was not oblivious to the present and, above all, to the post-war rush to

Harold Stewart with Professor Carmen Blacker and Masamato Tomoe, the proprietor of the Hotel Shirukaso. Photo courtesy of Gwen Smith.

modernise. Stewart raged against desecrating bulldozers and ugly ferroconcrete constructions, preferring the lost world captured in photographs of Shinmozen Street in the 1930s, when antiques, wooden houses and local costumes still abounded. Nevertheless, he found that these changes could not be ignored even in a poetic account of his spiritual quest set in the famous Buddhist sites of Kyoto:

> Yes, I hate cars and factories and high-tension pylons and pollution in poems as much as in 'real' life; but they are the 20th Cent's contribution to world culture and one *must* reflect the contemporary world according to the litterary [*sic*] crickets. I like Lamb's reply to that hoary chestnut: 'Confound the age! I'll write for antiquity!' Oddly enough, if you try cutting out the offending bits, the end is weakened. Opposites depend on each other (ADFA MS G233 1975).

Rather than reflecting a wilfully self-centred, imaginary world, Stewart's life-work is a response to the spiritual void felt in contemporary life, while, to deal with day-to-day existence, like the Japanese themselves, he developed the knack of focusing on what interested him in a prospect to the exclusion of its unprofitable or disconcerting aspects.

He also took a lively interest in local events and politics. He savoured to the full living in 'a place where every stone drips with history' (ADFA MS G233 1974), delighting in its rich annual calendar of festivities, as well as in rare openings of temples and treasure-houses. 'So many wonderful things happen here every day, let alone every week and month', he enthused (NLA MS 8973/16/6 Smith 1966). For years he watched unfailingly the *Gion Matsuri*, an annual pageant that unfolds in period costumes the city's past; and he regularly attended the monthly Kitano and Toji fairs. Similarly, he worshiped at the great Pure Land temples, at the same time conceding that local ceremonies, which entailed kneeling, were often 'the usual Japanese combination of exquisite aesthetic sensations and sheer agony' (NLA MS 8973/16/6 Smith 1982). The poet also followed closely changes in the political landscape, such as the scandals arising from Tanaka's interaction with the corporate world, and the shocks caused by the late influx of Japanese women into parliamentary life. Never a lover of bureaucratic Big Brother, Stewart applauded civil disobedience, whether in the Japanese Diet or the streets and byways:

> This week fishermen who have lost their livelihood through sea pollution by industry, tied their boats together and threw a cordon round the harbour, preventing all shipping from reaching Sumitoma's wharf, while an intrepid band stuffed the company's outlet pipes with sandbags so that their poisonous PBC effluents backfired into their own paint! The good old Samurai spirit is not dead yet! (ADFA MS G233 1973).

He was alert, too, to local oddities, especially those produced by borrowings from Western culture. Displaced Bambis and Santas inspired his mirth, whereas the decision of the city fathers to reproduce 'an *underground* full-size replica of the Sistine Chapel frescoes in ceramics' for easier cleaning left him gagging with disbelief, as Japan's rush to Westernise assumed surreal dimensions (NLA MS 8973/16/34).

Determined not to have his instincts cheapened by ephemera, Stewart immersed himself in Buddhism, as well as in the history and art treasures of Kyoto. To correspondents he asserted that it would require not weeks but years to visit the many sites of the town and surrounding district, in fact that half a lifetime would scarcely be enough. And he delighted in guiding acquaintances through its winding streets and disparate temples. Visitors who had the temerity to allow only one day to 'do' Kyoto were warned that, at its expiration, their strapping legs would be worn down to stumps and their bodies so exhausted that they would need assistance to board a *shinkasen* back to Tokyo for days of recuperation. This was hardly an exaggeration, as his curatorial commentary was relentless, his itineraries packed and demanding; however, all agreed that they were a remarkable, unforgettable experience. Many who met Stewart through friends' referrals became, in turn, friends and some even patrons of his creative endeavours, while he was often enjoined to share his learning with a wider public through a guidebook. Stewart himself had always balanced his sedentary habits with long walks, and he enjoyed chaperoning the uninitiated around his city of adoption until the early 1990s, when ailments and mounting years forced him to decline the duties of guide, interpreter and factotum.

The authoritative writer

This detailed knowledge, based on the attentive reading of English-language authorities and on an extraordinarily retentive memory, also infused his writing. It is most obvious in his magnum opus, *By the old walls of Kyoto: a year's cycle of landscape poems with prose commentaries* (1981), which consists of 138 pages of verse followed by 290 pages of elaborate notes, many of which constitute independent essays in their own right. Typically this commentary is a subtle mixture of personal reflections, historical data and *aperçus* of contemporary life, as in the long opening paragraph:

> Arashiyama, which means Stormy Mountains, a place of great natural beauty situated at the mouth of the gorges in the north-west of Kyoto, derives its name from the suddenness with which, on a previously fine day, a storm can descend from Nishiyama, the nearby Western Range. Between steep mountain-sides covered with dense forest, which in late spring puts forth a profusion of foliage in all the various tints and tones of green, a river flows through the gorges, its water of a deep jade caused by mineral deposits washed down from the declivities as well as by its reflection of their verdure. In this scenery of a typically Japanese character, the people of Kyoto can picnic, fish, swim, or row boats. Arashiyama, also known by the Chinese reading of its characters as Ranzan, is equally famous for the blazing autumnal colours of its maples and other deciduous trees; its monochrome delicacy under snow when a light mist weaves over the water; and its cherry-blossoms in spring when discreet splashes of the faintest pink appear among the young browns and greens of the newly budding twigs. In the late thirteenth century the former Emperor Kameyama, who was then living in his retirement villa on the present site of the Rinzen-ji Temple near the bridge, had these cherry-trees transplanted from Mount Yoshino, where about one hundred thousand still grow in four main groves, the most celebrated place in Japan for viewing cherry-blossoms and one often praised in poetry and painting (Stewart 1981:141).

Whether in writing or verbally, Stewart strove after comprehensiveness. With the sensitivity of an autodidact, augmented presumably by his lack of command of Japanese, he virtually overwhelmed his audience with authoritative detail, enriched by years of first-hand experience. There is no discernible chink in his learning, its visually awesome mass seems to defy question, with only the accompanying verse admitting spiritual failings that the protagonist seeks to redress:

> My stubbornness still struggles on uphill,
> Growing more breathless, more exhausted, till

> Obstinate efforts must admit defeat.
> At last I must resign my powerless will
> And wholly lean upon that Other Power
> For help, on whom my light and life depend
> (Stewart 1981:7).

But whereas these long notes have been generally appreciated, their authoritative nature acknowledged, a series of essays that appeared in the short-lived journal *Hemisphere* have been largely forgotten. Written to give his name further currency among those interested in Eastern culture and, as crucially, to increase his always meagre funds, Stewart also saw them as parts of a projected guidebook on Kyoto, which, as the accompanying editorial introduction remarked, offered directions 'not so much as in the usual guide book, but in a more leisurely, more neighbourly way' (Stewart 1979a:54). In later years Stewart was actually approached to write such a guide to the city but declined the offer, preferring to direct his energies into essential poetic labours. *By the old walls of Kyoto*, he often remarked, constituted in itself a thorough reference work on many of the city's Buddhist monuments and, in depicting its quester's experience at famous sites, provides an implicit itinerary others could follow. Later, with death approaching, Stewart did gather his *Hemisphere* pieces into a separate folder, which he hoped might one day be published as a less forbidding, less scholarly account of Kyoto's shrines and festivals.

His first published attempt at popular travel writing was a two-part article entitled 'A walk in old Kyoto'. Avoiding a prosaic opening, which might have begun 'Kiyomizudera, the Pure Water Temple, predates the Onin Wars', Stewart's article commences *in medias res*:

> Guarding the two-storeyed Main Gate of the temple are two roaring mythic lions of granite, post-war replacements for the ornate bronze ones which used to stand here but were melted down for their metal. This gate is the oldest structure still extant at the temple and dates from 1478. It is sometimes called the *Akamon* or Red Gate, because it was once coloured with vermilion, but this has long since faded to a more attractive greyish pink (Stewart 1979a:54).

His standpoint here, as throughout, is that of a visitor on foot, his tone relaxed but gently erudite. Dates are kept to a minimum without sacrificing an awareness of the long history of the temple and its complex interweaving with the life of the city. The information in the rest of the essay is dense and varied, with constant attention being paid to the choices, views and enticing, puzzling objects that present themselves at every turn.

> Returning now past the pagoda, on your right an ancient wisteria spread over a refreshment stall; while on your left the *Kyo-do* or Sutra Hall contains

both the sacred Buddhist scriptures and...two attendant Bodhisattvas, *Monju*, symbolising Wisdom and *Fugen* symbolising Compassion (Stewart 1979a:56).

The paired essays bring to life and render comprehensible, to Westerners, a bustling but mysterious section of the ancient capital. Stewart is equally informative about iconography ('the *Senju Kannon*, or Bodhisattva of Compassion with Eleven Heads and a Thousand Arms, to see and save all suffering beings throughout the universe' (Stewart 1979a:57)) and traditional delicacies, from the *yatsuhashi*, or 'eight bridge' biscuits (made of 'cinnamon-flavoured strips of rice-dough...and immortalised in Zeami's Noh play *Kakitsubata*' (Stewart 1979b:76)), to the time-honoured fare available to the bon vivant in a traditional tea-house:

> ...such as *amazake* or unfermented sake, a non-alcoholic but warming winter drink, which tastes rather like hot sweet barley-water and is spiced with a touch of ginger. With this is recommended a serving of *warabi-mochi*, a delicious jelly prepared from bracken fern shots...cut into cubes and dusted with a light brown powder made from roast soya beans sweetened with a little sugar (Stewart 1979b:80).

Street by street and through intersections the narrator's eye travels up the mountain's slope, as he comments on souvenir shops, shrines and crafts, such as the window display of a pottery master in the form of a miniature landscape: 'sketched in white sand on a black lacquer board or tray using only a feather and perhaps a pebble or two' (Stewart 1979b:77). Although individual store holders will change, the paired essays provided at once a snapshot of the area, as well as an enduring commentary on the kind of wonders it will presumably offer to future generations, because, as Stewart concludes, whoever ascends *Shijo-dori* leaves their century behind for another, and virtually timeless, world.

His ensuing articles in *Hemisphere* remained focused on renowned festivals and temples in Kyoto, with the exception of 'A retreat of *Rakan*', which deals with a site famed for contemplative calm and artistic achievement.[11] Two essays are devoted to Stewart's beloved *Gion Matsuri*, and sketch not only the origins and history of the festival, but also the art of float-making and, most difficult of all, the place held by its pageant and music in the mind of Kyoto's citizens. Sounds and personalised vignettes also distinguish his depictions of the Toji and Kitano fairs, as the narrator shares local incidents with readers continents away:

> In a booth opposite a plump matron has her hair done up in sausage-rolls with the plastic curlers which she offers as a boon to women with straight hair. In old Japan it was a disgrace for a woman to have naturally wavy hair, but now Western fashions prevail. Not to be outdone in demonstrating the use and durability of the goods which he has for sale, her neighbour, a young yokel down from the

mountains for the day, is wearing a pair of diaphanous panty-stockings—over the top of his blue jeans and gunboats! (Stewart 1975:16–17)

Curiosities are balanced by an eye for generic detail, that is, for scenes that are repeated in many similar situations. For instance, the 'still-bare bushes [that] seem covered with snow' beside *Kitano Tenmanga* recur wherever worshippers have rejected 'paper-slips foretelling bad fortunes' by attaching them to deciduous trees (Stewart 1975:19); the geometric elements used in garden design to represent the four elements also recur: cube, sphere, pyramid and concave disc for, respectively, earth, water, fire and air, balanced fittingly on 'a lotus-base' (Stewart 1977:35).

The poet

Submerged but pointedly present in the articles are gentle reminders of the author's other allegiance: poetry. The two-part peregrination through old Kyoto, for example, climaxes with glimpses of a replica of 'the retreat of *Matsuo Basho* (1644–1694), most famous of all haiku poets' (Stewart 1979b:81), and of a further thatched dwelling of a Heian noble who renounced the pomp and honours of palace life to devote himself to the wandering existence of a Buddhist poet-priest. More boldly, but without fanfare, the author interleaves other essays with his own unattributed verse in heroic couplets—his idiosyncratic rendition of a haiku. Stewart maintained that this was the most natural English form to capture the concision, discipline and insight that are features of the classical haiku; however, detractors claimed that his translations in heroic couplets reduced the distinctive voices of Japanese masters to a single, metrically predictable note. Unquestionable Stewart himself composed memorable vignettes:

> The many-layered maples still let through
> The splintered sun, but seldom splits of blue
> (Stewart 1977:37).

Apart from a condensing of effects superior to prose, at its best a couplet not only captures the components of a tableau, but replicates its changing tempo:

> Rapt by a little whirlwind, cherry-petals
> Revolve above the pond on which it settles
> (Stewart 1977:37).

Like so many of the scenes he described and the local arts he treasured, these essays contain diverse layers of personal reference, from his own silent demonstration of the superiority of prosody to prose, to occasional mute homage to potent influences on his life, as in the acknowledgment of Masaaki for photographs that adorn 'A retreat of *Rakan*'.

Stewart reached a large readership through his haiku translations, but longed to be recognised as a master in his own right. His *A net of fireflies: Japanese haiku and haiku paintings* (1960) became a financial mainstay, thanks largely to American sales, having been reprinted 25 times by 1986, after which it was reissued in a new gift-book format, while *A chime of windbells: a year of Japanese haiku in English verse* (1969) was reprinted ten times in less than a decade. This success arguably proved his mastery of the form, which was further demonstrated by embedding original compositions, under a pseudonym, among genuine translations. No one, he boasted, had spotted the difference, and his own couplets certainly reveal a sensitive observer of nature:

Sudden spring
With tender impact on the icy air,
The peach-buds burst: their silken petals flare
(Stewart 1960:17).

Or:

Summer watercolour
The iris standing in the marsh: so blue,
Its roots have drunk the sky's reflected hue
(Stewart 1960:40).

For instance, of the 80 translations in the first section, devoted to spring, in *A net of fireflies*, eight are Stewart's originals, which sit comfortably beside those of writers such as Issa, Buson and Basho, who is credited with 12 of the originals. Stewart's *go*, or studio-name, was Ho-o (phoenix), which also served as a punning gibe at specialists or other readers who imagined they could easily discern counterfeit from 'genuine' productions. Stewart, of course, no less than Basho or Homer, was not always at 'concert pitch': his couplets, translations or originals, can become metrically tedious, and some of his compositions are banally descriptive:

In the ravine
Wind-driven clouds above: the rocks that crown
The gorge lean over—will they topple down?
(Stewart 1969:109).

Rarely doubting his own genius, the poet left among his manuscripts a collection of hundreds of 'haiku', arranged according to a traditional seasonal structure and entitled 'Over the vermilion bridge'. The collection, however, never found a publisher, in part because Stewart was not a well-known author, and in part probably because of the shortcomings mentioned above. That he hoped for much more is betrayed by the manuscript's epigraphs: 'He was a man who used to notice such things' (Thomas Hardy) and 'And with a mighty meaning of a kind/That tells the more the more it is not told' (Edward Arlington Robinson). A seven-page introduction defends his choice of the couplet in preference to a pedestrian rendering of the haiku form that would otherwise 'read merely like three slack insipid snippets of prose' (NLA MS8973/7). The volume closes with 34 pages of notes and would, presumably, have been completed with illustrations based on Japanese watercolours, as were his other haiku volumes.

During nearly three decades in Kyoto, Stewart's private life remained an unhappy compromise, but artistically he blossomed. Sexual relationships were pursued furtively and denied publicly, while he profiled himself as the acolyte of notable authorities on Pure Land Buddhism, whom he assisted in translating key Buddhist texts. Yet aspects of his identity shifted. The wavering narcissist of 1963 was gradually replaced by a genuinely compassionate, less dogmatic believer, whose wrath was greatly subdued, his physical pride humbled by age. Stewart's faith became sincere and strong, and his arduous struggle to achieve it provided the subject of his first epic, *By the old walls of Kyoto*. Consisting of 4351 lines of poetry, divided into 12 cantos, it took more than a decade to complete and, according to its introduction, traces 'the poet's pilgrimage from the self-power methods of Zen to the Other Power teachings of Pure Land Buddhism' (Stewart 1981:xvi). Allegedly it gives 'a trustworthy account of the defeats and triumphs through which he passed' (Stewart 1981:xvi), and it includes even a glimpse of his unreclaimed Adamic self:

> How can I chasten with ascetic shame
> These flagrant loins that feather into flame
> And rouse the infernal fowl with spurs of rage
> Incarcerated in my body's cage?
> A middle-aged and moulting sensualist
> Whose cock-sure plumes have faded, I persist
> In passionate pursuits, which I disown
> After I fall a prey to senile lust.
> Revulsion turns away in self-disgust
> From stale temptations that I would resist
> And yet, despite my years, have not outgrown
> (Stewart 1981:20).

Nevertheless, it is 'trustworthy' only in the most general sense, for an exemplary paradigm has been imposed on his actual, zigzagging course to produce an ideal image of the poet-quester entirely focused on the need for inner growth.[12]

Drawing inspiration from the Japanese adage that only perfection is good enough, Stewart took immense pains with this epic poem. The temple sites depicted were revisited again and again to ensure minute accuracy, while he composed the cantos at a rate of two per year, then revised them, he claimed, with the same care he had lavished on his haiku translations, which could be recast more than 50 times to achieve his desired effect. This was flexible yet sonorous verse, honed to read with the ease and directness of prose:

> The last few flakes were falling as I strolled
> Nearer the village huddled up with cold
> Against Daimonji's foot, where in a fold
> Dwellings with wooden frames were weathered black
> But roofed with sheets of white, stepped up the lane
> That climbs between their shuttered shops to gain
> Ginkaku-ji's front gate. Though at the back
> The mountain's shaven brow loomed overhead
> Where Bon-fires at the end of summer glow,
> Winter's calligraphy had traced instead
> The character for 'Great' in strokes of snow
> (Stewart 1981:107).

Particularly impressive are its diverse moods, his deep learning conveyed with a deft touch and its many resonant scenes, such as his superb evocation of the great Zen stone garden, *Ryoan-ji*, in Canto II, or the celebration of his favourite statue of the Buddha, *Miroku Bosatsu* at Koryu-ji, in Canto VB:

> Transcendent Insight in perfection lies
> Behind those infinitely distant eyes
> With half-closed lids that gaze, serene, sublime,
> Out of eternal stillness into time.
>
> Such pure Compassion, human yet withdrawn;
> Nirvana still deferred, till he can save
> All whom ignorance, hate, and lust enslave
> (Stewart 1981:38).

The final canto, however, best encapsulates the distance travelled from the hubristic 'Young Phoenix', who 'had swallowed…the solar centre of the universe' to become 'radiant with spiritual glow of Wrath and Pride', to his later, wiser avatar:

> The sun goes down through vague diffusive veils
> In which its glow of rosy copper fails,
> While smoky lilac hazes dim and hide
> The scars where blind and backward progress gnaws
> The range, despoiled by mechanistic jaws;
> Till impious steel pagodas that bestride
> The ridge and stalk the ruined countryside
> And callous factories that spread abroad
> Their insolent chimneys, now can be ignored.
> My body, too, declines: its aging sun,
> The heart's creative fire, grows moribund;
> But I can call upon the solar fund
> Of Amida for strength, when I have none
> (Stewart 1981:137).

Only the truly humble and selfless can rely on Amida's intercession, which, beyond the 'insolent' errors of modern man, is still as assured now as centuries before. AD Hope, a critic rarely given to hyperbole, affirmed to Stewart that with *By the old walls of Kyoto* he had written the greatest poem in English of that century.

It was completed on 19 December 1977 and shortly afterwards Stewart began, or rather returned to, what became 'Autumn landscape roll: a divine panorama'. Already outlined in his Saionji application decades before, its composition became the focus and incentive of his remaining years, filling his thoughts and dictating a daily routine that began at 5 am with writing, followed by business and an afternoon nap, then more work at night.

The plot of his new epic was admirably simple and bold. It commences with a competition, sponsored by the emperor, between the two finest painters of the Tang dynasty: Lu Ssu-hsun and Wu Tao-tzu. The former relies on meticulous detail; the latter relies on few but suggestive brush strokes and is adjudged the winner. Indeed, so realistic are Wu's creations that they blur the distinction between life and art. A scroll, decorated by his brush, becomes a blank when its fish swims off, or a depiction of a thundering waterfall in a bedroom keeps its occupants awake. Similarly, Wu is accustomed to enter imaginatively into his landscape painting and one day never returns: 'Translated out of earthly space and time/Into an autumn vision more sublime' (NLA MS8973/11 II:419–20). Within it he encounters the seminal thinkers and faiths of that age and traverses the Buddhist cosmology from hell to paradise, while the tale ends with the erasure of earthly illusion and the return of creative insight to its infinite origin beyond Western dualisms:

Time at its terminating gyre will stop,
And since in essence they were never two,
The sea will slip into the shining drop,
Whose crystal instant holds eternity
(NLA MS8973/11 II:5230–33).

The Australian died a fortnight after finishing his second epic poem, to the end living proof of his own insight that strength could flow from opposites (see Ackland 2001:241–51). The religious commitment of this final manuscript poem of 5356 lines is apparent throughout, and summed up by its epigraph from Wu Ching's *Pilgrimage to the West*:

> I dedicate this work to the glory of the Buddha's Pure Land... May it mitigate the sufferings of the lost and damned. May all who read it or hear it read... finally be reborn in the Realm of Uttermost Bliss; and by their common intercession may they requite me for the arduousness of my task (NLA MS8973/11 II).

Harold Stewart taking Australian visitors on a tour of Kyoto. Photo courtesy of Gwen Smith.

Yet the prankster, the man who revelled in pseudonyms, dissimulation and disguises, remained a disturbing 'double' to the Buddhist poet-sage, and is still evident in the prefatory note to 'Over the vermilion bridge' that could have served as his epitaph:

> Almost nothing has so far been discovered about the life of our poet, who is known to posterity by his *go*, or studio name...But recent research has shown that he must have been born about the end of the fifth or beginning of the sixth year of Taisho [1916 or 1917] in one of the islands of Japan. In middle life he is said to have moved to Kyoto, where he lived in obscurity and where most of his haiku were written; but the date of his death has yet to be determined (NLA MS8973/7).

'Decently neglected'

Stewart, more than most individuals, was keenly aware of personal identity as self-fabrication. Consciously he had played on its mask-like aspects, as well as laboured to transform his primal self, while he would have appreciated the extent to which he, through his own life-choices, had helped 'author' his own obscurity.

The Australian poet had travelled east to find the mythical Pure Land, and struggled lifelong to transform his burning animal energies into higher forms. His trials led eventually to poetry of enduring worth, and to a Buddhist faith through which he attempted to resign himself to neglect and ignominy:

> I, who could not give up the world, go free:
> This irreligious world renounces me
> Ignored in peace and decently neglected
> Till I am safely dead, I lay no claim
> To rank, privilege, prestige, degree,
> Nor claim the flaring fraudulence of fame,
> But work unknown, my only wealth the Name
> (Stewart 1981:50).

Despite this acceptance registered in *By the old walls of Kyoto*, lack of recognition in his homeland weighed heavily on him. Also, extreme reticence about Australian homophobia testified arguably to the lasting hurt it had inflicted, as did his unflagging disdain for 'the lurky country', which he also dubbed 'darkest Oz'. Following the Buddhist injunctions of patience and conciliation did not come easily to him. Nevertheless, when he died on 18 July 1995, his bones after cremation were purest white, signifying to Buddhists a life of extraordinary merit. In Australia obituaries remembered him as a Buddhist recluse, and celebrated his co-production of a single day, the Ern Malley hoax. It was further evidence that his major compositions were still unknown, his work as an innovator and precursor within the Australia–Japan relationship unrecognised. This, however, is gradually changing as readers encounter the two final epics that are the *summa* of his life's intellectual and spiritual engagement, as well as the finest products of that marriage of Eastern and Western sensibilities from which, as AD Hope rightly surmised, would be born Stewart's most memorable achievements.

Notes

1. For a fuller account of the response to modernism, see Haese (1988).
2. For an overview of the problems addressed and solutions proposed by the traditionalists, see Guénon (1941; 1943).
3. His successful application was confirmed in the *Canberra Times* on 7 November 1958.
4. His original program specified concentration on Zen and Chinese, 'with perhaps some study of Japanese and Sanskrit' (NLA MS8973/13/2).
5. One poem is entitled *Prelude: 'give me new phoenix wings'*, and flight is a key motif in each of the collection's three sections.
6. Stewart encountered this work in the Richard Wilhelm translation, with a foreword and commentary by Jung (1931).
7. 'The apocalypse of the young phoenix', Riley Collection:26.
8. See Ackland (2001:181–3) on Stewart's continued double life.
9. Letter to Marion Riley, 10 December 1968, Riley Collection.
10. On the consequences of this and on Stewart's later accommodation see Ackland (2001:241–51).
11. The title, as Stewart explains, refers to small 'Buddhist folk-carvings in stone…of the *Rakan*, as the Japanese call the *Arahats*, who number sixteen, eighteen, or five hundred, and were those personal disciples of the historical Buddha able to attain Enlightenment during his lifetime' (Stewart 1977:41).
12. For further discussion of the poem's themes, see Green (1973; 1981).

6 A matter of perspective: two Australian-Japanese families' encounters with white Australia, 1888–1946

Pam Oliver

Japanese residents of white Australia occupied an unusual space. The laws controlling entry to Australia, from an official perspective, defined Japanese identity. This perspective is, however, misleading as it suggests the existence of an immutable position not given to interpretation. However, a much more nuanced, complex and, in some respects, unexpected picture of relations between Japanese and 'white Australia' emerges when the stories of individual encounters are examined (Oliver 2002).[1]

This chapter studies a period when racial and cultural identity in Australia is often considered to have been fixed, when people were either white or non-white and the biological theory of race was accepted as scientific truth. A belief exists that the sense of self in regard to race and nationality was not questioned during this period of history but developed in the post-modern era. However, such a binary approach to self and other was not as rigidly applied under white Australia as some scholars assume. In another study (Oliver 2002) I argued that in the period of Australian history when one theory of race was generally accepted, the difficulties of interpreting and applying it to a particular group or historical circumstance to decide who was 'one of us', that is, Australian, or 'other' were recognised.

Few studies address the question of the identity of Japanese in Australia. It is an exploratory field. Nagata maintains that the term 'Japanese–Australian' is 'almost never heard' in Australia. and that we lack the words to describe these people in a way that places them within a meaningful socio-cultural context. Terms used, such as 'Japanese in Australia', fail to convey the layering of culture and experience behind their identity (Nagata 1999; 2001).

Jones's (2002) study employs one of the few terms Japanese coined about their situation in Australia. She quotes Hama Yasutaro: 'I have been in Australia for so long that I now call Broome my number two home.' Japan was 'home' in the sense that Australians spoke of the British Isles as 'home'. This designation of place provides a useful insight.

Tamura (2003:81–2) places war brides in a borderland. In the public eye they saw themselves as representatives of their homeland. In their personal lives they tried to assimilate and to raise children 'in the Australian way'.

Nagata and Tamura touch upon the reception of this identity by the white community. Whites on Thursday Island, according to Nagata, respected Japanese. They were admitted to the local European school, while other Asians attended the Aboriginal school. This respect diminished with the war and some Japanese changed their names to hide their identity. The war brides, however, retained a sense of pride in their heritage. They often gained respect, although some suffered abuse from the white community.

These studies suggest a process of intermingling of the self-identity of Japanese and the ascribed identity by the majority white community. The identity of a person or group is influenced by many shifting factors. In a study of Australian responses to Japanese, Oliver (2002) discovered that 'white' Australians considered behavioural and cultural traits more indicative of identity than physical features. Contemporary events also influenced interpretation of behaviour.

This chapter examines the experiences of two families, their development of self-identity and the reception of that identity in Australia at local, state and federal levels. Today, questions such as whether it is possible to choose one's racial identity and have it accepted are seen as post-modern issues. It is clear from this study that it was a consciously examined question in the lives of Japanese people in Australia before the Second World War and for those white Australians among whom they lived. The inquiry includes the following: how did Japanese perceive their identity in regard to race and nationality? Were they successfully able to define an identity that worked for them? Were they able to have that identity recognised by white Australians? How did the shaping of their identity change over time in their eyes and in the eyes of those whose acceptance they sought? How far can it be established in the case of two families, as Curthoys (2000) argues, that white Australia did not address its racial others in a united or coherent discourse, but rather in separate registers at different times?

Questions of identity—theoretical perspectives

The debate concerning identity theory is too vast to be represented meaningfully here. For the purposes of this enquiry, some representative studies of important aspects have been chosen for their relevance to the Australian historical context and the stories of the Japanese residents. They suggest a means of analysis and a language which may further the work on Japanese identity in Australia and provide a way of situating Japanese experience within the wider context of thematic debates in Australian history such as race, white Australia and immigration.

This chapter takes the position that identity is not fixed but inherently fluid and even polyvalent in nature. Because the work of Nagata and Tamura suggests that Japanese in Australia had an identity that was not 'a perfect fit', Hall's work is useful. Identities, he argues, are constituted from within representations. They involve a certain suturing together of perceptions. The question is how we are represented and how that bears on how we represent ourselves. However, the notion of suturing or articulation leaves the person with a very fragile identity, suggesting a certain unworkability (Hall & du Gay 1996:3, 6). The chapter will consider whether this aspect applied to members of the families.

Scholars such as Powell (1999) call for a reconfiguring of identity, which, in the midst of a multiplicity of cultural influences, more closely resembles the 'lived perplexity' of peoples' lives. The writers in his edited volume consider the limitations of binary concepts, such as self/other, white/non-white, citizen/alien, foreign/native born. Boundaries, they argue, are not fixed but permeable. While subscribing to these views, this chapter uses the terms white, non-white, British, Japanese and European found in the archival material. Although they are intended by the original users to uphold a binary position, it is evident that the boundaries were permeable. The definition of terms and their usage was not an exact science. The white/non-white binary referred principally to skin colour. However, it is evident in the stories below that culture played a large part in defining whiteness. A white person with white parents could be classed as Japanese. A Japanese could be considered 'British', a term mostly used to refer to white Australians whose origins lay in the British Isles, or 'Australian', usually inferring a person whose cultural orientation was Australian more than anything else. 'British subject' could refer to non-white or white citizens born in the British Empire.

Powell (1999:5) further calls for a multiperspectivity in studying cultural identity, for the researcher to take account of the polyvalent nature of lived cultural identity and to perceive culturally distinct others more as fully constituted selves. He argues for the definition of culture to include not only issues of race, class, transnationality and hybridity but self-identity beyond biological identity. This presents possibilities for studying Japanese development of self-identity and the question of whether this achieved any degree of recognition from the majority white population in Australia.

The concept of hybridity, where the person is seen as different from either alternative, in this case Australian or Japanese, will be explored. The limitations of hyphenated identity such as Japanese–Australian will also be addressed. The concept of border crossing suggests boundary limitations and also a condition of mobility, where the person does not construct a place or condition of their own but experiences the uncertainty of the constant border crossing (Hall & du Gay 1996:91–2). These terms suggest discomfort in self-identity, a question that will be explored below.

Broinowski's work is useful as an exposition of the East/West binary. She argues that Australians perceived the 'East' from the perspectives of geography or history. To those who saw Australia's nearness to Asia as important for trade and culture, she argues that the East/West divide made less sense. They relied on a geographical perspective. Those to whom the East/West duality made most sense, and these she maintains were the majority, argued from history. Australia was British and white, with a thoroughly European orientation. For both, the Orient started across the channel at the end of the thin red line to Singapore. Some Australians perceived the Japanese as having an East/West duality in their identity. To these Australians the Japanese were perceived as the nearest thing to the white man, a superior type of Asian (Broinowski 1996:6–7). The geography versus history consideration is useful in looking at Australian perceptions of the Japanese and Japanese understanding of their own space and identity.

Race and white Australia

Racial theory today recognises that there is no scientific basis for the concept of 'race', even though a belief in embedded racial characteristics persists. Theorists are divided on whether an overarching theory of racism can be developed or even whether the term 'race' should continue to be used (Hollinsworth 1998:3–8, 29–43, 47, 60; Castles 1996:20, 22, 31–2; Malik 1996:2–7). In pre-1945 Australia, one basic theory of race existed.

Two widely known works shaped racial theory in Australia before 1945. These were used in an attempt to establish a clear line between white and non-white, mostly for the purposes of exclusion. The earliest, by Charles Pearson, influenced members of the first Federal Parliament of 1901. Pearson believed in the widely accepted doctrine of racial hierarchy based on skin colour (Pearson 1893:ch 1, 2; *CPD* 1901:4644–5, 5233). The second, Stoddard's influential work of 1920, argued that race not politics was the basic factor in human affairs. He divided the world into five racial areas based on skin colour. Stoddard added cultural characteristics to his biological markers. However, in his introduction he acknowledged that defining racial difference was difficult. Although the contrast between white and coloured in mental and spiritual endowments were 'definite', these aspects were 'even more elusive of definition' than physical characteristics (Stoddard 1920:xiv, 5, 10, 48–9).

These theorists had considerable difficulty in grappling with questions of national identity (Dixon 1995:137–47; Oliver 2003a; NAA: SP1714/1, N40344). Their ideas greatly influenced Australian officialdom in its interpretation of the information gained by studying Japanese activities before the Second World War, but it was not the only racial discourse of the times. Because it proved extremely difficult to apply the theories to intelligence information in particular cases, some officials, and many Australians who had Japanese colleagues or neighbours, recognised that Japanese could assimilate (NAA: C123/1, WOS; NAA: MP124/6, 462/201/753). The binary white/non-white was not entirely reliable. Japanese, it was observed, acquired competence along British models in many areas of life, particularly in education, technology and business. They could outperform whites. Some communities accepted this process of assimilation, as the stories below will show, as positive evidence of Japanese becoming Australian and welcomed them as citizens. Thus, an unofficial discourse of experience developed alongside the official racial theory but was not as well articulated.

Geography versus history

The importance of geography cannot be underestimated, especially in regard to Australia's northern coastline. Japanese settled from Cossack to Townsville and all ports in between. Although white Australians divided the continent up into colonies before Federation, the Japanese had a different sense of geography. The important divider was not political boundaries but that of sea and land. White north-coast dwellers shared similar views. Singapore was the other end of the sea lane connecting Australia to Asia, as much as a thin red line dividing Australia from Asia. Japanese on the north coast looked inwards to the Asia-Pacific region throughout which their countrymen had spread and their ships and merchants travelled for trade and commerce.

Japanese first worked on luggers along the north of Australia in the late 1870s in a pearling industry controlled by white pearling masters. The first indentured labourers (indents) hired for a specific period of time for work in pearling arrived at Thursday Island in November 1883. Others were recruited at Yokohama and Kobe from June 1885 by Streeter and Co, the largest of the Western Australian pearlers, and by Fearon & Low, who recruited for Thursday Island and Darwin. In the 1888–89 season, the centre of pearling activity moved along the sea lanes to Broome following the development of deep-sea diving apparatus and the discovery of seemingly limitless pearl beds in that area. At the peak of the industry in 1913, there were 1166 Japanese indents at Broome and 574 at Thursday Island (Sissons 1979a; Moore 1994:121).

Prior to Federation, Japanese indents entered Australia to work on cane fields in Queensland. Other individuals travelled rural Australia or settled, for example, in Sydney, Newcastle, Brisbane, Melbourne and Geelong, where they were mostly engaged in the fledgling Australia–Japan import/export trade that developed after 1896 (Nagata 2001:85–90). Such individual Japanese were subject to very few entry restrictions until the late 1890s. After 1901, the passing of the Immigration Restriction Act meant that people of 'colour' could not enter Australia without passing the Dictation Test. By 1904, certain categories of Japanese entrants were exempt, including merchants, tourists and students. Such people could enter for 12 months on a passport but required permission for an extension of their stay. The new immigration laws changed the nature of the Japanese 'community'. The number of indentured labourers in pearling declined but the number involved in the import and export firms increased, particularly in Sydney, Melbourne and Brisbane.

The Muramatsu family

Sakutaroo Muramatsu[2] arrived at Cossack from Kobe in 1888 in the early stages of the pearling industry. Information relating to the family's emigration and business life in Australia is recorded in his son Jiro's diary. Other members of the family included Tsune, who lived in Broome in the early 1890s, and Jiro's younger brother, Saburo.[3]

At age 14, Jiro records how his father returned to Japan and brought him via Singapore to Broome, arriving on 10 December 1893. At Broome, the family lived in a mixed-race population in which non-whites were the majority. In April 1894 the family moved to its thriving general store at Cossack. Here Jiro began his business life. Sakutaroo made annual visits to Japan, lasting about three months. During his 1895 absence, Tsune arrived from Broome to assist Jiro with stocktaking.

On 20 June 1895, Jiro travelled to Melbourne to continue his education at St Francis Xavier College as a boarder. He joined 166 boys at the Jesuit-run school (Dening & Kennedy 1993:63). Jiro's guardian, H Furusawa, the consul at Melbourne, paid £16 16s per quarter in fees and additional expenses for piano lessons and books (Xavier Archives, ledger 1886:195–6). A tribute to Jiro in the *Xaverian* (1910:18) indicates his adjustment to Australian school life and the positive attitude of others towards him.

> Jiro Muramats! What a boy of '97 but remembers him well...though he knew very little English on his arrival, still in a short time he picked up the language marvelously well. His kindly and gentlemanly disposition, together with the whole-hearted way into which he threw himself into his surroundings soon made him a universal favourite. It used to be the fun of the world to see him going

head over heels into a game of football. In class he held his own, and the writer will long remember the tussle between Jiro and himself for the mathematical prize of the Sub-Matric. Jiro finally won, and the roof nearly went off the Speech Hall as he mounted the stage to receive his prize.

Xavier's records do not mention that Jiro was Japanese. To the school he was a boarder from the West. His friends were Australians. Jiro particularly mentions Francis O'Keefe, or Frank, a close friend, who studied at Xavier from 1893–96 and entered the Jesuit novitiate in 1898. Frank was a well-known personality. He travelled to Ireland for priestly training and returned in 1906 to Xavier, with which he was associated in some capacity for the rest of his life.

With Frank as his travelling companion in school holidays, Jiro travelled extensively and met British and Japanese of high social status. In Sydney, they visited Alexander Marks, the Honorary Consul for Japan, Consul Gitaki, and representatives of the recently opened trading house F Kanematsu (Australia) Ltd. This firm became one of Australia's biggest trading houses engaged in the Australia–Japan trade. Jiro also visited large regional towns in Victoria and South Australia. In 1898 he travelled overland to Adelaide via many country centres. He met the Japanese consul, John Langdon Parsons, in Adelaide on 24 January 1898. In February 1898 Sakutaroo's illness cut short Jiro's time at Xavier. His father died before Jiro reached Cossack. The *Xaverian* (1898:52) recorded the event.

Jiro maintained contact with school friends, especially Frank, into the 1920s but returned to Melbourne only once from June to August in 1899. During this stay, he applied for naturalisation. Initially, the application was refused, along with a number of Polynesian applicants, because they were 'people of colour'. Alexander Marks intervened on Jiro's behalf and he took the oath of allegiance before Marks on 17 June 1899 (NAA: A712/1, 1899/K6473). Pending Federation and changes to immigration laws probably influenced Jiro's decision to naturalise at this time. It was not only a commitment to life in Australia but also a measure that would assist his business.

In 1905 Jiro married Hatsu, who had arrived in 1895. Their daughter was born in July 1913. Jiro presents in documents as a confident businessman able to move in European and Japanese circles. His stated identity as a naturalised British subject was respected until 1915. After this date, he faced difficulties under state laws that discriminated against naturalised non-white British subjects. He fought at local, state and commonwealth levels against legal restrictions to his business expansion and the limitations on his political rights gained by naturalisation. Jiro's fight to have his identity accepted is discussed below.

Establishing a business identity[4]

Jiro's business was based initially on the store in Cossack. He was a partner in the firm J & T Muramats, which was responsible for the family's interests in Australia. From 1906 he commenced pearling at a time when the industry at Broome was increasing steadily. By 1908 Broome had the same predominance of Japanese indents as Thursday Island. Jiro's actual business records are sketchy. Few are extant for the period from 1910 to the late 1920s because the majority of his records were destroyed when Darwin was bombed in 1942. However, security service investigations into assets of Japanese in Australia provide substantial information.

After 1906 Jiro gradually acquired pearling boats and permits to hire indentured labourers, including Japanese and kupangers. By 1915 Jiro's influence in pearling at Cossack became so extensive that white pearlers saw him as a threat. There is strong evidence that Jiro had ten boats in 1912, when Asiatics were prevented by Western Australian law from obtaining any further licences. When it is considered that in 1909 there were 113 pearlers in Western Australia, of whom 48 owned only one boat and only six pearlers owned eight or more luggers (Moore 1994:130), the threat posed by Jiro becomes clearer. Further, there is no evidence of any other Japanese in Western Australia or the Northern Territory who actually owned luggers. Through the 1920s and 1930s, Jiro continued to purchase boats and expand his fleet along the northern sea lane to Darwin.

Jiro's operations followed practices more representative of European traders. As a point of comparison, small Japanese concerns in Sydney, Townsville and Cairns, for example, while selling some general goods, imported specialty Japanese items and in this way complemented rather than competed with white storeowners. Jiro's activities place him in competition with white owners and pearlers.

It is significant that Jiro did not trade with Japanese firms in Sydney, Perth and Singapore but used local Australian firms or British and German firms. His commercial correspondence for 1924–26 record, for example, sales of shell to Otto Gerdau Ltd, a firm based in Singapore and New York, which realised £340 in November 1923. He placed orders for a wide variety of goods during the 1920s for small quantities of shoes, clothes and food items and large quantities of meat probably intended as goods for the store and provisions for crews. By 1935 purchases reached £1214. These were placed with Fremantle merchants including Bateman Ltd, ships chandlers and general importers, and D & J Fowler, grocers. In Singapore, he traded with Guthrie & Co and Otto Gerdau.

His banking was not with the Yokohama Specie Bank of Sydney, which most Japanese firms used, but with the Union Bank of Australia in Broome.

Jiro acquired a large amount of Australian property. By 1935 he owned six properties in Cossack. In November 1941 his holdings in Darwin were worth in excess of £11,000. He owned shares in paper mills to the value of about £700. His credit notes in New York exceeded £25,000. These acquisitions represented considerable personal success, which could have been even greater had his position as a master pearler and successful businessman not been challenged twice. On both occasions the issue hinged on his identity.

Challenges to Jiro's identity[5]

The first challenge occurred in 1915 when Jiro's pearling rival, Geoffrey Taylor, left for the First World War. As the Collector of Customs at Cossack explained to External Affairs:

> ...this Japanese already has more influence than he should have over Cossack pearling matters and judging from statements made by white pearlers, they have been compelled to leave Cossack as their Japanese workers are more loyal to Muramats, their rival, than to themselves.

Although naturalised, Jiro was too successful and his non-white background became an issue. He sold his boat *Ivy* to Taylor, who obtained permits for six indents before paying Jiro. In Taylor's absence, Jiro supplied stores to the boat and took its shell. The ownership reverted to Jiro and he unsuccessfully claimed the six permits. Instead they were held in Taylor's name for his return or until six months after the peace. If Taylor did not resumed pearling, they were to be issued to a white pearler or cancelled. In 1920 Jiro again unsuccessfully claimed the permits and £150 still owning on *Ivy*.

The question of permits arose again in the 1930s. This dispute with the Commonwealth and Western Australian governments lasted several years. The key issues were the numbers of boat licences and indent permits Jiro could legally own as a non-white British subject. He wanted to increase his Western Australian fleet while retaining all his rights at Darwin. Questions relating to historic state boundaries and laws were crucial.

Jiro knew how to lobby. He was well known in the Department of Home Affairs in Canberra. His Member of Parliament at Darwin, Nelson, and the Chief Pearling Inspector, WL Stanley, supported him. However, Jiro sought to develop a business based on shipping across Australia's north coast at a time when Japan had invaded Manchuria. Fear of Japan's southward expansion and sampan activity in the Pacific was causing Australia anxiety. The question of whether a person could have his or her identity accepted was important. Jiro raised the issue in his dispute with the government.

In 1932 Jiro sought to transfer crew permits from unseaworthy vessels to two new luggers. The request was denied. The initial reply by an Acting Secretary of Home Affairs in the absence of the secretary, Quinlan, was based on racial grounds. Permits by transfer were not granted to non-European applicants. However, when Quinlan returned, he stated in an unofficial letter of 1 April 1932 to his Assistant Secretary that he knew Jiro's pearling activities well and resented the manner in which Jiro worked around regulations. He was unhappy that Jiro and his manager, McKay, transferred some boats to Aru Island in Dutch territory in order to increase their pearl take. Quinlan ignored the fact that white pearlers had done this since 1905. He wrote further:

> I feel inclined...to give him in future the minimum concessions possible in every direction, and my attitude would be to refuse this present application and give him as much trouble as possible, even if we have to change our attitude later on. It won't do him any harm to wake him up to the fact that we have some powers and intend to exercise them.

Jiro responded with an angry letter to Nelson on 19 April 1932. Further letters raised two questions relating to his national and racial identity: 'After granting me all the rights, capacities and Privileges same as natural born British subject by naturalization, Has the Minister power to make distinctions between white British race and naturalized British subjects?'

He further argued that in Western Australia there were only two coloured British Indians with pearling licences in Broome allowed to work one boat each. There were no coloured naturalised British subjects pearling there except him. He only had three of the ten licences he was entitled to in Western Australia. No naturalised person held a licence in Darwin, so he was the only person affected. He wondered if the minister would permit him to purchase a further seven boats, as he wanted to increase his fleet in Western Australia.

Nelson made further overtures to Quinlan. However, his department considered it undesirable for a 'naturalised British subject of Japanese race' to have control of a fleet of 15 vessels. Quinlan wrote in internal memos that he was unhappy at Jiro's stand against the limitations on shell in Darwin, which he saw as a further attempt to circumvent regulations. Quinlan decided to refuse the application initially, 'leaving...Muramatsu to submit reasons in support of the application if he wishes to press it'. However, the reply to Nelson stated that Jiro could transfer his permits to the new boats but could not increase his fleet without permission of the Western Australian authorities, who were concerned about over-fishing of shell. The minister was not disposed to permit Jiro to increase his fleet in Western Australia while retaining his fleet at Darwin.

Jiro Muramatsu, 1920. Photo courtesy National Archives of Australia (NAAWA: K1145, Muramatsu, Jiro).

Jiro's response to Nelson is poignant: 'I will not be able to enlarge my business seems to me a very unfair treatment, why Government, in the first place, granting me all the rights same as natural born British Subjects? [sic]'.

The Chief Pearling Inspector at Darwin supported Jiro in July 1932: 'It would appear that the practice of...refusing the permits to other than white naturalised British subjects excludes such a man as Mr Muramats...' He further argued in a letter to the minister that there seemed no reason for the distinction between white naturalised subjects and non-white British subjects. Muramatsu was 'a gentleman of culture and a law abiding citizen and lives permanently in Darwin. As a reputable and extensive producer and trader, he is a valuable citizen to any country, and deserves encouragement rather than repression.'

By September 1933 Jiro had gained permission for some of his permits and an agreement for further consideration when pearling conditions improved. It is not clear whether he ever achieved his aim of 15 boats from these extant records.

Clear distinctions were made between naturalised whites and naturalised 'coloureds' in Western Australia and Queensland. The Commonwealth Government recognised this but was less inclined to use racial arguments. Because of Jiro's opposition to regulations, the government was not willing to increase his boat permits to 15. By 1933 the official letters rely on the argument that Jiro opposed a conservation policy supported by pearlers in general. However, Customs at Darwin pointed out that Jiro was the only master pearler who had obeyed the regulations in regard to not working indents on shore. In a handwritten note in August 1933, the minister said he would treat Muramatsu as being fully entitled to consideration as a British subject. Commonwealth officials were wary of using race overtly as an argument to deny Jiro his requests, but for a few this was a good reason. Naturalised or not, he was Japanese-born and not all officials recognised him as a true British subject on a par with Indians.

The challenge to his political rights[6]

In 1923, displaying his knowledge of the law and ability to manoeuvre his way through the political and legal systems, Jiro appealed to the High Court for the restoration of his right to vote in Commonwealth elections. Again differences in state laws in relation to Asians who had naturalised before Federation affected Jiro.

The legal situation was as follows. Under Section 41 of Federal Constitution of 1901, naturalised people eligible to vote before 12 February 1902 could enrol to vote in a Commonwealth election if they were already enrolled to vote in elections for the more numerous House of Parliament of the state in which they lived. Further, Section 39 of the Commonwealth Electoral Act stated that no Aboriginal native of Australia, Asia, the Pacific or Africa could vote unless eligible under Section 41. Western Australia and Queensland passed further legislation to prevent non-whites from enrolling as voters even under Section 41.

Jiro had naturalised in Victoria but lived in Western Australia. The Western Australian Electoral Act of 1907 excluded non-whites, but in Jiro's case the Police Magistrate at Roebourne had approved his enrolment for state elections in 1922. As a result, Jiro argued that he was entitled to Commonwealth enrolment under Section 41, but the Commonwealth Electoral Officer, HR Way, dismissed the application under the 1907 Western Australian Electoral Act.

Jiro appealed to the High Court in 1923 on the grounds that, being on the Western Australian roll, he had the right to vote in Western Australia and to enrol for Commonwealth elections. During the hearing, it was argued that under the Commonwealth Electoral Act he had the right to be on the Western Australian roll but was disqualified from voting as an aboriginal native of Japan. Consequently, he could not vote in Commonwealth elections. Changes to the Nationality Act in 1920 meant that non-whites could naturalise if they were British subjects but under the Electoral Act they could not vote. This anomaly lead to investigation of the rights of aliens and naturalised subjects state by state.

The grounds on which Jiro appealed are interesting. He argued that, although he was born in Japan, he was not an aboriginal native of Japan. He was supported by the Magistrates' Court at Perth, which sought a 'definite and authoritative decision on the question as to what constitutes an aboriginal native of any country within Section 35 of the Commonwealth Electoral Act 1918–22'.

The High Court argued that Jiro was an aboriginal native of Japan even though the Perth Magistrate had ruled that he was not. Aboriginal, they stated, was properly defined as those who lived in the country before Europeans settled. It was used from a 'European perspective'. Jiro had argued that he was not Ainu; however, the High Court ruled that the Japanese race that Jiro belonged to resided in Japan before Europeans settled in Japan in the 19th century. Ainu were only aboriginal natives of Japan from the Japanese perspective, not from the European point of view. Seeing that Jiro admitted he was born in Japan, he was, from a European perspective, an aboriginal native of Japan. Further, he had not demonstrated that he was not an aboriginal native of Asia or the Pacific. The Solicitor General ruled that, although Jiro was a naturalised British subject, he was also an aboriginal native of Asia. His case was dismissed.

Jiro was interned in December 1941. He died in 1943. Hatsu returned to Japan and filed with some success for compensation for confiscation of their property. The compensation hinged on whether Jiro and Hatsu were recognised as British subjects. Naturalisation was an important marker of belonging in Australian eyes. Jiro recognised its importance and used it well as a bargaining tool when he could not function as he wished in society. Jiro presents as a man whose sense of self identity was well developed.

Jiro maintained firmly that, although Japanese-born, he was a naturalised British subject. At the very least, Australia had no right to distinguish between naturalised persons of colour. Neither should it have made distinctions between white and non-white naturalised persons. For this stand he received considerable respect. He certainly demonstrated his expertise in the law and posed questions that white Australia refused at times to address.

The Nakashiba family[7]

John Iwamatsu Nakashiba was born on 12 December 1874. He arrived in Australia about 1890 at Thursday Island and worked as a houseboy. Although he retained stronger links with Japanese people than Jiro, he had Europeans in his immediate family and a large measure of support from the white community. Despite the fact that he was not naturalised, the white community in which he lived recognised him and his brother, Bunsuke, as valued citizens. Unlike Jiro, he was not a successful businessman, except in the years when he relied on family members to run aspects of his business. He became bankrupt three times.

In his early years in business, John diversified successfully and his growing prosperity was not resented. There were no limitations placed on the expansion of the business by local authorities. In 1906 John owned a store in Cairns that sold some general goods but basically relied on importing and selling Japanese goods to tourists and Japanese residents in the area. In 1912 he opened a fancy goods business in Brisbane in partnership with Mr Asajiro. Nakshiba's interest in the store was valued at £1360. He was also a partner in a registered firm of boat builders at Cairns and was employed as an interpreter by the Customs Service. He held a seven-year lease on a sugar farm of 45 acres on the Mulgrave River. During John's prosperous years in Cairns, his firm Nakashiba Bros was managed by Bunsuke, who arrived, aged 15, in 1907. Bunsuke worked in the business until 1921, except for a period between February 1910 and August 1912 when he travelled to Japan to complete his education.

The respect in which the family was held is demonstrated by the reaction of the people of Cairns to the pending deportation of Bunsuke and his brother-in-law, Warkichi, in 1921. At this time, Bunsuke applied to bring his Japanese wife to Australia. This sparked a routine Department of Home and Territories investigation. The application was refused on the grounds that Bunsuke had harboured a prohibited immigrant at Cairns. He was asked to leave the Commonwealth. The immigrant was his brother-in-law, who had landed at

Cairns from Thursday Island 13 years before and who had been part-owner of the business since 1917.

The pending loss of Bunsuke and Warkichi to the business community at Cairns sparked a public outcry. Thirty-six business and professional people petitioned the Minister of External Affairs for an extension: '[Bunsuke] has always borne the best of characters and is esteemed as a citizen and business man, and we pray that...you will in your clemency re-consider his application and grant him a further exemption as allowed by law.'

The Acting Consul General and the President of the Senate, as well as the Nakashibas' (British) solicitors, argued that the brothers were not conscious of having broken the law. Further, the government had made no allowance for the fact that 'blood was thicker than water'. Nakashiba Bros was a large business in the town, which was not in competition with Europeans. Its closure would greatly affect Japanese banking and commercial interests.

A further argument presented by white traders was that John and Bunsuke had done no more than reputable, wealthy British interests on Thursday Island who had harboured Japanese indents for years and engaged them on shore despite regulations. The implication was that the Department of Home and Territories turned a blind eye to British activities but acted unfairly against the Nakashibas.

The Nakashibas enjoyed comfortable relations with white citizens of Cairns. Unlike Jiro, they were not in competition with Australian interests but tapped a different market and brought wealth to the town. They were respected as individuals to the point where residents were prepared to afford them the right to ignore or work around regulations, just as British businesses did. Despite this recognition of a de facto citizenship, the Department of Home and Territories was not impressed. It believed that in 1917 John had assisted illegal boat arrivals on his property at Cow Station, about 32 kilometres from Cairns. Further, it argued that the Nakashibas 'knew the law'. Bunsuke was given six months to leave and departed on 21 September 1921 for Aru Island.

John married an Australian born in Brisbane of German parentage. Their son, S——, was born in Cairns on 8 July 1924. Two daughters followed. When John was declared bankrupt at Cairns as a silk merchant, the family moved to Thursday Island, where John engaged in pearling interests and a drapery business. He went bankrupt in Thursday Island and moved to Darwin to open a general haberdashery and commissioning agents business, the NAD Co.

In Darwin, John was the president of the Japanese Society and was regarded as the leader of the community. The masters of Japanese luggers visited him while in port. The company's main activity was to act as agent to various companies and societies in Darwin but it did not prosper financially. John became knowledgeable about and influential in the pearling industry. In 1937 he lobbied for a pearling base for Japanese luggers at Darwin. Articles in the paper contain announcements he made about developments in the pearling industry. On 9 September 1938, for example, he reported the transfer of operations by Japanese-owned luggers along a stretch of 200 miles of the Arafura Sea to promising new beds off Melville and Bathurst Islands. John's growing power within the Japanese community caused friction between members of the Japanese Society. In July 1941 he claimed a right to consular powers. When this was refused, he tendered his resignation as president and secretary of the Japanese Society. By late 1941 his influence also caused concern in Military Intelligence circles that believed he was an agent of the Japanese government.

Just exactly what John's position was in regard to the Japanese in Darwin was only clarified after his internment. From 8 December 1941 to June 1942 the Navy requested his release from internment because he had acted as an agent for Naval Intelligence. For several months prior to the outbreak of war, John was commissioned by Intelligence and secretly supplied information regarding Japanese activities to the Staff Officer at Darwin at some personal risk. Intercepted correspondence at Darwin showed that Japanese residents suspected he was a British agent. Military Intelligence refused to release him because he was not naturalised. It tried to find suitable employment for him so his family could be released as well, but he was not suited to work as an interpreter with the Allied Translator Interpreter Section. He remained interned and cruelly treated by other Japanese, but work was found on a farm in Victoria for his wife and two daughters. The Army attempted to find suitable work for S—— but this proved more difficult. In May 1945 he was released to Manpower in Queensland, a department that organised government works during wartime.

Peter Nakashiba[8]

Sometime in 1908 John adopted a child. In 1911 he sought permission to take Peter to Japan for his education. The official debate over whether this child should be permitted to go to Japan was eventually brought to the attention of the Prime Minister. The issue was his identity.

The first questions relating to Peter's identity were his natural parentage and the legality of his adoption. The adoption papers had been signed by the 'alleged' Japanese father. It was 'understood that the reputed mother' was a half-caste Aboriginal. Customs doubted the veracity of this story and advised the Commonwealth Attorney General:

> I have taken particular notice of its eyes and their conspicuous blueness and the total absence of the slit-like, half closed appearance which is a sure indication of the presence of oriental blood and which is the peculiar characteristic of that race, lends strength to the entertained doubt as to the veracity of the statements shewn [sic] in the birth certificate.

No white child could leave Australia without an accompanying white parent. The Acting Prime Minister, WM Hughes, ordered that the child was not to leave the Commonwealth. Further, Customs should determine whether the child was white or not and, if 'it' was white, 'it' was to be 'brought up accordingly'. By October 1911, the Premier of Queensland stated he was of 'the opinion that the child is of unmixed European blood'. Government officials directed that the child be placed in an orphanage. This does not seem to have happened and John did not go to Japan.

Thus, from early in life Peter lived in the shadow lands. Suspected by Japanese in Japan and Australians in Australia, no-one trusted him because his identity could not be grasped. From the records, an often very unhappy and illusive person emerges.

The story of his early life became a crucial text for Australian military, security and civil authorities from 1941. Peter was certainly illegitimate. He was most likely the child of a wealthy businessman and a white woman, the result of a short liaison.

Most agreed Peter looked white but he was not trusted. His friends at Charters Towers School from 1921–27 reported to Military Intelligence in 1941 that he was pro-Japanese. After matriculating at Sydney University, Peter worked on a farm in the Ingham district and then met and married a British girl at Thursday Island. The couple settled in Sydney and changed their name. But between 1930 and 1934, Peter joined his step-parents in Darwin where he worked as an interpreter. According to a Darwin police officer who had known him in Cairns, ' he was a good style of a man and showed no signs of being Japanese'. This interesting remark suggests that some white Australians saw identity as more than skin deep.

Peter travelled to Japan in the mid-1930s and returned in 1937. In 1938 he interpreted in the lugger cases in the High Court in Darwin. This case eventuated when Japanese owners of several luggers, urged by local white Darwin residents and the Japanese community, sued the Commonwealth Government for the wrongful arrest of the luggers off the northern coast by the patrol boat *Larrakia*, which maintained they were illegally in territorial waters off an Aboriginal

John Iwamatsu Nakashiba and his adopted son, Peter Nakashiba, Darwin, 1937. Photo courtesy National Archives of Australia (NAAACT: M119, 74).

reserve. John and other Japanese in the town hired Australian lawyers and arranged funding through Mitsui & Co of Sydney. After the cases, which the Commonwealth Government lost, Peter obtained a position in the Tokyo Trading Company in Japan. Although the Japanese congratulated him for his win, he was not well received by his work mates. He was also jailed in Japan, like other Europeans at the time, and interrogated and suspected of being a spy. Further, his position in this Japanese trading company, a subsidiary of the South Seas Development Company involved in Japan's southward expansion, also aroused suspicion in Australia. Longfield Lloyd, of the Australian Legation in Japan, spoke to Peter at the Australian office in Tokyo. Peter was disturbed that his firm was seeking to involve him in espionage. Lloyd reported that Peter appeared to be a 'very miserable man'.

Peter offered his services to the Australian forces through the legation in Japan, and on his return to Sydney in March 1941 he gave information to intelligence and enlisted in the Militia 16th Machine Gun. Because the army did not altogether trust him and his behaviour had become unreliable, he was kept under strict observation from the time of his arrival back in Australia. His usefulness in intelligence was recognised but the Militia felt by September 1941 that he was too difficult to control to serve as an agent. In January 1942 Northern Command remarked that some of Peter's previous reports about Japan's intentions had turned out to be fairly accurate. He was requested by the Allied Translator Interpreter Section and worked for them during the war. However, Peter's misery increased through the war years. His wife divorced him in 1946 and successfully sued a newspaper for inaccurately reporting that her husband was Japanese.

Conclusion

These families demonstrate that there is no single concept that describes adequately the identity of Japanese in Australia. If we are to develop methods and a language for the development and recognition of Japanese identity in Australia, then we need to consider the sense of self-identity of individuals. The individuals above lived in different spaces and received differing degrees of recognition of their self-identity at different stages of their lives.

Jiro was comfortable in the space he defined for himself. His was not a hyphenated or hybrid identity. He could not be said to dwell uncomfortably in a borderland. He is what would be called today a truly bi-cultural person. Until 1915 he experienced acceptance for his firm self-identity as a Japanese-born naturalised British subject. The circumstances of history resulted in challenges to the space he wished to occupy. His business competition threatened white pearlers three years after restrictive laws were passed against 'coloured' businessmen in Western Australia. His fighting spirit, evident in the struggle to regain his voting rights and expand his business at a time of Japan's southward advance, although respected, was resented. The major issue for authorities was not so much race but who was in charge, who developed policy.

John Iwamatsu Nakashiba, in contrast, never naturalised. He was perceived as having a Japanese identity but being a 'good citizen'. He did not compete with Australians, but complemented white business. He broke regulations when it suited him and for this he commanded a degree of respect from white traders and opprobrium from officials. John kept his real allegiance secret. Whites in Darwin were certain he spied for Japan. Japanese colleagues discovered he was spying for Australia. Although he was culturally more Japanese than European, in the end it was his allegiance to Australia, despite his lack of naturalisation, that was recognised and which assisted his family in wartime. He does not fit any of the theoretical models but perhaps it can be said that his 'number two home' gradually became 'number one' by 1941.

Peter failed to achieve a workable self-identity. He approximates Hall's identity formulated through a suturing of perceptions. Born white, illegitimate and raised by Japanese, even a name change did not establish him firmly in a white community that did not trust 'white Japanese' who moved so easily between two cultures. The Japanese did not trust him either. As a result, others ascribed to Peter the identity they were most comfortable with and this varied over time. His case demonstrates the importance of an individual's cultural behaviour in the recognition of identity and suggests that race is far more than skin colour.

White people reached a comfortable position about the identity and trustworthiness of individual Japanese when they knew them and when that person had a firm sense of self. At this point stereotypes were challenged. Officials were inclined to respect naturalisation as a marker of belonging but reacted adversely when naturalised non-whites demanded their rights. The attitude of the Department of Home Affairs was that rights were there to be bestowed at the government's bidding or even rescinded. They did not like challenges to regulations, particularly from a non-white naturalised person. Jiro was correct that he did not necessarily have the same rights as others in all circumstances. This reveals perhaps more about Australia's whiteness than it does about Japanese identity, but it also provides supporting evidence for Curthoys's position that white Australia did not address its racial others in a united or coherent discourse but in separate registers at different times.

In research into Japanese identity, it is important to look beyond state boundaries in studying individual stories and family histories. These families originally settled in Queensland and Western Australia and lived in Darwin in the 1930s, all in areas along the northern sea lanes of Australia, which connected them to Asia and the Pacific. Political boundaries partition the natural geographic areas which affect people's lives and identities. As researchers, we need to look beyond the limitations of traditionally defined spaces and consider the influences of connections into the wider diaspora to which immigrants are subjected.

Notes

1. Acknowledgment: the author acknowledges the support of the Northern Territory History Award scheme for funding for this research.

    The introduction in Walker (1999) also argues for a more nuanced approach.

2. The names in this section are as they appear in NAA files. Real names are used for deceased family members. Initials are used for family members who may still be alive.

3. Information about this family can be found in NAA: PP302/1, WA17964, Battye Library MN1216, ACC 3700A, and NAA: A712/1, 1899/K6473.

4. Information for this section is found in NAA: A433/1, 1941/2/2244; NAA: A7359/101, 9; NAA: A1379/1, EPJ1396; NAA: F1 1936/271; NAA: F1 1938/402; NAA: MP1103/2; Battye Library MN 1216, ACC 1019A/1-52 and ACC2628A/1-12.

5. All quotes in this section are found in NAA: A433/1, 1941/2/2244.

6. Information relevant to this section can be found in NAA: A406/62, E1945/1, part 1; NAA: A10078/1, 1923/10.

7. Information relevant to this section can be found in NAA: A1/15, 1921/24449; NAA: A1/15, 1911/16228; NAA: A367/1, C68609; NAA: A367, C65778; NAA: BP242/1, Q24264; NAA: MP729/6, 63/401/518.

8. Information relevant to this section can be found in NAA: BP242/1, Q24264.

7 The Hirodo story: a three generational family case study of bi-cultural living

Graham Eccles

Shigeyoshi Hirodo, a 24-year-old commerce graduate, set foot on Australian soil at Sydney's Circular Quay for the first time early in 1908. He had arrived in the bustling harbour city to begin a two-year wool-classing course at Sydney Technical College in Oxford Street. It was a trail-blazing enrolment; no Japanese had previously sat the course. It changed the lives of three generations of the Hirodo family and was to result in unexpected influences on official responses to international events.

For the rest of his days, the greater part of Hirodo's life and career would encompass two countries. His involvement in the wool trade, particularly after he became managing director of a major Japanese wool-buying firm, benefited both Australia and Japan at trade and political levels. He raised his family of six children in both countries and they became bi-cultural in an era when such a concept had not been articulated. However, Hirodo's influence as one individual is also an example of situations in which Cinthia Enloe argues that 'the international is personal' (Mackie & Jones 2001:4). As head of his firm's Australian operations, he was in a position of sufficient power by the 1930s to influence bilateral trade negotiations between the two countries. His son, in the 1950s and 1960s, was also to find himself unexpectedly part of major bilateral negotiations.

This chapter examines the Hirodo family's experience of living across a continuum involving two nation states. It examines individual impacts on international trade, as well as the influence of global events on a significant trading family. It also contributes to a growing number of case studies that explore positive experiences of Japanese families who lived and worked in Australia and Japan in the 20th century during the white Australia era. It provides one of the few available personal accounts in English of the experiences of war and occupation in Japan of Japanese children born in Australia.[1] As a case study of a trading family, its intention is demonstrative rather than theoretical. The encounters of the participants are often against the grain of what might be expected given the policies and attitudes prevalent at the time. The family members do not fit defined paradigms or dwell in borderlands. Shigeyoshi Hirodo was never legally Australian but had recognised de facto resident status under the immigration changes of 1904, which permitted merchants to enter the country. Yet despite his seemingly precarious situation in the face of the white Australia policy, Hirodo and, later, his Australian-born son, Kenji, exerted influence in the affairs of two nations.

Only a small number of studies of trading families who lived in Australia exist. The field is still exploratory. Jones (2002), in her study of Western Australian Japanese, and Nagata's (1996) work on Queensland Japanese include some merchant families. Oliver's work on the Japanese trading company network provides further stories (Oliver 2001:17). This case study of the Hirodo family aims to add to this small but growing body of literature.

Early encounters with white Australia

Shigeyoshi, who came from the village of Hirodo, once steeped in samurai tradition, had anticipated putting his commerce degree to work in Japan. With this aim in mind, he was surprised to receive contrary advice from Japan's then Minister for Education, Mr Kikuchi, whom he had approached for career advice. Because of Japan's future wool needs, he was advised to go to Australia and learn all he could about the versatile fibre. The minister's desire for young men to go abroad to study was also part of a growing trend to find out more about modern overseas practices and to use the research to develop industries, especially in primary resources. Shigeyoshi could hardly reject such words of wisdom from so important a figure (Hirodo 25.3.2004).

Financed by his father, a brewer of sake and soy sauces in Hirodo, he arrived in Sydney determined to complete the wool-classing course in one year. Then he would launch his own trading company in competition with the growing number of Japanese-owned firms opening in Sydney. This ambition was a reasonable one. As Oliver has demonstrated, the Japanese trading company network was at a stage of expansion in the years leading up to the First World War. Two other immigrants, Hideo Kuwahata and Hirokichi Nakamura, had arrived in Sydney to open their own trading companies. From 1888 Kuwahata became the first and largest Japanese ships' providore, in addition to engaging in the importation of exotic Japanese garden plants and general fancy goods, which he sold in his shop near today's Circular Quay. He helped many young Japanese men find work in Sydney. Hirokichi Nakamura arrived with his abacus and no English in 1897 but, just before Hirodo arrived, he had his own flourishing import–export business. These young men grew up in a Japan that had developed a culture of self-reliance and initiative (Samuel Smythe's book *Self help* was a best seller in Japan (Oliver 2006)). In this climate of personal initiative, Sydney presented a well-established business climate for Japanese firms, especially after the opening of the direct shipping link with Japan in 1896.

By the time Shigeyoshi was entering his training, large firms from Japan had also taken advantage of opportunities becoming available for international trade. For example, F Kanematsu (Australia) Ltd had opened its doors in 1890. Its owner had established Nichigō Bōeki Kanematsu Shōten in Kobe after three years of intensive research into the possibilities for trade with Australia. His assistant Toranosuke Kitamura was to become the managing director.[2] In 1890 the Sydney branch shipped the first direct consignment of wool by a Japanese firm from Sydney to Japan. The branch also imported various kinds of Japanese goods from porcelain to bamboo curtains. By 1901 the large family *zaibatsu* firm of Mitsui & Co, which had been established in the 1870s in Japan and expanded to Shanghai, London and New York, also opened in Sydney to trade in wool, timber, silk and wheat (Oliver 2001:17–19).

This climate of individual enterprise within not only an Australia-wide network but a growing world-wide network indeed presented Hirodo with great opportunities for his future. It provided pathways across the Pacific and expanded the space merchants and their families could expect to inhabit over a working lifetime of travel through an international network beyond the narrow confines of any national identification.

This wide area of endeavour in which the Japanese firms were trading assisted Shigeyoshi to gain his degree in wool-classing in Sydney. He needed work experience on a sheep station, which was no problem for his fellow students, all of whom were white. But for a young man of Asian appearance it was an obstacle that the college had not previously encountered. Despite overtures to a number of property owners, the college could not place him. Mindful of the prevailing white Australia sentiment in the bush and the violent clashes a decade earlier with the pioneering shearers' union, station owners wanted no trouble in their shearing sheds.

Shigeyoshi, in desperation, sought help within the Japanese trading network in Sydney and approached Toranosuke Kitamura, the manager of Kanematsu. In his approach to Kitamura, two things worked in Shigeyoshi's favour—he once had been offered a job with Kanematsu in Kobe and, like himself, Kitamura had graduated from Tokyo Commercial College. Having established his firm as a leading buyer of Australian wool, Kitamura's contacts in the industry were impressive. To assist Shigeyoshi, he enlisted the support of Henry Luke White, who, with his three brothers, ran Belltrees, a vast, 220,000-acre sheep run in the Upper Hunter region of New South Wales (Hirodo 2.4.2004).

The White family did not hesitate to accept Shigeyoshi for work experience. The Whites, like a growing number of Australian sheep farmers, had strong connections to Japan, having exported hundreds of sheep to that country, as well as a number of thoroughbred mares. (Years later, Shigeyoshi would tell his family that 'I owed my career to Mr Kitamura and Henry Luke White'.) Several months later he graduated from college with his diploma, achieved in just one year, as he had set himself, a remarkable feat for a young foreigner in a strange land (White 1981:16, 26, 56; Oliver 2001; Belltrees Archive, White).[3]

The goal of starting his own trading company, as other young Japanese in Sydney had managed to do, became impossible when his father was unable to provide the necessary finance due to business difficulties brought on by an economic downturn in Japan. With his own finances running low, he again turned to Kanematsu for help. He obtained employment as a clerk in the firm's wool department. Although he could not foresee it, that position would be the start of almost a century of involvement in the Australian wool industry by Shigeyoshi, his son and grandson.

Shigeyoshi adapted quickly to the office routine and the daily activities on the show floor, where hundreds of bales of wool were displayed for the buyers to sample. It was here that his fellow Australian and international colleagues nicknamed him 'Sam' to avoid problems with pronouncing Shigeyoshi. Thereafter he always referred to himself as Sam Hirodo.

Sam's experience of settling in Sydney and his involvement with both the Australian and Japanese communities did not end his direct involvement with Japan nor confine him to Australia. He had been a clerk at Kanematsu barely two years when he was asked to be the Australian correspondent for the Japanese newspaper *Mainichi shinbun*, of which Fusajiro Kanematsu had once been owner and editor. Further, by the time war broke out in 1914 and Sam Hirodo had achieved the status of wool buyer, he was entrusted with vital overseas business trips to purchase wool. The British government acquired all the Commonwealth's merino and crossbred fleece in 1916, which meant that Australia's wool auctions were suspended for the remainder of the war and that Japan could not purchase the Australian wool it required.

With stockpiles running low, Japanese mill owners faced imminent closure unless wool could be found. Sam was dispatched on board a British cruiser to South Africa, the first of three visits to that country, where he bought sufficient supplies to keep the mills viable. That first passage aboard a warship was obtained through top-level diplomatic activity between Japan and a sympathetic British government. It was also an early indication of Hirodo's status and value to his government. As wool sales did not resume in Australia until 1920, he also went to South America to supplement the South African purchases (Hirodo 2.4.2004).[4]

Family life in white Australia

Sam's circumstances, along with those of his firm, had changed by 1923 when he finally returned to Australia as chief wool buyer for Kanematsu. By the 1920s, Kanematsu was among the top four Japanese trading companies in Australia and its employees were benefiting handsomely. In 1907 Fusajiro Kanematsu had made the company a joint stock venture between himself and his handful of subordinates. Kitamura built on this by gifting shares to each employee who had been with the company for three or more years, an enlightened approach for the times. By the time Sam returned, the company had just been floated as a separate entity in Australia and registered as a company in New South Wales (Purcell 1980:208, 241–3). As chief wool buyer, Sam became largely responsible for the firm's wool trading, which for the year ending 1923 amounted to 60,288 bales with a value of £1.16 million.

Sam had married in accordance with the tradition of arranged marriages while in Japan. His seniority in the firm meant that his wife was of similar social status. Chiyo Kawai was the eldest daughter of a bureaucrat in the Ministry of Transport. Sam brought her and their first-born child, a son, Michio, with him. Merchants of reputable Japanese firms with sufficient seniority had no difficulty bringing wives and children to Australia under the exemptions granted by the Commonwealth. The family settled in a house in the fashionable suburb of Cremorne, overlooking Mosman Bay and The Heads beyond. The North Shore suburb and adjoining Mosman were popular with many of the more than 319 Japanese families living in Sydney at this time (Oliver 2001:2). It was here that the Hirodo family expanded considerably. Chiyo gave birth to two daughters, Shizue and Kameko, and another son, Kenji. Two more daughters, Yoshie and Naoe, followed.

All six children attended local schools. Michio was enrolled at Sydney Church of England Grammar School (Shore), the older girls at Loreto Catholic School in nearby Kirribilli and the youngest children at the local state-run Mosman Primary School. As a consequence, all the Hirodo children grew up to speak English fluently. Indeed, they could utter only a few Japanese words or phrases. Kenji would recall later that their childhood in Sydney had been a delightful experience.

> The Japanese community between the wars was considered a part of the social fabric of Sydney and as a result we played with the neighborhood kids after school and at weekends without detecting the slightest hint of racism (Hirodo 21.7.2005).

Pressures of work meant their father rarely interacted with them apart from weekends. Monday to Friday, he would catch the first ferry to Circular Quay before they had risen and was rarely home at night before they were back in their beds.

Managing director of Kanematsu

During the 1930s, Sam Hirodo achieved a status that was unusual for a Japanese resident of white Australia. He was in a position of power, which enabled him to play a key role in bilateral relations. The respect that he had gained from many Australian business leaders and politicians through his work at Kanematsu facilitated the significant contributions he made to trade negotiations before the Second World War. Sam had been appointed a director of Kanematsu prior to Kitamura's death in 1930. Now, as managing director, his workload became even greater as he took charge of a company that had become the world's biggest buyer of wool for a nation that, by the end of the 1920s, was the biggest wool consumer. By 1931–32 Kanematsu's sales turnover for all goods was second only to that of its rival Mitsui & Co of Sydney, reaching £3 million in that financial year. By 1936 Kanematsu's sales of wool had soared to 245,538 bales valued at £4.14 million (Purcell 1980:252). As head of such an influential company, Sam's stature in the industry and the local Japanese community grew enormously. He also was quite prepared to speak strongly, when he felt it necessary, on behalf of Japan and for the need to improve bilateral relations.

On his return from a business trip to Japan in 1931, he was most forthright when he informed a reporter from the *Brisbane Telegraph* that, unless Australia was prepared to execute a trade treaty with Japan, Japan would reluctantly be compelled to seek other fields for its wool requirements. He was quoted as saying that the balance of trade between the two countries was four times in favour of Australia.

> No one will dispute that Japan is the backbone of the Australian wool sales and when Japan is off the market a slump in wool prices takes place which is a serious thing for the Australian wool growers. Japan desires Australia to execute immediately a trade treaty, with a revision of the tariff so that Japan could secure a portion of Australian trade. The Japanese manufacturers are anxious to secure a reasonable volume of trade so that the unfavourable balance could be reduced to some extent. Japan does not want to flood the Australian market, but she certainly wants fair treatment seeing she is the backbone of the wool industry in Australia (Mese 1968).

In 1934 Sam was called back to Japan for talks with both his firm and the government, which wanted his evaluation of the vast flocks of sheep that had been established on stations in the newly acquired territory of Manchukuo, the occupied former Chinese province of Manchuria. He was apart from his

Sam Hirodo with a thoroughbred horse bought by Kanematsu on behalf of the Japanese government in 1934. Photo courtesy of the Hirodo family.

family for almost six months and, soon after his return, found himself a key player in the resolution of the damaging trade diversion dispute between Australia and Japan.

The dispute flared while both governments were discussing the creation of a Treaty of Friendship, Commerce and Navigation. Australia sought to divert some of its trade away from Japan in favour of a protesting British government concerned at the loss of trade to Japan, which had occurred during the 1930s. A sticking point in the negotiations between Australia and Japan was the mutual requests for tariff reductions on items vital to each nation's trade. To the dismay of the Japanese, the Australian government delivered an ultimatum on 20 February 1936—slash imports of cotton and rayon piece goods to 'satisfactory levels' or duties would be levied to achieve that effect.

Japan retaliated swiftly, ordering Japanese buyers to boycott the Australian wool sales while applying an import licensing system and a massive surtax on Australian exports to Japan. This dispute has been written about by others, thus I will concentrate on Sam's role in the background negotiations for a settlement through his role within the Japanese Chamber of Commerce in Sydney (Sissons 1975; Tsokhas 1989).

Sam Hirodo, his wife, Chiyoko, and friend Hatsue Nagahata, with the Hirodo children, Michio, Shizue, Kamiko, Naoe, Kenji and Yoshie, in the garden of the family's home in the Sydney suburb of Mosman. Photo courtesy of the Hirodo family.

As the two governments sought to find a face-saving resolution to the dispute, Sam Hirodo, as chairman of the Japanese Chamber of Commerce in Sydney, found himself in backroom discussions to break the impasse. Over the next three months he became, arguably, the key figure in resolving the dispute. Sam cabled his head office in Kobe that 'if Japan undertook to admit 500,000 bales of wool annually the Australian graziers and Members of Parliament would secure a quota for Japanese textiles of 150 million square yards [of cotton and rayon cloth]' (Sissons 1975:9).

Sam's plan was the result of discussions with the Director of the Council for Scientific and Industrial Research's Animal Health Laboratory in Sydney, Dr Ian Clunies-Ross. The two men had become acquainted through membership of the Japan–Australia Society, which was:

> the premier organisation in the promotion of Japan-mindedness…whose Australian members represented the leaders of pastoral, finance, retail, brewing, mining and shipping capital. While the expansion of trade was uppermost in the Japan-mindedness of most of the society's Australian members, Japanese intelligence saw these leading Sydney business figures as 'potential co-operators in an expanding Japanese empire. Japanese intelligence (or consular staff)

cultivated these business leaders and provided business deals and trips to Japan. Throughout the 1930s the Japan-mindedness of a dominant strata of Sydney's business world deepened (Cottle 2001:9).

The Hirodo–Clunies-Ross friendship had led Sam to provide valuable assistance for the scientist's trip to Asia to investigate whether sheep populations in North China, Mongolia, Manchuria and Korea threatened the Australian wool industry. It was over dinner many months later that Sam told Clunies-Ross about his idea for a solution to the dispute. Impressed, the scientist contacted Charles Hawker, a prominent government backbencher who had accompanied him on the Asia trip. Over the next few weeks, Sam became the 'middle man', passing information and advice to Japan through the Japanese Consul General, Kuramatsu Murai, and to the Australian government through Clunies-Ross via Hawker.

According to Sissons, Sam at one stage must have been a very busy man with the number of messages passing through him. By 4 December, with the Japanese woollen mills desperately needing their buyers to re-enter the auction rooms in Australia, an agreement appeared to be within reach. But the minister in charge of the treaty negotiations, Sir Henry Gullett, who wanted Japan to take 514,000 bales while accepting only 122.5 million square yards of textiles, was not impressed with the suggested agreement.

> On the 6th, Clunies-Ross was writing to Hawker...Hirodo when I asked him what had happened told me that the last and final thing to impede a settlement was that having settled the quota and the duties Gullett has insisted on them agreeing to buy 500,000 bales. I do not know whether the latter was aware that they had re-opened negotiations on the understanding that a basis of approximately 125,000,000 yards against 400,000 bales would be acceptable but I feel I have been placed in a false position and that Japanese have grounds for being aggrieved...Hirodo has now cabled proposals for disguising the acceptance of 500,000 bales against 122 million yards, namely that for the last six months of this selling season they should take the full 500,000 or a total of 750,000, thus making it possible to publish in Japan a quota over the two years of about 400,000 bales...The final settlement signed on December 26 was not greatly different from what Clunies-Ross in the letter quoted above described as Hirodo's proposal (Sissons 1975:37).

Over the next two years, Sam readied himself for retirement. By now a wealthy man and nearing the mandatory retirement age of 55, he yearned to buy a sheep property in New South Wales where he would be content to see out the rest of his life. But first he wanted to take his young family back to Japan, not only to familiarise them with their cultural roots but also to learn to speak and write Japanese. It proved a fateful move.

Encounters in war-torn and occupied Japan

The move to Japan and the onset of war affected the Hirodo family in different ways from those of other Japanese who had not resided in Australia or been born there. It was particularly exacting for the genuinely Australian Hirodo children. Their wartime encounters with both Japanese authorities and later Australian occupational forces demonstrates the unusual and almost impossible-to-define space and identity that their lived experience placed them in.

The family left Brisbane by sea on 3 January 1938 and on arrival in Japan the children were amazed to witness several hundred people gathered on the wharf to greet their father, who clearly had achieved a level of importance at home that was unknown to his family. He took his wife and children back to his ancestral village and stayed long enough to see the children enrolled at school before returning to Sydney to install his successor and attend a number of farewell functions in his honour.

The measure of respect Sam had attained during his work in Australia is evident in the honours accorded to him not only at the official functions but also in the media coverage of his departure for Japan. At the final function, held at Aarons Exchange Hotel, representatives from all sections of the wool industry gathered to farewell him. He was presented with an inkstand of Australian timbers decorated with a kangaroo and a gold plate recording that the gift was 'a token of regard from friends in the wool trade'.

In an article about the occasion published in *Country Life* on 29 July 1938, the chairman of the New South Wales and Queensland Woolbuyers Association, DAS Campbell, stated that Sam's personality was one of character and ability, and the trade had been built up by men of his quality and could only be maintained by those who lived up to the highest traditions of the trade, 'as Mr Hirodo had done'. He added that his loss would be a serious one, because the trade could not afford to lose men of his calibre, but his influence would remain after he had gone.

Three weeks later, after Sam left Australia, the *Monthly Trade and Shipping Review* wrote:

> The retirement of Mr Shigeyoshi Hirodo, familiarly known as 'Sam', brought to a close a very interesting and illuminating career, and his presence will be greatly missed by not only those in wool and shipping circles, but all those who knew him. He was a man of outstanding character and ability, with a charming personality and generous nature...His career was a very brilliant one, and his name will go down as one of those great personalities who have contributed much toward the building up of the great volume of trade between Australia and the East (Mese 1968).

Back in Japan, Sam set about ensuring his family's financial security for the years ahead. He bought three vast tracts of land, two of them covering 100,000 hectares bordering airfields. The other purchase close to the new family home about 50 kilometres from the centre of Tokyo comprised about 100 hectares of paddy field land with a small mountain in the middle. Here he built and rented what his family recalls were 60 houses that provided a regular income stream. He was even able to afford to pay for the children of relatives to attend private schools. He felt confident his family would be comfortable for the rest of their lives. But a succession of world events, with Japan's invasion of China, the outbreak of war in Europe and Japan's attack on the United States at Pearl Harbor, soon shattered the family's belief in its future security.

Japan's entry into the Second World War meant that many Japanese families, who had not wanted to leave Australia before war was officially declared, found themselves interned for the duration of the conflict. They forfeited homes, other possessions and even their bank accounts under National Security (Enemy Property) Regulations. Sam Hirodo had left behind a credit balance of £373 15s 10d on the books of F Kanematsu (Australia) Ltd, which he would never be able to reclaim (NAA: A1379/1, EPJ122; Nagata 1996).

As the Japanese forces pushed southwards, daily life in Tokyo was different from anything the Hirodo children had experienced previously. At times their common English tongue threatened to land them in trouble with the authorities. Kenji, by now 15 years old, was shocked when he and his Japanese–Australian school friends found themselves in strife for conversing in English during a regular train ride to school.

> '…Because some of us had either been born abroad or raised from a young age outside Japan, we did not speak Japanese well and so we naturally talked to each other in English,' Kenji recalled. 'Ten of us had grown up in either Sydney or Melbourne because our fathers had been diplomats or in the trading companies. We had no idea we were drawing attention to ourselves until the day a swarthy official-looking fellow walked up and warned us against speaking in the enemy's tongue. 'Cut it out or I'll arrest you!' he barked. Not knowing much Japanese at that stage to converse comfortably in the language, we thereafter travelled together hardly saying a word (Hirodo 10.4.2004).

Still, speaking English fluently had its advantages. According to Kenji, the authorities gave the Japanese people only limited information about the war's progress. However, the family was broadly aware of developments in the Pacific. They possessed an illegal medium-wave radio capable of receiving many United States broadcasts, particularly at night when the air was still and cool. While local broadcasts spoke about glorious Japanese victories at Guadalcanal and in the Coral Sea, the family knew differently.

As the war turned sharply against Japan, life in Tokyo became more perilous each day. American B29s pounded the city with bombs and, according to Kenji, the night sky would be lit so brightly by the explosions 'that you could read a book quite easily'. So hazardous had life become that Sam moved his family back to Hirodo village. They were far away when the American Air Force launched its most devastating attack on Tokyo on 9–10 March 1945. For three hours, 334 low-flying aircraft dropped 1667 tons of napalm and oil bombs, resulting in a firestorm of terrifying proportions, which consumed some 16 square miles of the city's built up area. An estimated 80,000 to 100,000 citizens died, some 41,000 were injured and almost one million rendered homeless (Weinberg 1994:869–71).

Although much of the city was laid to waste, Japan remained firm until early August, when American President Harry S Truman gave permission for atom bombs to be dropped on Hiroshima and Nagasaki. Japan surrendered five days later. For the next 12 months, as the Allied Occupation Forces took control under the direction of American General Douglas MacArthur, the Hirodos remained in the country before returning to Tokyo.

> Our house was left untouched by the firestorm but three of Dad's rental homes were not so fortunate. Still, he was grateful that most of his property remained untouched by the terrible scorched earth destruction we could see in the distance (Hirodo 2.4.2004).

However, Sam's relief was short-lived. As part of a plan to democratise Japan and wipe out centuries of rural serfdom, the Allied Council for Japan introduced a sweeping land reform program that stripped the big landholders of their properties, limiting them to just over 12 acres each. Sam's vast holdings evaporated overnight and, along with them, the wealth he had accumulated so carefully.[5] Dashed, too, were his dreams of eventually returning to Australia to buy a sheep station (Hirodo 2004:T2; Davies 2001:296–7; Dower 1999:76, 82, 244, 251, 352).

The three younger children returned to school, while the two older girls married young men from Kobe. To supplement their husbands' meagre incomes, both women worked on the switchboard at the British Embassy. Their older sibling, Michio, who had been nicknamed 'Midge' by classmates at Shore, his exclusive public school in Sydney, obtained a job as a translator at the Canadian Embassy, a position he retained until retirement. During his final year at Seikei College, Kenji regularly wagged school to act as an interpreter for the Australian contingent, a position he obtained largely by accident. He met a young corporal in the street one day who was taken aback by Kenji's ability to speak English with an Australian accent. They met frequently and the young soldier was often invited to the Hirodo home. Not surprisingly, he mentioned Kenji's dual language skills and background to more senior officers, who inquired if he would accept a translator's job. Kenji was assigned to Camp Commandant Major James Hoare who, among other tasks, 'acquired' houses of imposing quality for senior officers and suitable employees to staff them (Hirodo 2004–05 tape 4).

A recipient of one of the virtual mansions was Colonel Eric Longfield-Lloyd, who had been appointed Australia's first trade commissioner to Japan in 1935. He returned to Japan during the Occupation as political advisor to William McMahon Ball, a British Commonwealth member on the Allied Council. Kenji recalled:

> I mentioned Longfield-Lloyd's name to Dad who was pleasantly surprised as they had been friends back in Sydney. As a result, Mum and Dad met up with him on a number of occasions before he returned home (Hirodo 2004–05 tape 4).

It was during this period that the Hirodo children's previous encounters with Western culture in Australia led them to a religious conversion that ultimately found the entire family embracing Catholicism. All four girls had become strongly attracted to the Christian religion through their education at Sacred Heart Convent and were determined to join the Roman Catholic Church in spite of their father's strong opposition. One daughter, Yoshie (later called Christine), made her feelings clear by taking a job alongside an American air force chaplain who became a frequent weekend visitor to the Hirodo house. Sam's youngest daughter, Naoe (Theresa), was so devout that eventually she entered the Sacred Heart Order. One Sunday the chaplain, Father Wilders, baptised all six children as Catholics. To their delight, Sam agreed to convert as well, but only after the death of his childhood friend, a Buddhist priest in Hirodo. As a nun, Theresa rose through the ranks of Sacred Heart to become Mother Superior, at one stage teaching English to the present Empress, Michiko.

With his rental income severely reduced, Sam returned to the workforce, accepting a position in a small textile firm, Suita Shoji, whose owner had ambitions to become a major player in the processing of wool. Sam established a wool-buying department for the firm and soon afterwards convinced his youngest son, who also had obtained a commerce degree, to follow him into the industry.

Kenji Hirodo: post-war encounters—a question of citizenship

In 1951 Kenji Hirodo retraced his father's experience of arriving at Circular Quay in Sydney by ship. Possibly he was the first Japanese to be admitted on an Australian passport after the end of hostilities. He immediately enrolled in the wool-classing course at Sydney Technical College, as his father had done 43 years earlier.

Planning a return to Australia required a resolution of the question of Kenji's actual legal position in regard to his identity and citizenship. He was born in Australia, but wartime and post-war changes to immigration law altered the position of Japanese in Australia, including Australian-born children. Their legal status was not clear-cut. However, according to Kenji, the assistance of members of the Australian Occupation Forces eased the process. Obtaining the necessary documentation posed few problems for him, as he had inquired about his citizenship status while working at Australian headquarters in Tokyo. On the advice of the commander-in-chief of the Australian arm of the British Commonwealth Occupational Forces, Lieutenant General Horace 'Red Robbie' Robertson, Kenji had his name struck off a Japanese family register that had been completed and filed in Hirodo village by his father on their return to Japan. Officially, he was no longer a Japanese citizen. Before leaving Japan, Kenji's bona fides as an Australian was confirmed by Australian consular official Ted Weatherstone, who believes Kenji may well have been the first Australian-born Japanese to be allowed to re-enter the country.

> If not, he certainly would have been among the earliest. Under the 1948 Citizenship Act, I issued a number of visas to Japanese during the Occupation but the Act would not have had a great deal to do with Kenji's desire to return to Australia. He would have had an entitlement anyway (Weatherstone 2004).

Proving one's self to be a citizen of the Commonwealth while residing in occupied Japan had other benefits. Once their birthright was established, Australian-born Japanese could shop at Tokyo's famous food emporium, Meiji-ya, which had been allowed to reopen as the city's ration centre. In a country where millions of people struggled to stave off starvation, accessibility to the centre was a godsend.

Once back in the country of his birth, Kenji was awarded his wool-classing diploma after completing the two-year course in just 12 months, exactly as his father had done in 1908. Almost immediately he joined the Bradford-based firm Biggin and Ayrton, a job arranged by Sam, who was buying wool through the firm on behalf of his new employer. For a number of years after the end of the Occupation, both Japanese and German trading companies were prohibited from directly participating in Australia's wool auction rooms, reluctantly buying their wool through local agents. Even then, the Japanese mill owners had such specific requirements that their buyers needed to visit Australia to ensure the agents met the orders correctly. Much to Kenji's delight, Sam Hirodo unexpectedly found himself back on Australian soil along with a number of his old pre-war colleagues from Kanematsu's rival trading companies.

However, it was a vastly different environment to the one they had previously encountered. Anti-Japanese sentiment was rife throughout the country and finding temporary lodgings was difficult. Sam and others found refuge with a Mrs Youdale, a widow who ran a five-bedroom boarding house in Edgecliff, close to the city. Because her tenants were polite, clean and paid on time, Mrs Youdale was happy to rent her rooms exclusively to visiting Japanese businessmen. What some of her neighbours thought of her actions can only be imagined (Hirodo 2004 tape 2).

Although he spoke perfect English with an Australian accent and, indeed, considered himself Australian, Kenji could not hide the colour of his skin and encountered his share of confrontations with the local populace. He recalls drinking after work one evening in a Kings Cross bar with fellow employees from Biggin and Ayrton when a returned serviceman demanded to know why he was in the country. The crowded bar fell silent. Physically, Kenji was no match for the threatening stranger but he held his ground and explained his background in fluent English. Surprised, the drinker shook hands and walked away. Some of the patrons quietly applauded.

By the end of the record 1956–57 wool season, Kenji Hirodo was a happily married man with two young children. Several years earlier, Sam had determined his son should take a wife as he had done in the time-honoured way of an arranged marriage—even though the family had converted to Catholicism. He returned to Japan to wed Masako Kake, who took the name of Christina. After their honeymoon, Kenji brought his bride to Sydney and resumed his career as a wool buyer.

Around the time of the 1956 Olympic Games in Melbourne, father and son found themselves working for the same company when Sam's firm was taken over by Itoman, a medium-sized textile trader, which signed a joint venture agreement with Biggin and Ayrton.

Shortly afterwards, the landmark Australia–Japan Agreement on Commerce was signed in the face of strong criticism from a still unforgiving Australian community. By 1960 Australia had agreed to the conditional export of iron ore. However, an inability to buy the vast quantities of ore needed for massive expansion of its industries frustrated Japan to the point that Shigeo Nagano, president of the Fuji Steel Company, led a goodwill mission to Australia on behalf of the Tokyo Chamber of Commerce (Terada 2001). It was probably the most powerful and influential group of Japanese business leaders to have visited Australia—the aim being to persuade the government to re-negotiate the Commerce Treaty and allow Japan to buy greater quantities of iron ore.

It was at this point that Kenji found himself involved in bilateral negotiations, as his father had before him. Nagano, a consummate diplomat, who often described himself as the 'steel man', left nothing to chance and, as a result, Kenji Hirodo was seconded to the delegation. Nagano felt he needed someone on his team who could ensure cultural and language differences would not lead to misinterpretation by the Australians. He wanted someone by his side who understood the Australian manner of speech and customs intimately. Inquiries through the Australian Ambassador in Tokyo led to a telephone call to the president of Itoman in Osaka and a further call to Kenji in Sydney. He was on the team. To avoid any embarrassing gaffes and so he could deliver speeches in an Australian way, Nagano insisted Kenji vet and read out loud to him every speech that Nagano had to deliver.

By the time the mission ended, Kenji felt he had played a small but valuable part in the often-secretive discussions with Australia's politicians and business elite. The delegation returned to Japan confident that its quiet diplomacy would bear fruit. Two years later the treaty was re-negotiated and the restriction on iron ore exports eased substantially. The economies of both nations benefited massively in the years ahead by this change of heart.

Not long afterwards, Kenji was approached again to assist with Japan's trade expansion—this time by using his contacts in the wool industry to help raise the image of vehicle manufacturer Toyota in rural New South Wales. The company's main focus in Australia at that time was selling its LandCruiser four-wheel drive workhorse but, in the face of stiff competition from the more popular Land Rover and Willys Jeep vehicles, sales were not encouraging.

> Japan's Deputy Consul-General in Sydney, Mr Tachibana, called me up and outlined a strategy that would involve me addressing Rotary meetings in country towns and offering growers advice on wool quality and how to prepare their clips to obtain the high prices being offered by the Japanese buyers in Sydney. I would also offer to visit their properties, but I was not to breathe a word about the LandCruiser. Only if they accepted my advice and it proved profitable would I ask them to return the favour and buy Toyota. It proved to be a very successful tactic (Hirodo 16.5.2005).

By June 1964 there was almost 4000 Toyota commercial vehicles in Australia, half of them LandCruisers (Davis 1999:55). By the end of the 20th century, Toyota had cemented its place alongside Holden Ltd and the Ford Motor Company of Australia Ltd as makers of the nation's most popular motor vehicles.

Third generational change in a bilateral environment

When Sam died from cancer in the late 1960s, Kenji was left to carry on the much-respected Hirodo name in the wool industry. But he would now do it from Japan. Itoman appointed him to run the company's entire wool operations from its Osaka office and, by the time Kenji was 40, another promotion found him running a newly formed department called General Merchandise. This had the effect of putting his involvement with wool on hold—at least with Itoman.

Meanwhile, in Australia a revolutionary way of accurately measuring the value of raw wool through instrumentation, a process called objective measurement, sent shock waves through the wool-buying fraternity. As companies and mill owners gained confidence in the new scientific method of testing and valuing wool, the vast majority of buyers were cast aside like dag ends on a shearing shed floor. But the writing was on the wall for many of their employers, too. Some of the more famous trading houses were forced to close their offices as the mills turned to Australian agents to buy and ship their wool requirements as a way of cutting costs. Even the great spinning and weaving mills were not immune to the many changes suddenly engulfing the world of wool. The growing affluence of Japanese society meant there was no longer reliance on wool for warmth and comfort. Synthetic fibres were in abundance, homes were being built along Western lines and air-conditioning was affordable to many. Many mill owners had to turn to production of cotton goods to stay afloat.

Kenji Hirodo's company was hit hard by the changes, suffering massive losses on its textile trading that led to the closure of his department. Instead of waiting to be sacked, he started looking for a new position and eventually found himself opening an office in Japan for GH Michell & Sons, one of the world's biggest raw wool processors headquartered in Adelaide.

He negotiated employment terms that would allow him to work until he was 65 and then retire with his wife to Australia to see out the end of his days. As an Australian citizen, he knew he would have to return eventually, having been able to remain in Japan through the granting of four-yearly business visas. But well before his retirement, Kenji convinced his son, Paul, who had graduated in economics from Gakushuin University in Tokyo, to follow him and, of course, his grandfather, into the wool trade. Kenji had other plans, too—he was keen for his son to succeed him in Michell's Japan office. He suggested to the company's hierarchy that they consider training him as a wool buyer and in other aspects of the business in Australia, and then send him back to Japan as his understudy. To Kenji's delight, the company agreed. A third generation of Hirodos was thus poised to enter the wool industry. A year later, Paul Hirodo joined Michell in Adelaide. He was nearly 25, coincidentally the age his grandfather and father had been when they started their careers in wool.

By the time Paul was 28, his father had set in train plans for him to take a bride in the traditional way and Paul returned to Japan to meet a number of young ladies who might be suitable. Eventually, he married Chiyo Yoshida, the daughter of a businessman and, following their honeymoon, flew with her back to Australia. Three years later, Chiyo gave birth to a son, Jamie, in Melbourne, thereby establishing a third generation of Hirodos to have been born in Australia.

Conclusion

The Hirodo story is but one case study of a Japanese merchant family that embraced both Australia and Japan. Many more remain to be told. Given the size of the Japanese trading network that spread, as shown above, across four continents between the 1870s and the 1940s, the Hirodo family, who lived an international lifestyle across three generations spanning 100 years, belonged to a large community of merchants and traders.

The business life that dictated the family's movements across the globe followed the economic and diplomatic fluctuations of the relationship between Australia and Japan. This also meant the international situation called for the personal involvement of members of the family at key periods, such as the 1936 trade diversion dispute and the 1957 negotiations for the first trade treaty between Australia and Japan after the Second World War.

Inevitably, this international lifestyle impacted on the family's domestic circumstances. However, they managed to live an integrated life that was neither totally Australian nor Japanese in identity. Because they could shift comfortably within the geographic and cultural millieu that encompassed the trading space in which they lived, they were, like many wool families, bi-cultural in their personal lives. All three generations of the Hirodo family resided from time to time in Australia and Japan. All three male heads of the family married according to Japanese tradition but brought up and educated their children—for at least part of their young lives—in Australia.

In addition, this facility in shifting along such a continuum placed them in the position, both before globalisation and during it, to make their mark on international events rather than to simply be shaped by them. Sam Hirodo and his son, Kenji, had their fortunes and futures marked by the events of the Second World War. The family's economic circumstances were affected by both the confiscation of enemy property in Australia and the measures for the democratisation of Japan undertaken by the Supreme Command for Allied Powers in the years after the surrender of Japan. However, the personal networks they had been part of survived to assist them to recover after the Second World War. Their identities, both as well-known trading people and well-respected company family members, assisted in the reconstruction of their lives on both sides of the conflict.

The ability to continue moving along the continuum of the Australia–Japan relationship even through the difficult years of the immediate post-war era was assisted not only by their reputation but also by the general acceptance merchant families had achieved in Australia and Japan. When they returned to Japan prior to the war, the parents were able to assist their Australian-born children to adjust to an unfamiliar environment. Later, the family was able to retain acceptance with Australian people. For example, Kenji was recognised as Australian in Japan by British Commonwealth Occupational Forces personnel. He was able to overcome the prejudice of many Australians when he returned because of his prior knowledge of Australia, its values and lifestyle.

This complex identity within the family has continued in recent years. In 1991 Kenji handed the Japanese operations of GH Michell & Sons to his son and prepared once again to return to the land of his birth. Kenji and his wife had planned to retire in Sydney, where his daughter, Kathy, and another son, Stephen, were living with their children—but his involvement in the Japanese passion for golf drew him to Melbourne and its famed sandbelt golf courses. Today, Kenji Hirodo is a respected member of three golf clubs—Metropolitan, in the city's eastern suburbs, and Peninsula and The National, which are both on the Mornington Peninsula and boast five courses between them. Having played the game for over 50 years and usually *six* times a week since retiring, he estimates he has completed well over 12,000 rounds of golf—surely a feat worthy of a place in the *Guinness book of records*. However, this passion for his life in Melbourne does not preclude his responsibilities as the head of the wider Hirodo family in Japan, where his surviving siblings and many of their children live.

Kenji's son, Paul, an Australian citizen, also plans to retire in Melbourne with his wife in the not-too-distant future. His time of working for Michell in Osaka is coming to an end. It is possible Kenji will have his son for company on the fairways of Melbourne as this part of the extended Hirodo family moves along the continuum back to Australia. Through this continuing involvement, even in retirement, in the Australia–Japan relationship, Enloe's argument that the international is personal can truly be reversed for the Hirodo family.

Notes

Acknowledgment: research for this chapter was commissioned by the Hirodo family and funded by the Australia–Japan Foundation with the support of the Chancellor of Monash University, Jerry Ellis.

1. Recent publications include Jones (2002) and Mackie & Jones (2001).
2. So deep was Kitamura's attachment to Australia that when he died in Japan many years later, some of his remains were brought back to Sydney and buried in South Head Cemetery (Sono 2000:127).
3. For other examples of Australian relations with Japanese wool buyers, see NAA: SP1098/12.
4. See, for example, NAA: A433/1, 1940/2/2351.
5. Although sources on land reform record that the system of land ownership was feudal and the arrangements between tenants and owners was long-standing, Sam Hirodo's experience demonstrates that new owners could buy in quite easily, as well as lose fortunes in property as a result of the provisions of the Supreme Command for Allied Powers.

8 Ten years in a Victorian jail: the convict as the 'other'

Hideko Nakamura

In an era of globalisation, as people move freely around the world, one consequence is a significant rise in the number of foreign nationals experiencing imprisonment or detention. According to the Ministry of Foreign Affairs of Japan, 186 Japanese nationals were in foreign prisons on 1 April 2005. This figure was provided by a ministry staff member who did not have specific statistics for past years, but who admits that the number has increased dramatically over the past decade. However, the stories of these Japanese people in foreign prisons have rarely been told. Prisoners of other nationalities are in a similar, unpublicised situation, with notable exceptions such as Schapelle Corby, an Australian citizen arrested in Bali in October 2004 on a charge of possessing cannabis.

The frequent movement of people from one nation state to another, especially for the purposes of business and travel, poses challenges for justice systems. It raises issues of perceptions of the 'other' in human rights situations, especially where questions of defence in criminal procedures are involved. Whereas we are familiar with travel and tourism relationships with the 'other', closer encounters between 'self' and 'other' in bureaucratic and other internal national systems are less well-understood spaces. Further, when that engagement with the 'other' occurs within criminal investigations and court procedures, media influences social perception of the cases, and makes interrogating such encounters even more problematic.

This chapter focuses on a criminal case in which five Japanese tourists were arrested in Melbourne in June 1992 and later convicted for allegedly smuggling approximately 13 kilograms of heroin in their suitcases. It examines the media portrayal of the case, in order to illustrate how the tourists' identities shift in relation to state authority as well as public opinion. Identity, in this case, is defined as the labelling attached by society to the individual, or group of individuals. Since a prisoner has limited control over his or her own life and is labelled a convict, a prisoner is deprived of most of the role enjoyed by a free individual. Moreover, if a prisoner is a foreigner, he or she is perceived as 'the other' and tends to be devalued. Compared to the Corby case, where she is treated as one of 'us' by the Australian public and media and thus attracts considerable attention, the five Japanese were ignored by Australians. However, their stories featured repeatedly in the Japanese media from the late 1990s until the time when four of them were deported from Australia late in 2002. The Japanese media counted them as 'one of us', Japanese, just as the Australian media picture Corby as 'one of us', Australian.

'It is extremely regrettable that I couldn't clear my name while I was in prison'; 'I was humiliated' (*Asahi shinbun* 2002; Green 2002b). These words were uttered by two Japanese, formerly imprisoned in Australia, at a press conference held at Tokyo International Airport when they arrived back on Japanese soil in November 2002. Together with three Japanese men, they had been in a Victorian jail for more than ten years after their arrest in June 1992. The five Japanese had been sentenced to 15 to 20 years in jail. Four of them were deported from Australia on parole, after spending ten years and five months in prison. Three and half years later, the last person, who received a longer sentence, was repatriated in May 2006. During this period, their identities shifted from that of 'ordinary' Japanese citizens to criminals. The case is now known as 'the Melbourne Case' in Japan, so named by the Japanese lawyers of Osaka who supported the five.

The Melbourne Case was widely publicised in Japan because attorneys, in Osaka, formed a group to support the prisoners in an appeal to the United Nations Human Rights Commission in August 1998.[11] The media provided wide coverage of the prisoners' stories and, as a result, Japanese audiences now know the case well. In contrast, the Australian media did not report it, except for features in the *Age* (Green 2002a; Rule 2002). This is strikingly different from the Corby case, which has stirred up a virtual media frenzy. Yet, interestingly, Honda Chika, the only female among the former prisoners, has recently been dubbed the 'Japanese Corby in Australia' (Faine 2005; McCutcheon 2005).

Similarly, the Japanese language media in Australia, for example the monthly newspaper *Nichigo Press*, was indifferent to the case until its later stages.[22] Why was this? Was it because of some language or cultural barrier? Was prejudice at work? From the outset these differences put the five Japanese at a distinct disadvantage, and helped undermine their credibility and, ultimately, their dignity as free individuals.

The following essay explores the case from the prisoners' perspective, while at the same time drawing on court documents and media reports to demonstrate the gap between the prisoners' views and the public's perception. At issue here is not the innocence or guilt of the Japanese involved, but whether their rights were fully upheld by the Australian authorities. Were they inevitably placed at a disadvantage as alleged drug offenders? Their status as foreigners was crucial. This arguably created many opportunities for misunderstanding and misrepresentation. And it affected the public perception of their identity. In short, Australian society labelled them as 'criminal', a verdict which the Japanese concerned could not, and did not, accept.

Nor were they assisted by the Japanese community in Australia, which was initially concerned lest the case create a bad image of Japan, such as was already emerging in newspaper articles with headings such as 'Yakuza link suspected in tourist heroin haul' (Taylor 1992; Takagi 2000:168).[33] Later, once the details of the case were revealed by other sources, and supporters of the prisoners portrayed them as ordinary Japanese, the Australian Japanese community perception altered. From reviewing the evidence afforded by prisoner and expert opinion, it is clear that language and cultural differences were key factors in producing distorted public perceptions, and that unforeseeable changes of identity occurred in those who had to negotiate a long period of imprisonment.

What is the Melbourne Case?

On 15 June 1992, seven Japanese tourists, three women and four men, left the Narita International Airport for Melbourne via Kuala Lumpur, where they stayed overnight. While they were dining at the Sakura Japanese restaurant, four of their suitcases were stolen. A guide who welcomed the Japanese at the airport, aided by several Malaysian men, had placed their baggage in a van and accompanied the Japanese tourists from the airport. Upset by the theft, the Japanese hardly slept that night. Next morning fortune appeared to smile on them when a Chinese Malaysian, called 'Charlie', apologised for the incident and provided new suitcases. He explained that the original suitcases had been found; however, they were slashed and thus needed replacing. Charlie was a friend of Katsuno Yoshio, who acted as a tour leader.

The group arrived at the International Terminal at Melbourne Airport on the morning of 17 June with these new and 'heavy' suitcases. One of the tourists, Yoshio, was stopped and questioned by immigration officials because his visa had been cancelled. An immigration officer found that he possessed others' air tickets, and eventually the 'heavy' suitcases were checked by X-ray at Customs. Nearly 13 kilograms of heroin (65% purity in 142 packets) were discovered concealed in the layered lids of the suitcases.[44] From that moment the Japanese were treated as suspects and criminals, with the exception of two women whose bags were not stolen. These two were repatriated without being charged.

A Malaysian man was also arrested and tried with the Japanese at the County Court of Victoria, between February and June 1994. The man had been on the same flight from Kuala Lumpur and was suspected of acting as an overseer to the Japanese. The request from their legal representatives for separate trials was rejected because of cost and inconvenience (County Court 1994:64, 1524). Evidence submitted by the Crown consisted mainly of police interviews of the suspects, along with the testimony of nearly 100 witnesses who were called to the trial. The jury's verdict was guilty for all the suspects. It took the jury a week to finalise the verdict, which may suggest that its members had difficulty reaching a consensus. The judge later sentenced each suspect. Honda Chika later complained that 15 years in jail was equivalent to a murder conviction. The Japanese were told by other inmates, and even by their legal representatives, that if they had admitted their crime, the sentence would have been much lighter.

Dissatisfied with the judgment, they appealed the verdict. A Supreme Court hearing was held in November 1995. All their appeal grounds were rejected except for those of Katsuno Yoshio, who had received insufficient notification of his rights during the police investigation. Yet in 1996 the County Court again found him guilty, but reduced his sentence from 25 years to 20 years. The prisoners were all assisted by Legal Aid and, since the budget was limited, the Legal Aid lawyers did not conduct their own investigation to support the prisoners. Meanwhile, a support group was formed, which funded High Court appeals.[55] These appeals were also rejected in 1997 (for four prisoners) and in 1999 (for Yoshio).

Gradually the support activities attracted some expert attention through networking. A Japanese international law academic advised the prisoners to submit an application to the United Nations Human Rights Commission. With the assistance of a group of 52 lawyers in Osaka, the application for the individual communication was sent to Geneva in August 1998. Because Australia had signed the Optional Protocol for the International Covenant on Civil and Political Rights in September 1991, to ensure the right of individual petition to the United Nations (Charlesworth 1991:428), the Japanese prisoners were able to make an application against Australia. However, Japan had not signed the protocol, despite strong demand for ratification by human rights activists and experts. The Japanese media became aware of this move, and began to change their views about the prisoners from that of criminal to that of victim (*Asahi shinbun* 1998). The final outcome of the United Nations appeal is yet to be concluded.

Some personnel from the Japanese media visited Melbourne to meet the prisoners. *Yomiuri TV*, in February 2000, and *TV Asahi*, in August 2001 and November 2002, reported the case, respecting the voices of the prisoners. Some viewers criticised the Ministry of Foreign Affairs for not trying to protect the Japanese nationals while they were in custody.

In spite of the efforts by experts and supporters, the Japanese could not clear their names, and four of the prisoners were deported to Japan in November 2002 on parole. The *Age,* a Melbourne-based newspaper, showed on its front page a large photograph of the female prisoner, Chika (who shed tears at a press conference in Tokyo), with a headline, 'Deportation ends 10 years of purgatory' (Green 2002b). Although the Japanese were arrested, tried and imprisoned in Australia, their existence was hardly known to the Australian people until recently. They were a forgotten minority. They were non-English-speaking foreign-national prisoners. They were the 'others'.

What are the issues of the case?

The case became more complex than it initially seemed, not only because the Japanese denied any involvement in the illegal importation of heroin, but also because they were dealing with the Australian justice system, which was totally unfamiliar to them. For example, Japanese courts do not have juries. Legal representatives in Australia advised the Japanese prisoners to avoid choosing older people as jurors because the older generations tend to hate Japanese people because of their memories of the Second World War. Moreover, these lawyers did not encourage the Japanese to testify in court, believing that cross-examination would be unbearable for them, and that some of the testimony would have a negative impact on other suspects. All that the Japanese prisoners could do was to depend on their legal representatives, who rarely visited their prison prior to the trial. Lack of communication between the Japanese and their legal representatives was obvious. They were helpless, with little autonomy. Chika wrote in her statement that she met her lawyer twice before the trial, and on one occasion there was no interpreter present (Melbourne Jiken Bengodan 2002:20). Thus the communication gap between the Japanese and the lawyers was a serious problem. Being a suspect who cannot speak English is itself a great disadvantage, which may lead to mistakes with fatal consequences.

Further problems surrounded the case, such as cultural misunderstanding, inadequate interpreters, lack of support from the Japanese government and the selection of evidence. These factors placed the Japanese prisoners in a powerless position and greatly affected the outcome of the court judgment. Recognition of language and cultural barriers is vital to an understanding of the issues of a case. Such barriers often generate prejudice and are apt to be ignored, even in a multicultural society like present-day Australia, as this case demonstrates. As Paul Wilson (1991:4–5), a prominent criminologist, argues, wrongful conviction occurs in the Australian criminal justice system for a variety of reasons, such as over-zealous police conduct, incompetent investigation and media stereotyping. All these factors were associated with the case, in addition to the cultural factors mentioned above. Although misunderstandings may be inevitable when two cultures encounter each other under any circumstances, the mainstream culture is usually predominant, so that the behaviour and attitudes of the minority culture may be considered 'wrong' or 'strange', and lead to stereotyping.

Language difference constitutes a fundamental obstacle and challenge. The role of interpreters, therefore, is critical in many situations where people with non-English-speaking backgrounds are involved (Laster & Taylor 1994:111). Laster and Taylor (1994:137) stress the importance of the provision of interpreters as a human right for suspects with non-English-speaking backgrounds. However, massive problems surrounded language and the role of interpreters in the Melbourne Case. Two studies on the problem of interpreters in the case were conducted: one by supporters of the prisoners in 1998 for the mercy application, and the other by language experts in 2000 for the submission of a supplementary report to the United Nations Human Rights Commission. Both groups used a similar methodology. They listened to interview tapes, recorded by the police, to check whether each English translation in the transcripts of interview was accurate or not. Through this process, researchers found a number of misinterpretations, confusion created by interpreters and inappropriate additional questions or explanations added by interpreters. Misinterpretations involved various problems: there were simple mistakes in numbers and choice of words; interpreters did not always understand police questions and consequently distorted these; and interpreters did not fully interpret what suspects explained.

Serious mistakes made by interpreters affect the credibility of the accused. In the Melbourne Case, the police gained a negative impression of the accused when a serious misinterpretation occurred. For example, because of mistakes made by the interpreter, it was hard for the accused to make the police believe that the suitcases had been stolen and replaced by new ones. Later, in the courtroom, the Crown persistently argued that the clothes inside the suitcases must have been damaged when their original bags were slashed. The police were suspicious about the story of the stolen suitcases (County Court 1994:878, 1527). The prosecutor addressed the jury: 'the Crown asks you to look at them [interview tapes] because we say that the more you look at them the more you realise that each one is telling you a pack of lies' (County Court 1994:1047). The

Osaka lawyers claim that the theft of the luggage is an indispensable element by which to test the reliability of the testimony of each of the accused

How was the theory of a 'concocted story' created? When the Federal Police interviewed one of the suspects at the airport, a man from a travel agency was used as an interpreter. He was not qualified. His English and Japanese language ability was limited. When an interviewer asked about luggage, the interpreter could not handle the interviewer's questions. Thus the suspect's responses did not make sense to the police and eventually the interviewer was upset with the suspect, saying to the interpreter, '[t]ell him, I think he's talking rubbish, tell him, he's talking rubbish' (Melbourne Jiken Bengodan 2002:139). The fact that his bag had been stolen in Kuala Lumpur was not conveyed properly to the interviewer.

Further, the police needed seven interpreters for the suspects and employed some unqualified interpreters. Chris Poole, one of the interpreters, commented that there were not enough interpreters available at that time, and that coordination for the arrangement of the interpreters was not well managed (*Southern Sky* 2002). The National Accreditation Authority for Translators and Interpreters controls the accreditation of interpreters in Australia. A candidate must pass Level 3 to deal with legal matters. Of several interpreters employed for the police interviews, only two had Level 3. Under these circumstances, is it justifiable to conclude that the Japanese were simply unlucky when they were arrested in a foreign country?

Moreover, when the competence of an interpreter is problematic, the emotion of a suspect may be disregarded. A Japanese broadcasting company, *TV Asahi*, found a videotape containing a recorded interview where Chika, in tears, repeatedly claimed that, had she known there was heroin inside her bag, she would have reported the fact much earlier. Yet the interpreter could not understand her, asking her to repeat her response. She repeated the same answer slowly, trying to make the Australian interpreter understand. However, the interpreter told the police he was not certain what she had said. Japanese viewers understand why she cried at the interview, but their Australian counterparts did not because her words were completely lost and her emotion was not conveyed adequately. Later Chika told supporters that the interpreter looked up a dictionary for simple words such as elder sister (*ane*) or salesman (*eigyō man*) (Chika 2002).

In brief, the police, prosecutors, judges, jury and even the defence lawyers had to rely only on the portion of English conversation spoken by the investigators and the interpreters. This encouraged a different version of the story to be produced: namely, that the accused fabricated the story of switching the luggage, and that the five Japanese were aware of the illicit drug importation (Silvester 1994). Even though the crucial role of interpreters was pointed out by the defence lawyer at the Magistrates' Court, the problem was not recognised as vital by others involved in the legal proceedings.

Japanese experts, who acknowledged that similar problems occurred in Japan among foreign nationals, revealed the seriousness of the linguistic problems in the case.[65] Watanabe Osamu, a law professor, gives an example where a foreign national was charged with murder because the police were confused when the suspect used the terms 'brother' and 'sister', even though they were not real brothers and sisters (*Asahi shinbun* 2000c). The suspect's lawyer did not trust the person until he fully understood why the suspect used 'brother' and 'sister'. In some cultures these words are used as a mark of respect when referring to seniors. Watanabe argues that such linguistic misunderstandings in criminal matters may lead to miscarriages of justice.

How has the identity of the Japanese been depicted and shifted?

The five Japanese maintained their innocence. They believed that they were innocent victims, while the court ruled that they were criminals. As their story was publicised, people's perceptions also changed, thanks in large part to the media. Some newspaper headings illustrate the change. Soon after the Japanese were arrested, the *Herald Sun* (1992) reported the case with the heading, 'Mafia alert on $30 million bust'. Similarly, in the *Age* an article bore the caption, 'Yakuza link suspected in tourist heroin haul' (Taylor 1992). On the other hand, the Japanese media reported the case moderately. *Asahi shinbun* (1992) used the headline, 'Trafficking 13 kilogram heroin to Australia—five Japanese arrested in Australia', and named four of the men.

The five Japanese felt isolated until Stephen Young, a Christian priest who speaks Japanese fluently, started visiting them two months after their arrest. Young's regular visits eased the distress of the prisoners, who found it hard to trust anyone. One of the men, Katsuno Masaharu, rejected Young to begin with. One day Masaharu happened to read a Bible that had been left on a table in his room. Then he accepted Young. The prisoners began to study the Bible, as the priest learned about the case. He then became their spokesperson. Young informed the Japanese community in Melbourne about their circumstances, which led some Japanese to support the prisoners. Sometimes they went to the County Court to watch the trial, while Young attended on many occasions to monitor proceedings. He acted, too, as a volunteer interpreter between the prisoners and their defence lawyers. As communication improved, the lawyers encouraged the prisoners, saying that they would soon be freed.

The jury's verdict of guilty, therefore, was unexpected for the prisoners and their supporters. A newspaper article in the *Age* (Silvester 1994) detailed the case under the title, 'Six found guilty on heroin charges'. Although the article mentioned the switching of luggage in Kuala Lumpur, it included a negative depiction of the Japanese as Yakuza, toe-tapping and chain-smoking while waiting for luggage at the airport. As convicted persons, their full names were printed. The Japanese newspaper *Asahi shinbun* (1994) reported the verdict in a small article containing all the male names. The case drew a local Australian audience, but little attention in Japan. From this point on, their legal status was no longer that of 'suspects' but of 'convicts'. Active support continued, however, after they lost the County Court trial.

Supporters held regular meetings to devise strategies for further appeals. They also took turns to visit the prisoners, attempting to meet and talk with them most weekends. Even after the male prisoners were moved to Fulham Correctional Centre near Sale (220 kilometres from Melbourne) in May 1997, they had visitors at least twice a month on average. The supporters visited the Consulate-General of Japan and sent letters to major Japanese newspapers to inform them about the case and the prisoners' situation. The Japanese media did not at first respond. The staff of the Consulate-General replied consistently that they had done their best, in accordance with their 'manual' for protecting Japanese nationals, and could not do much more. They rarely visited the prisoners until the later stages.

It took several years for the prisoners' voices to be heard. *Asahi shinbun* (1998) published an article on the appeal to the United Nations Human Rights Commission, using the word 'innocence'. In *Sunday Mainichi* (2000) the case was featured under the title, 'Seven years in prison when touring overseas, the rescue project by 52 lawyers of Osaka'. The Japanese media were interested in the case during the late 1990s and early 2000s. Often the word 'innocence' was used, together with statements raising the problems posed by language and cultural barriers (*Asahi shinbun* 2000a; 2000b). All the male prisoners agreed to their names being published, but Chika kept her name out of the press until after she was deported. She was concerned about the feelings of her family, especially of her mother, who was afraid of her daughter being considered a criminal by the public. Katsuno Masaharu always claimed that he had no reason to hide his name. He acted as a spokesperson for the prisoners every time they met media representatives or the Japanese lawyers from Osaka.

Visitors learned that each prisoner was an ordinary human being like him- or herself. They came to understand that the relatives of the prisoners were suffering as well. Most visitors were moved by Katsuno Masaharu's strong insistence on his innocence. The parents of the Katsuno brothers regularly helped their grandchildren because of the absence of their fathers. Masaharu often described the relatives as victims, too. Masaharu's son, who is now in his early 30s, suffered from depression for several years. Chika's elder sister needed tranquilisers in the early days. Japanese people tend to feel ashamed if a family member is involved in a criminal act, and do not want to talk about it publicly. The relatives of the Japanese prisoners also had to endure the stigma involved when a family member is labelled as a 'criminal'.

As parole for four of the prisoners was nearing, the Japanese media became enthusiastic. *TV Asahi*, in particular, researched the case thoroughly and aired a special program on 24 November 2002, soon after the four returned to Japan. The program demonstrated various problems that the ex-prisoners had faced, such as inadequately trained interpreters, the judge's comment on the reasons for the refusal of separate trials, and the failure to investigate the involvement of 'Charlie', whom *TV Asahi* interviewed on the telephone. Both Chika and Masaharu were invited to *TV Asahi's* studio and encouraged to speak. They showed determination to prove their innocence.

About three months prior to the parole, the *Age* featured the case with the headings, 'After 10 years in jail, a new fight for innocence' (Green 2002a) and 'How four suitcases of heroin turned a five-day dream holiday into 10 years behind bars' (Rule 2002). In the latter, Andrew Rule interviewed Chika and talked with some supporters. He eventually formulated a version of the story which differed from that of the Australian authorities. Rule outlined the 'event' from the prisoners' perspective. He described the prisoners as ordinary Japanese. He further pointed out:

> Had the Japanese been able to support their story in any way, they stood to get the benefit of the doubt. It would be reasonable to believe they would accept new suitcases to replace stolen ones. But the Japanese were being defended by Legal Aid lawyers who couldn't communicate with them easily, let alone afford any independent investigation in Malaysia to substantiate their story.

Most Japanese media welcomed the return of the paroled prisoners and sympathised with them. The first press conference was packed with nearly 200 people, including supporters and lawyers. They now enjoyed the status of free people. Their identities shifted from that of 'victims' or 'sufferers', or even 'fighters', to that of innocent people in the eyes of the public. Christian supporters in Japan welcomed them as 'people who encountered God'.

As mentioned above, the Melbourne Case reveals serious dilemmas faced not only by naïve people but also by ordinary people, who may become suspects or criminals in a case. This is an important issue in an era of global travel, when people move frequently and rapidly from one nation state to another. Although the five Japanese were tried together and convicted together, as if they were a team, each needs to be examined separately. Each has his or her own independent story, even though they experienced the same incident and spent more than ten years in Australian prisons.

Conflicting identities—a case study

What did this ordeal mean to the prisoners? The recasting of their identities was not their choice, but was the outcome of complex legal procedures, including interrogations and the trial. Insight into the important issue of how the prisoners experienced the case, and how they understood the experience of being treated as criminals, can be gained by examining Masaharu's case. He was one of the most articulate, recording his views in numerous statements, reports, letters, testimonies, messages and notes while he was in prison. These written sources bear witness to his despair, anger and hope.

One statement detailed his account of the case. It covered how the tour was organised (Charlie invited his friend, Yoshio, and asked him to collect tour members); why he joined the tour (his other younger brother, Mitsuo, was asked to join by Yoshio, then Mitsuo invited Masaharu); how the expenses were paid (Masaharu was told that one of the original members cancelled his tour, so Masaharu did not have to pay); how the tour members met at the airport (seven members got together and introduced each other); how he met Charlie and his fellows (they helped to carry the tourists' luggage soon after they arrived at Kuala Lumpur airport); how he was told that their luggage had been stolen (right after they left a restaurant, Charlie rushed up to the Japanese to tell them their suitcases had been stolen while they were dining); how he spent the night at a hotel (he lay on the sofa sulking, and heard later that their suitcases had been found and would be delivered next morning); how he found a new suitcase (he checked inside the bag and found sake, packets of cigarettes and some books were missing); what he did during sightseeing (he was trying to buy a lighter bag, but he could not find one); how he waited for his luggage at Melbourne Airport (an officer grabbed his arm when he was trying to look for Yoshio, who had been stopped by an immigration officer); and what he saw inside their suitcases when a custom's officer opened them with an electric drill (small bags of heroin were found in the lining of the lid. The moment, to him, seemed unreal like a dream. His status of free tourist turned into that of a suspected smuggler.)

The tourists were taken to Swanston Hotel, where they had bookings. There the police conducted an undercover operation, in an attempt to capture the recipient of the heroin. Masaharu and others were asked to 'co-operate' in the police operation. He states:

> I thought our position were witnesses and co-operators of the investigations. Since I was thinking that, I even remarked on the method of investigation to the police. I did not know or realise that we were being arrested (Melbourne Jiken Bengodan 2002:33).

He believed he was assisting the police. He did not imagine that he was a suspect at this stage. They were never told that they were being arrested. The line between co-operators and suspects was unclear for a while. As a result, the Japanese waited and waited for release—Masaharu was undoubtedly confident of release soon after the police interviews were concluded. Masaharu further argues:

> At the interview with the police, there was an interpreter beside me, but I had never been told, or had it explained to me, that I would be or was arrested for such and such reasons. Also I was never informed what would happen to us in the future. So that is one of the reasons why I could not understand that I had been arrested. If I was to be arrested and held in custody, at least they should have declared so. Isn't this a duty that the police should never neglect? Moreover, since I was an alien whose customs and languages are different, I wanted more care. Concerning this incident, I was not only unaware of being held as a suspect, but I also thought I was a victim: therefore I had no idea that I was arrested (Melbourne Jiken Bengodan 2002:33–4).

Article 9 of the International Covenant on Civil and Political Rights states that 'everyone has the right to liberty and security of person. If arrested, a person has a right to be informed of reasons for the arrest and of any charge against them.' The right to be informed was not properly upheld. Masaharu saw himself as a victim, not a suspect, and his suffering commenced. He rejected his new identity.

The term 'identity' is fluid. It can refer to nationality, ethnicity or gender, as well as to role or position in society. It usually connotes a sense of belonging, or position, in society (Morris-Suzuki 1998:205). As Kathryn Woodward (1997:29, 35–6) suggests, however, identity can be understood as a concept of 'other' and difference. Through his new identity of 'convict', Masaharu arguably becomes different from 'non-convicts', and becomes the 'other'. Yet he refused to acknowledge this identity. It was imposed from outside to justify his imprisonment, through legal procedures exercised by the state. As Tessa Morris-Suzuki (1998:199) explains, 'identities flash between polar points of positive and negative, shaped by both the need to be "one with" and the need to be "distinct from"'. Convict is the 'other' and distinct from non-convicts who are good citizens.

Almost always a power relationship exists in labelling a certain group of people. Jan O'Herne (1994:137), survivor of the Japanese military sexual slavery system during the Second World War, insists that the term 'comfort women' is never correct, insisting that the women 'were war-rape victims, enslaved and conscripted by the Japanese Imperial Army'. Unlike the label 'convict', the term 'comfort women' was used to camouflage the real nature of the system. Thus the system appeared to be legitimate. But now it is revealed as a crime against humanity. Vera Mackie (2000:39) proposes the term 'women subjected to enforced military prostitution' as an alternative to 'comfort women'. For her, the term characterises 'the *institutional* aspect of this form of violence'. Masaharu, like Jan, could not accept the title of 'convict'; he, too, felt himself the innocent victim of a state-orchestrated crime.

Masaharu always stresses that the case will not be concluded until his innocence is proven. While in jail, another identity shift occurred. The former conservative, Shinto believer converted to Christianity. In the depths of his despair he encountered the Bible and understood himself to be one of God's 'elect' (from his Christian testimony written in April 1993). Before the incident he had been proud of himself as a Japanese 'samurai' and respected the Emperor. Amid the confusion of arrest followed by imprisonment, he found in Christianity a reason for living. Two months after the guilty verdict he wrote an 11-page letter to his parents acknowledging the comfort received from God and those who believed that what he said was true. Presumably he needed to think that he was one of the 'elect' to compensate for the imposed, demeaning identity of 'convict'. He, however, had to endure humiliating prison life, where he experienced a number of heart attacks.

Since returning to Japan, Masaharu has encountered difficulty in finding his own place. His relatives do not understand his inner struggles. He does not want to recall his past, when he was labelled a 'convict'. He prefers to think ahead. He says to himself that he has to fight for the new identity of an innocent man.

Conclusion

Masaharu's story is an example of shifting identities experienced by one of the Japanese ex-prisoners who was categorised as a 'convict'. Even though the media may depict them as 'victims', the taint of convict will remain until their names are cleared. What does this shift in identities mean for the ex-prisoners? Chika often mentioned that her time, as far as Japan was concerned, had stopped, which implies that her identity as a Japanese woman—a daughter and sister—had been affected. Her identity, born of belonging to her family, had been taken from her by her imprisonment. Yet it strongly stayed within her, for she always insisted to her supporters that she wanted to go back to Japan.

These identity changes are traceable back to the fact that the Japanese were arrested and tried under the Australian justice system. It remains a moot point whether the Japanese were fairly treated under this system. As the Osaka attorneys claim, there are grounds for claiming that their human rights were violated in the course of legal proceedings, especially during police interrogation. Some of the interpreters employed by the police could not handle the interviews. Inappropriate interpretation led to misunderstandings, putting the Japanese in an increasingly vulnerable position. In short, language barriers may lead to suspects from non-English-speaking backgrounds being classed as criminals. It is hardly an exaggeration to say that criminals are created by a deficient system, where a suspect from a non-English-speaking background cannot fully make others understand what is happening. As the International Covenant on Civil and Political Rights proclaims, highly qualified interpreters need to be provided for suspects from non-English-speaking backgrounds. Moreover, the role of interpreters as an important profession should be recognised to guarantee services of high quality for users. For, as the Melbourne Case categorically demonstrates, cultural and language barriers play a significant part in the outcome of court decisions.

As we have seen, the Japanese prisoners experienced conflicting identities through their depiction by the Australian justice system and the media. Clearly the imposed identity of 'criminal' diminished their dignity. Their resistance took a variety of forms, such as writing, working hard in prison, being a model prisoner and praying to God. An imposed identity cannot easily be altered. It is a boundary that divides people: us/them, Australian/Japanese. Lastly I would emphasise that the case is not only a story of the Japanese prisoners, but also an Australian story for Australians in the sense that they need to be aware of indifference to the 'other'. As Morris-Suzuki (2003:240) argues, 'without listening to the voice of the "other", people belonging to a dominant culture cannot understand how their thoughts and discourse are created and maintained'. The Melbourne Case provides a variety of sources for constructing a different version of a story.

Notes

1. On behalf of the prisoners, a group of lawyers from Osaka sent an application to the United Nations Human Rights Commission in August 1998 to appeal against the Australian Court decision on the grounds of violation of human rights, particularly the right to free access to an interpreter and the right to a fair trial as cited in the International Covenant on Civil and Political Rights. Article 14 (1) of the Covenant states

    [a]ll persons shall be equal before the courts and tribunals. In the determination of any criminal charge against him, or of his rights and obligations in a suit at law, everyone shall be entitled to a fair and public hearing by a competent, independent and impartial tribunal established by law. Further, 14 (3) (a) [t]o be informed promptly and in detail in a language which he understands of the nature and cause of the charge against him; and (f) [t]o have the free assistance of an interpreter if he cannot understand or speak the language used in court, are directly related to their appealing points.

2. *Nichigo Press* (2002) features Honda Chika's story. Two journalists visited the Dame Phyllis Frost Centre (a women's prison in Victoria) and interviewed Chika, who was about to be deported. Chika talked about the incident, prison life, an attempted suicide, a nervous breakdown and her conversion to Christianity.

3. The reason the term 'Yakuza' was used was that one of the tourists, Katsuno Yoshio, had been a member of a Yakuza group. However, Yoshio had terminated his membership two years prior to the incident. Yoshio admitted to some criminal acts while he was involved in the Yakuza group, but claimed that he had no knowledge of the importation of heroin (personal conversation with Yoshio, date unknown).

4. Three identifiable fingerprints were found, but none of them belonged to the accused (County Court 1994:39).

5. The Japanese, except Yoshio, appealed to the High Court in June 1997. Yoshio appealed in September 1999.

6. In Japan, police interviews with suspects are not usually tape-recorded. It is much harder for a third party to substantiate the validity of the interview.

9

Theatres of discipline in the age of consensual euphoria: performing globalisation and 'empire' in recent contemporary performance in Australia and Japan

Peter Eckersall

This chapter explores the notion that inter-cultural theatre—including theatre exchanges and dialogue between Australia and Japan—is now a facet of the global cultural economy. In light of this, I analyse two case studies; works by the Melbourne-based Not Yet It's Difficult performing group—of which I am the dramaturge—and Tokyo-based Gekidan Kaitaisha. Analysis shows that the contemporary arts relate to social conditions that are markedly similar in Australia and Japan. For the theatre to respond to this situation, various strategies of resistance that mimic and hyper-inflate the disciplinary society that has in many ways come to organise our way of life are identified in the works of the companies.

As Lo and Gilbert state, inter-cultural theatre 'is a hybrid derived from an intentional encounter between cultures and performing traditions' (Lo & Gilbert 2002:36). Also a genre of the arts that has arisen in the context of globalisation, the authors argue:

> This neoliberal embrace of cultural difference celebrates the possibilities of cultural fusion and the construction of radical subjectivities beyond national and ethnic boundaries. Intercultural practice in this sense is deeply imbricated in globalization and the perceived deterritorialization of social, cultural, and political boundaries for those in the developed world, even if this is not often acknowledged by the critics and practitioners themselves (Lo & Gilbert 2002:40).

An unspoken flavour of inter-culturalism is its largely Western-centric centres of activity and interests (Lo & Gilbert 2002:36; Eckersall 2004). Consequently, the idea that there is now a more intensely political experience of inter-culturalism needs to be addressed.

Inter-cultural relations and the intensity of empire

Since the 1980s experimental theatre in Australia and Japan has shown a diversity of changing aesthetic forms, requiring new kinds of commentary and analysis. Some discussions of the changing faces of theatre are worth recalling.¹

Turning briefly to Japan, the popularisation of theatre in the 1980s, that is often called the '*shōgekijō* (small theatre) boom', has been described as a 'bubble theatre' of euphoria (Eckersall 2000), theatre that rejected ideology and language (Uchino 2000:87), and a 'ludic theatre' of speed and nostalgia (Rolf 1992). *Fin de siècle,* cyberpunk-like representations in theatre have also been identified, as in Uchino Tadashi's discussion of Japanese theatre's fascination with images of Armageddon (2000) and my own reading of 'Japan as dystopia', explored in a discussion of the work of Daisan Erotica (2000). Alternative theatre in the 1980s has been read critically as a site of production that was, to some degree, subsumed by a culture hell-bent on the erasure of history and the enduring celebration of an 'endless present'—to borrow from HD Harootunian's (1993) notion of Japanese post-war capitalism as an 'undifferentiated process of identity formation' and sameness.

Social changes in Japan after the 1980s are also an important factor in thinking about Japan's contemporary cultural production. As Uchino Tadashi wrote:

> Ten years have passed since Aum Shinri-kyo—a cult group sometimes dubbed 'the last underground theatre company,'—attacked Tokyo's subway lines with sarin gas in 1995. In the same year, Japan also experienced the Hanshin Awaji Great Earthquake. Many cultural theorists are currently looking at 1995 as an historical watershed in Japan's socio-psychological milieu (Uchino 2006).

In this milieu, cultural critics in Japan point to a misplaced sense of elation that permeated through Japanese society and culture after the 1980s and is riding in the face of deep evidence of economic decline and rising social problems.

This chapter is concerned in particular with such trends in Australia and Japan as global entities (more about this soon) and the evidence for a countervailing response in the domain of contemporary theatre production. Although it has become difficult to see places where this response can be found in the arts, the analysis below suggests that not all theatre has been reified, as one might conclude from viewing the mainstream alone. We might productively consider the evidence for theatre's recent struggle with the social-political world. In particular, forces of globalisation combining seemingly utopian perspectives on the borderless world but inter-relating with the rise of ecstatic and euphoric images of nationalism, coupled with neo-liberal fundamentalism and the rise of the consumer society[2], have been the subject of sustained critique in theatre and art.

The rising pressure of these forces has overwhelmingly changed the nature of cultural criticism. Although an argument that develops from the work of cultural comparisons between Australia and Japan, as noted, the arts are now evidently working between spaces of a globalised cultural economy and politics. Consequently, interactions that formerly happened in a bilateral context are now shaped by an imbricated and inter-flowing matrix of power. A study of the history of Australia–Japan contemporary theatre exchange (Eckersall 2004), for example, noted the influence of Japanese underground (*angura*) styles of theatre—including a heightened physicality and self-consciously 'East–West' aesthetics—on Australian contemporary performance from the late 1980s to the mid-1990s. In particular, the study noted the heavy imprint of the physical performance genres of *butō* and the style of theatre devised by Suzuki Tadashi and known colloquially as the Suzuki Method (Eckersall 2004:35). The study was critical of the exchange system, noting that in the Australian attempts to revive an avant-garde theatre culture, 'an engagement with Japanese histories and contexts of work is absent' (Eckersall 2004:38). The study concluded, moreover, that Australian and Japanese theatres were no longer in close bi-cultural relations. In essence, the global cultural economy requires rapidly changing performance dynamics. The 'Japan boom' of the 1980s and early 1990s, when Japanese performance was a fashionable wave, was over and the global arts market—Australia and Japan included—moved on to promote some other forms of presentation.

A further factor influencing the cultural dynamics of exchange mechanisms was the changing relationships between art and politics and art and society as explored by theatre makers. The memory of the radical avant-garde of the 1960s that held power over the contemporary theatre scene even into the 1990s rapidly declined from that point. As the playwright–director Kawamura Takeshi notes, change was necessary and inevitable:

> Given what was happening in the world around us and the magnitude of historical events that we saw, it seemed to me that this kind of theatre making based on story was no longer able to address the questions that were being asked. Another kind of theatre making was becoming necessary (Kawamura 2004).

Kawamura sees a global historical frame of reference influencing his ideas for new forms of art and culture. This means that in thinking about cultural relations between Australia and Japan it is now necessary to locate the bilateral dimensions of arts exchange within the contexts of globalisation politics.

To this end, the 'theatres of discipline', discussed below, open critical spaces of resistance in societies that are products of advanced capitalism. It is argued that common factors in all such states are a tendency among ruling powers to frame socially controlling and authoritarian disciplinary mechanisms within a fiction of nationalism, social progress and of what is termed 'consensual euphoria'. Therefore, there is no comparison of difference to be made between Australia and Japan now; both are subsumed into the matrix of empire. Rather, the comparison (more a sharing of information) might lie in making clear the mechanisms and strategies of resistance in art—how does theatre identify, criticise and, therefore, resist the powerful mechanisms that dominate in the world? This is perhaps the most productive task, and the only one available, for a comparative theatre project in the present time.

Global–local formations of power: always being inside

The facts of global–local performative moments in politics, the media and inside powerful corporate institutions have become increasingly prominent topics in social debates across the world. Australia and Japan are interesting sites to consider in this regard. Both have experienced dramatic and lasting social and political changes under the rubric of globalisation. Since the early 1980s, they have experienced economic deregulation and rising neo-conservative political orders. Yet neither is a dominant or secure power amidst globalisation's flows; both sit under America when it comes to war, both anxiously debate issues of cultural imperialism. But despite this world disorder, current political rhetoric generally discourages critical reflection and is euphoric. A prescient insight into this trend (rationalised as a system for the maintenance of political power) is offered in Guy Debord's seminal work *The society of the spectacle*: 'THE SPECTACLE MANIFESTS itself as an enormous positivity, out of reach and beyond dispute. All it says is: "Everything that appears is good; whatever is good will appear"' (Debord 1995:59).

As a means to power, such moments of euphoria are thought by their critics to ride over more dystopic and critical assessments of social development. Viewed from a counter-perspective, the general contrivance of public displays of commitment to this global–national combination, and political rhetoric that divides the world into forces of good and evil ('us' and 'other'), instil in the minds of the community at large images of general euphoria and national cultural essentialism. Such momentum towards homogeneity in the workspace and in society-at-large is what some have termed the 'identity trap' (Uchino 1999). Although it is noted below that the identity trap is found in many places, in Japan *Nihonjinron* has been constituted as a powerful force in Japanese social construction and identity formation. Recent events demonstrate how national–imperial symbols such as the *Hinomaru* have been revived as euphoric statements of Japanese power in the region.[3] For mainstream/conservative political groups in Japan, this momentum is a cause of celebration: for their opponents on the left, or among the remnants of the progressive counter-culture, this trend is cause for alarm.

Australia has likewise witnessed the rising sense of national cultural essentialism. Through debates about Australian history, the desire to imprint euphoric and uncomplicated versions of Australian nationhood has been witnessed in the so-called 'history wars', for example.[4] For critics such as the sociologist Ghassan Hage (2003:31), though, the preoccupation with euphoria hides darker realities: 'At the border, the protection of hope sometimes unleashes aggression, hatred and mistrust.' As will be discussed, this observation comes alive in theatre's critique of refugee issues.

In fact, it is argued here that the politics of euphoria in an age when the capacity for progressive society to evolve is anything but euphoric is a situation that is overwhelmingly experienced in Australia and debated in contemporary alternative Australian theatre culture. Australian Prime Minister John Howard's vision for Australia as 'comfortable and relaxed' (a post-election statement outlining the mindset of his first period of government in 1996) has been criticised among progressive scholars as a statement masking the deliberate erasure of cultural complexity and sophistication in the Australian cultural landscape. The subsequent transformation of Australian society under the rule of conservative forces is understood by all political factions to be a calculated manoeuvre designed to 'resist' (or, from the perspective of the right, to 'correct') the very kinds of identify confusion, plurality and intelligent debate that have been at the centre of Australian arts since the 1970s.

Furthermore, it is clear from these examples that national cultural essentialism and consensual euphoria are not the forces of ordinary disciplinary power as might be represented by police and military institutions (although we are seeing more of this kind of power recirculating through society and on display since the second Gulf War). Rather, they are a post-modern formation—the power of the 'superflat' (to use provocatively visual artist Murakami Takashi's theory of the banality of power in its contemporary representational forms). According to Murakami, 'Society, customs, art [and] culture all are extremely two dimensional' (Brehm 2002:36).[5] We might read into Murakami's large-scale images of cartoon figures the suggestion that power is euphoric and yet embedded in everyday forms of representation, production and consumption. Obligation to power has become everyday; even if it feels not quite right, people always have the superflat to keep their attention diverted from perceptions that are more oppressive and the general anxieties of their world. The sociologist Zygmunt Bauman, in his assessment of present-day society as experienced among developed nations such as Australia and Japan, has aptly coined the term 'ambient uncertainty'. This term well describes the superflat matrix (Bauman 1998).

As befitting the term superflat (which is a theory of art delivered in slogan format and uses English), these performative expressions of nationhood unfold in the context of globalisation. Hardt and Negri in their work *Empire* define globalisation as 'a *decentred* and *deterritorializing* apparatus of rule that progressively incorporates the entire global realm within its open, expanding frontiers' (Hardt & Negri 2000:xii). *Empire* develops a comprehensive critique of the politics of globalisation and argues that the rise of global capitalism, media, American hegemony and multilateral non-government organisations and the decline of civil society are inter-connected and form the basis of a new modality of power, a new 'empire'. This observation has profound ramifications for the field of cultural production; also, for our clearer understanding of the status of national culture. In the world of *Empire*, cultural production can be seen to both support (as in national performative events such as military parades and media images of disciplinary institutions such as refugee detention camps) and resist (as in alternative theatre and art) the 'apparatus of rule'. Moreover, 'resistance' might also be co-opted as 'support'. In *Empire*, cultural production is constantly at risk of being subsumed into some other commodity matrix; for example, the Arts Festival, the celebrity avant-garde, the blockbuster art show, arts as media sensationalism and so on. The cultural agencies of *Empire* might use alternative theatre as a panacea, as a way of demonstrating the continued existence of debate and diversity, although within proscribed limits. It is therefore important to consider how alternative theatre responds to—and participates in—the real world politic of globalisation. It is, further, important to examine where the limits of co-option are. In particular, as the disciplinary formation of globalisation becomes intense, we might study how its mechanisms might be dealt with—or be understood in theatre works.

Theatres of discipline

Here I propose the frameworks of *space*, *race* and *surveillance* to underpin the regime of globalisation and prosecute the sense of consensual euphoria in the world as evident points of discussion in recent avant-garde theatre in Australia and Japan. These performances, I further argue, are *theatres of discipline*, which alternately outline and resist the age of consensual euphoria and explore the modalities and border-regions of its power.

Theatres of discipline are theatre events that evoke a sense of, and put on display, the disciplinary formations of power transformed in the theatre space as modes of dramaturgical and aesthetic representation and expression. In the artworks discussed below, space, race and surveillance are political themes that develop as dramaturgical modes exploring the rise of consensual euphoria. Such theatre productions are often controversial. They risk the invocation and even celebration of power in their aesthetic forms in order to engage with audiences in debates about the substance of power. As noted above, theatres of discipline are not removed from the wider cultural forces in society, rather they respond to the proposal that in *Empire* there is no longer an outside. In the same vein, Phillip Auslander reasons that in post-modern theatre the 'conflation of the cultural and the economic renders "critical distance" impossible—the cultural can no longer presume to stand back from the economic/political and comment on it from without' (Auslander 1997:59).

In other words, theatres of discipline recognise and debate a significant problem for art in a globalised world; that it cannot be separate from the mechanisms and wider systems of representation and communication that are embedded in its contexts of production. Nor can a national theatre project maintain a progressive or radical stance when the nation itself has become a site for the degenerative performance of *Empire*. Rather, we might study how such disciplinary formations from the world might be addressed in theatre as sources of comment on the cultural spaces within which theatre works. In doing so, we might also learn more about trends in art in Australia and Japan and about how art struggles to productively engage with the cultural sphere—even if that proposition is now more complex than in the past.

Gekidan Kaitaisha and the politics of bodies in *angura*

For Shimizu Shinjin, the director of Japan's Gekidan Kaitaisha, 'ideology is a shadow' of action. The possibility of action—specifically performative acts that might be seen as moments of theatrical resistance—has become an unworkable proposition for this company. Shimizu proposes that the contemporary body has yielded to the demands of Foucault-like disciplinary regimes and is waiting for instruction. This is a body at sea. It is unable to rise above the waves and gain a sense of its position; the undercurrent is too strong, the space too bent on the body's erasure. The autonomy of the performers—who seem more like subjects in a social science experiment than actors—appears to be undermined and overrun by the space itself. As Stephen Barber writes, Kaitaisha's work emphasises 'imagery of incessant corporeal struggle—always placed in intimate juxtaposition with images resonant of urban media power and its implications for the human body, for sexuality, and for the spectator of the performance...' (Barber 2002:176–7).

Gekidan Kaitaisha, or 'theatre of deconstruction', describes itself as a maverick performance group and is certainly one of the most important companies to emerge from the Japanese underground theatre scene. Shimizu wants his work to be 'based on an acute criticism of society which…translate[s] to social issues including racism, identity in the refugee context, political pretension and hypocrisy' (Barber 2002:178–9). The corporeal struggle that is the essence of its performances, while not literal or symbolic, is a manifestation of the disciplinary forces in society that compel the members of this company in their daily lives. Being marginal in and to the Japanese context of empire, and Kaitaisha's deep commitment to the experimental off-centre theatre world, is the site of their subordination, as it is also the source of their potential liberation. Kaitaisha's invigorating vision of the world, as seen and, most importantly, embodied and experienced through subjective actions in performance, is perhaps on one level a revision of the 1960s counter-culture experiential political strategy for the Japanese avant-garde. But their understanding of 'corporeal struggle' has advanced beyond notions of subjectivity and selfhood alone. It is now centrally informed by a view of the way that power has shifted since the end of the Cold War and has become an all-encompassing and performative experience.

In explaining this stance, we might remember that sustained and intense explorations of corporeality have been a cornerstone of the avant-garde theatre (underground theatre, *angura*) in Japan since the 1960s, with precedents for this going back as far as the 1920s. Hijikata Tatsumi, Suzuki Tadashi, Kara Jûrô and Terayama Shûji are a quartet of well-known *angura* artists associated with the rise of the new and exciting physicality of theatre in 1960s Japan. The performing body as a site for the exploration of society during this period of social upheaval was a device for aesthetic innovation and a central metaphor for a society undergoing change. With few exceptions, contemporary Japanese theatre since that time has become known worldwide for its unique physical-aesthetic forms and has enjoyed widespread popularity among theatre audiences across the globe.

Kaitaisha's work displays hallmarks from Hijikata Tatsumi's dance performance *ankoku butō* (dark soul) (Broinowski 2003) and suggests an alternate critique of the recent history of theatrical representations of the body in the Japanese avant-garde. Kaitaisha's work asks that we reassess the politics of corporeality in such art. Hence, in the era of hyper-capitalism in Japan in the 1980s, Shimizu asserts that the performing body came to be seen as aesthetically driven and exotic. Consequently, the capacity for the body in performance to explore socially critical transformations was negated.

In fact many 1980s performances from the Japanese avant-garde became transfixed and constrained by slow, undulating aestheticism and Zen-like corporeal contemplations of an almost mythic, otherworldly space. Typical in this regard were the 1980s performance works by the hugely popular *butō* group Sankai Juku (based in Paris, although conspicuously Japanese). Such works featured the distinctive, passive naked and shaved *butō* body performing in Zen-mystic spatial designs such as beds of water or sand gardens. Sankai Juku's popular 1986 work *Unetsu* featured smoothly impassive bodies that seemed to glide across a bed of water. The stage surface was lit brilliantly to convey a sense of transcendental passage between solidity and fluidity. The performance offered experiences of profound emptiness and suggested the subtle contemplation of a certain beautiful strangeness. Unlike earlier *butō*, the emphasis in this hauntingly aesthetic work was not on the exploration of notions of cultural deformity or darkness, but on purity, harmony and the oriental sublime. Bodies moved as if propelled by the gentle forces of the oriental cosmos.

Another popular and enduring work of note was Tenkei Gekijō's *Mizu no eki* (*Water station*, 1981). The central dramaturgical premise was a parade of slow-moving silent figures gathering water from a village tap. The author and director of *Mizu no eki*, Ōta Shōgo, describes the work as:

> A broken faucet centre stage. A thin line of water from the spout. The sound of water. The variety of people as they come by, approach, touch the water, and pass on. In this composition, silence breaths as living human time, not as form (Ōta 1990:150).

Understandably, critics have sometimes compared the play's rhythm to that of *nō* theatre and the recourse to pre-modern images and sensibilities might hold nostalgic, otherworldly and culturally distinctive associations for viewers. Mari Boyd suggests that the 'seemingly trivial events [in the piece lead] to a new perception of life' (Ōta 1990:153).

In these suggestions of traditional aesthetics, the senses of Zen-like transcendence and quasi-mysticism come to the surface. A global audience enthusiastically consuming these images that denote the pre-modern and phantasmic transforms theatrical space into an aesthetic construct. Japaneseness is conceived in pseudo-contemplations of some hidden, awesome power. 'To end the world in order to imagine a renewed sense of [national] community' (Uchino 2000:89) is the goal of Uchino's understanding of what he terms 'Theatres of the private' of the 1980s. 'This is not a theatre of Cartesian subjects but of premodern undifferentiated selves in which spectators are supposed to contribute a full range of sentiments,' writes Uchino (2000:87). We might be seeing the origins of a post-modern and apolitical avant-garde *orientalia* in the corporeality of these 1980s *angura* works.

According to Shimizu, no such introspective possibilities for the performing body can be justified. He notes, 'It was a shock for theatre that a war without bodies...raised the curtain of the 1990s' (Kaitaisha 2001:71). In other words, the body since the 1980s has been conditioned by capitalism and war and is conditioned by an industrial–military-like sense of space and identity. Accordingly, Shimizu argues we must retrain and compel our imagination to be able to see the bodies that have been evacuated from the scene by media and ideology; by forces of globalisation, or empire. These suggestions have only intensified in the present-day so-called 'war on terrorism', a war that by all accounts is a performative enterprise. In response to this, Kaitaisha's work in recent times has consisted of scenes that it calls 'reconstructions', 'meditations' and 'testimony' that document 'how that last decade fell into political disorder' (program notes).

Into the century of degeneration

Kaitaisha's *Bye bye: into the century of degeneration* (1999)[6] was a work that aimed to explore this reality. Drawing together the threads of its performance activities over the 1990s, the work demonstrated the sense of corporeal struggle so aptly described by Barber above.

A sense of impending and implicit violence hung in the atmosphere as the piece unfolded. Disturbing and provocative moments in the performance included a sequence in which a woman was lifelessly and repeatedly passed from one expressionless male provocateur to another. Another sequence, which was repeated a number of times, evoked a sense of the refugee when performers wandered the vast, empty space of the stage as if compelled by some unknown or lost map of the world. Like a herd, they gathered only to be sent off on a new directionless intensity or path. As the critic Nishidō Kōjin suggests, Shimizu regards Japanese bodies as 'the bodies of cattle' (Nishidō 2004:147). Meanwhile other performers repeatedly slapped their thighs in a visceral performance of violence enacted on the flesh (*nikutai*).[7] The bandaged and damaged bodies of the performers evoked a powerful sense of pain and loss. In an extraordinary sequence in the work, the performers were suddenly transfixed, no longer able to move except for the minutiae of primal muscle tremor. A massive, almost overwhelming, projection of warfare played across the whole stage. Graphic images of Zero fighter planes, marching columns of Japanese soldiers and bodies amidst the violence of battle washed over the disabled and traumatised bodies of the performers, who were propelled towards erasure as if by some disciplinary–military vortex. The scene went beyond conventional notions of performance and its intensity almost belies description. But what is clear is the impression of dissolution and how immensity and pain rejected the representational aestheticism of 1980s Japanese theatre.

The conflation of space, race and surveillance is terminal in this work. There seems to be no further room to manoeuvre, as each principle element of the staging is complete in its ability to dissolve the body (*ningen jokyō*) and its presence in the space. 'There is nothing but *kaitai*', Shimizu says, nothing but deconstruction (Kaitaisha 2001:83). This might help to explain these deprived and empty bodies inhabiting the space without intention. For Shimizu, and his group, this is not symbolic or a theatrical metaphor, it is simply the expression of the way things are; in his words, 'the body brings something to light' (Shimizu 1996). By this act of 'testimony', *Bye bye: into the century of degeneration* sought to demonstrate (or became the consequence of) the ideological transformations and momentum towards global power and empire.

Not Yet It's Difficult

Not Yet It's Difficult (NYID), a performance group at the centre of an Australian avant-garde, explores Australian spatial and cultural reality in performance. Like Kaitaisha, NYID is an experimental and independent theatre company.[8] NYID explores theatre and performance by extending the dimensions of theatricality into physical and mediatised, non-traditional performance environments. At the same time, NYID often comments on theatre as an institution through its generally meta-theatrical style.[9] We might say that NYID is a theatre of discipline that revolts against the consensual euphoria and disciplinary functions of mainstream Australian society and culture.

NYID's *Scenes of the beginning from the end* (2001)[10], performed in multiple sites within a large multi-storey car park, traverses the mindscapes of contemporary Australian spatial and political experience. It referenced the fact that space is a contest in Australian life, helping to forge expressions of identity, economy and power. In *Scenes* bodies were propelled from the central Australian desert, passing through the iconic endless suburbia of Australian lives and finally arriving at the city and the domain of the global surveillance economy. As Peta Tait writes, '*Scenes of the Beginning from the End* consists of intersections of live bodies and filmed (e)scapes, physical talk and verbal football; cars as cultural fantasies of freedom set against fears of social monitoring' (Tait 2001).

Desert suburbs city

Scenes explored the experience of the white settler population of Australia clinging to the edges of the landscape; meanwhile the cultural imaginary of the centre is harsh, striking, fought-over and alien. People seem drawn to its vast possibilities and repulsed by it emptiness in equal measure. The desert is a conflictual space: land claims by Indigenous traditional owners conflict with mining rights; vast faming tracts, military bases and refugee camps make claims on the land; tourists in four-wheel drive vehicles and global backpackers driving old Holden cars traverse the scarred landscape in search of the 'real' Australia. In the desert part of *Scenes*, a single projection of a compressed journey from the outback, travelling through the hinterland and finishing at the Melbourne suburbs, formed a background for the performers. They began with choreographed movements sensitive to the central Australian landscape; forms were low, archetypal and contained. However, as the video images brought us to the suburbs, the bodies were seemingly urged into the space proper. They were literally propelled into the suburbs, their running bodies pushed as if by the dystopian suburban life force. At the conclusion of the scene, the audience was moved to a sequence of locations designating suburbs.

The suburbs build fences against the memory of the interior. Drawing on representations of the suburban mindscape, NYID staged a 'Neighbours-party' as a social 'dreaming' for an endless suburban labyrinth. The locus of the scene referenced the television show *Neighbours*, Australia's longest-running suburban soap opera. Set in the imaginary Melbourne suburb of Erinsborough, *Neighbours* is the model representation of average Australia. However, the dramaturgical frame extended and subverted the superficial harmony and Anglo-Australianness of the *Neighbours* stereotype: a pre-recorded sequence, which was played on video monitors in the space, used actual scripts from the television series. Yumi Umiumare and Kha Viet Tran, Japanese and Vietnamese-born actors, performing in their native languages, played a scene featuring the well-known 'stock' *Neighbours* characters of 'Charlene' and 'Scott'. This was looped and repeated as a kind of contemporary neo-conservative nightmare: where banal 'Aussie' soaps, which come to be venerated institutions for their capacity to speak in apolitical and euphoric terms to the 'average Australian', are 'occupied' and 'overrun' by the voices and faces of the racial–cultural other. Montages of scenes from the suburbs drawn from Australian theatre, film and literature helped to extend the sense of ambivalence of the Australian suburban experience. The piece suggested that before the politics of ambient uncertainty took root in Australia, we were invited to be 'comfortable and relaxed': suburbia is the space of this indifference.

Scenes from the beginning from the end. Photo by Lyn Pool, courtesy NYID.

A driver-point-of-view image of a commuter train's journey from the suburbs to the city marked the transition to the final site of performance. Once again, the audience was required to move from one performance site to the next. Arriving at the final space, the audience was divided. One group was removed from the live performance inter-actions and watched the whole of the final sequence via a large video projection screen. The group was given comfortable seats and served snacks. The other group experienced the final section of the performance first-hand. During the course of events, some members of the audience were subjected to surveillance, interrogation and punishment.

In iconic terms, the city has been a subject in many artworks. NYID explored its manifestation of the contemporary world of *Empire*. Hence, this section of the performance was designed to create in the audience an overwhelming sense of the intrusion of surveillance and disciplinary regimes. NYID has long incorporated images of surveillance into its work: David Pledger, NYID artistic director, comments:

> All of this technology is completely and utterly possible and in between that spectrum of looking at someone when they're not watching you, and that kind of organisation of power and capital, are these multiplicities of mediation which determine the way that we organise ourselves in space, our emotional lives, our thinking (Murphet 2001).

In *Scenes,* images of the surveillance of the city and a visual referencing of the journey through the city to the venue of the performance were projected onto the large video screens. Smiling operators at computer terminals gradually switched between surveillance images of the city, the car park venue and, finally, real time images of the audience. Ben Zipper's review comments:

> ...in a performance that picks up on earlier themes of work versus home, intimacy versus pop culture, independence versus mass persuasion...a new theme—corporate surveillance—is overtly introduced, through screen imagery of public cameras filming private lives. By the end a few audience members have signs hung around their necks, saying for example, 'I once imagined I was thinking. I atone for my transgression' (Zipper 2001).

These people were removed from the space and the remaining audience watched a final scene in which punishment in the form of beatings was acted out behind silhouette screens on the bodies of those taken away. With these

Scenes from the beginning from the end. Photo by Lyn Pool, courtesy NYID.

disturbing images, and their effect on audience members captured on cameras and replayed on projection screens, the piece concluded.

At the time of the first performances of *Scenes,* in May 2001, reviewers seemed to think that the dystopian tone of the surveillance scene was too overt. In response to the evident didacticism, Ben Zipper called the scene 'insulting'. Peta Tait, while positive overall, thought the work had 'Echoes of Foucaultian regimes but not punishing dismemberment in this Australia' (Tait 2001). In the scene of the city, media technology is depicted as an organising principle of politics and an instructional device. The mindscapes of Australian space are transformed into the corporate mediascapes of contemporary Australian existence. And we can no longer pretend that such images are only a fiction: in the present-day unfolding of 'wars on terror', such images of discipline are no longer the product of invention.

Closing: the theatre of discipline in an age of consensual euphoria

The goal of discipline is self-discipline. Alphonso Lingis writes:

> Surveillance registers the transgression as soon as it is initiated, indeed observes every possibility of transgression and every temptation to transgress, and neutralises them in advance. It differentiates individuals, makes comparisons possible between the levels, abilities and performances of different individuals, and between the different stages in the evolution of an individual...The disciplined body is individual in his or her school record, examination results, aptitude tests, military record, employment record, prison record and medical file (Lingis 1994:59–60).

As these performances by NYID and Kaitaisha show, surveillance and differentiation, as described by Lingis here, together with the performative acts of deterrence explored in these works, are bases of a new power structure in Australian life and the cornerstone of Shimizu's dystopian critique of Japan. In this way the disciplined body in these performances can be figured as a corporeal expression of empire.

Shimizu notes that in his view the appearance of the refugee camp, seemingly a *sine qua non* of globalisation, is more than a detention centre for the stateless and dispossessed. Its primary function is disciplinary, designed to foster in the minds of citizens a fear of difference and rejection by the state. (A secondary function is the fact that these camps are usually privatised arms of state security and are run for profit.) Shimizu argues, 'in the case of Japan, in the midst of globalisation there is rising nationalism, which means excluding the outside' (Kaitaisha 2001:75). He further argues that globalisation was 'conceived to allow for the possibility of differentiation', but in reality 'forces a homogeneous norm' (Kaitaisha 2001:75). As a result, in his company's performances, 'power has come to control the body even more tightly' (Kaitaisha 2001:75).

NYID's treatment of space, race and surveillance in *Scenes* reminds us of the fact that such politics of differentiation are alive in Australian society as well. 'Excise' is the word used in the Australia *Border Protection Bill 2001*, which removes Australian territories from the legal definition of Australia for the purpose of defining the locus and responsibilities for refugee groups.[11] In election mode in October 2001, the Prime Minister said to the parliamentary press gallery, 'those people will never set foot on Australian soil' (Rundle 2001:3). As Ien Ang (2000:xiv) has noted:

> [When] (mostly Asian or other non-European) refugees arrive on Australian shores, the deep-seated fears around the violability of the nation's borders in the Asian region are brought to the surface, with [then Federal Minister for Immigration and Aboriginal Affairs Phillip] Ruddock responding to the often near-hysterical mainstream public opinion by emphasising the criminality of their entry and increasing border surveillance.

Such performative inter-actions of globalisation and neo-liberalism with nationalism and parochialism have been widely commented on and constitute a vision of empire. By Pledger's understanding of surveillance mechanisms, we are reminded that we are being protected and we are being watched at every possible moment. To paraphrase his comments cited above, 'that kind of organisation of power...determines the way that we organise ourselves in space, our emotional lives, our thinking'. The intersection of formations and practices of space, race and surveillance in this sense supports an increasing and overriding spirit of authoritarianism and decline of democracy across our world.

Buffering dystopia, however, in the broader context of globalisation, the singular vision of national cultural essentialism is experienced as a form of consensual euphoria. In this context, notions of race pride are brought to bear in the revision and nostalgic celebration of mythical performative images of nationhood and citizenry. For example, the transformation in Australia of the annual Anzac Day ceremony (marking the deaths of soldiers in the First World War) into an ideological performance text is now used to suggest the unique qualities of Australian identity. Submitting to the authoritarian rule of national military fervour becomes a text that demonstrates one's commitment to nationhood. As in *Scenes,* the body is propelled towards the normative by the intensity of the images of its mediatised surroundings. Performative exploitation of state rituals as normative acts is also evident in Japanese society. Kaitaisha reminds us how warfare has been carefully constructed in Japan textbooks to ensure Japan is not excessively seen as an aggressor. Indeed, as we have seen, history texts in Australia and Japan have been a site of considerable political debate and have in some instances been euphorically revised to instil a sense of enduring prosaic identity, lack of reflection and blamelessness. Consensual euphoria is endemic; to critique and to suggest an alternative is to risk censure and exile (for example, the use of the terms 'un-Australian', 'elite' or 'outsider', or, in Japan, *soto*, a social concept that is widely noted as a powerful agency of value integration in the formation of the social world). Thus, in the suburbs of NYID's *Scenes* everyone is lost together and nobody minds. We might say that in Australia *and* Japan, consensual euphoria seems to ride over other more dystopic turns of events: the loss of freedoms, widening income disparity, the privatisation of public space and amenities, the rise of cults, the escalation of 'fear' politics and so on.

In the field of cultural production there are consequently powerful issues and forces that artists must address. The experimental theatres have always been associated with notions of critique, resistance and alternatives, but this has become a difficult proposition for the avant-garde. In Uchino's terms, 'It is this urge to erase history…that all cultural productions…have to resist' (Uchino 2000:93). Perhaps above all else, the performances discussed here open-up something from the world to the gaze of art. These works might show us the space of empire, a space that is neither comfortable nor euphoric, or the warm embrace of nostalgia. Rather, it is a space of discipline and hegemony exposed through theatrical acts—themselves acts of discipline. All the same, they are processes of agitation and protest. NYID and Kaitaisha show that bodies are under control and without will. In an age of empire, such notions as resistance might seem quaint and improbable but we can conclude that the alternative theatre continues to claim this critical space with notoriety and effect.

Notes

1. The 1960–75 era of dramatic transformations in art and politics (experienced in Japan and Australia alongside Europe and America) prefigures the analysis here of the 1980s theatre. I note how post-modernism and globalisation reoriented the social and cultural environments of the 1980s.

2. With regard to corporatist ideology and the rise of the consumer society, John Clammer (2000) writes:

   > Consumer capitalism creates new subjectivities. It does so by shaping taste, identity, and life style options; by creating needs, desires, and images of things, services, places, and foods; and through its impact on concepts of the perfect body via ideas of diet, health and fitness, body shape, colour and decoration. It operates most powerfully through the media and advertising, and in so doing profoundly influences emotions associated with subjectivities.

   Although his comments refer to Japan, they apply more broadly and are relevant to Australia.

3. The *Hinomaru* is Japan's national flag. In 2000 the government legislated that the flag must be raised and the anthem sung in all schools and at events of national prominence.

4. For an informative, comparative study of history wars in Australia and Japan, see Yonetani (2004).

5. Superflat is further described as: 'devoid of perspective and devoid of hierarchy, all existing equally and simultaneously' (see 'BT' 2000).

6. *Bye bye: into the century of degeneration* (1999), premiered at Setagaya Public Theatre, Tokyo. Artistic director: Shimizu Shinjin. Cast: Hino Hiruko, Kumamoto Kenjiro, Nakajima Miyuki, Moriyama Masako, Nomoto Ryoko, Yamagata Mitsuko, Takata Miho, Hasegawa Tomoko, Urasoe Hisfumi, Koike Shunji, Aota Reiko, Tsuchimoto Tadashi, Tano Hideko. Technical management: Hata Takeshi. Lighting design: Kawai Yuji, Sound design: Mizutani Yuji.

7. Flesh in the sense that *ankoku butô* creator Hijikata Tatsumi used the word *nikutai* (meat) in opposition to *shintai* (body) to describe the visceral intensities of the performing body in his influential performance *Nikutai no hanran,* usually translated as *The revolt of the flesh.*

8. NYID and Kaitaisha collaborated on an inter-cultural theatre exchange project called *Journey to confusion* (1989–93). For information and documentation see Eckersall, Uchino & Moriyama (2004); Eckersall (2005).

9. The idea of meta-theatre derives from the Greek *meta*, meaning beside or after. It is a post-modern formation of theatre that is alive to commenting on theatre's essential theatricality and changing contexts of production. NYID's meta-theatre has sometimes been termed 'theatre about theatre'.

10. *Scenes of the beginning from the end* (2001) premiered at the Public Office Car Park, Melbourne. Artistic director: David Pledger. Cast: Cazerine Barrie,

Paul Bongiovanni, Tony Briggs, Natalie Cursio, Tamara Saulwick, Louise Taube, Greg Ulfan. Dramaturge: Peter Eckersall. Technical manager: Paul Jackson. Lighting design: Shane Grant.

11 The Bill proposed 48-hour mandatory detention of Australians without charge and the power to ban organisations that the attorney-general (a government member) deemed to be supportive of terrorist acts or groups. Greens Senator Bob Brown (2002) regretted 'the creation of new offences of terrorism that could encompass some union activity, civil disobedience and dissent'. In response to bombings in Bali, Madrid and London, further extensive powers of surveillance and detention are currently being passed in the parliaments of the United Kingdom and Australia.

Bibliography

Publications and interviews

Ackland, Michael 2001, *Damaged men: the precarious lives of James McAuley and Harold Stewart*, Allen & Unwin, St Leonards.

Akabane Kinuko 1956, 'JR Black' in *Kindai bungaku kenkyū sōsho*, volume 1, Shōwa Joshi Daigaku.

Age 1935a, 'The mind of Japan', 12 August.

—— 1935b, 'Japanese mission', 15 August.

—— 1935c, 'Envoy formerly at Washington', 7 September.

Allen, Christopher 1997, *Art in Australia—from colonization to postmodernism*, Thames and Hudson, London.

Ang, I (ed) 2000, *Alter/Asians: Asian–Australian identities in art, media and popular culture*, Pluto Press, Sydney.

Arahata Kanson 1965, *Kanson jiden*, volume 1, Chikuma Shobō, Tokyo.

Argus 1940a, 'Italian honour for Australian', 29 May.

—— 1940b, 'Must achieve harmony: Australia–Japan', 16 July.

—— 1940c, 'Australia and Japan', 27 July.

—— 1941, 'To fill post here', 17 April.

Asahi Shinbun 1891, 24 March.

—— 1992, 23/6/1992;

—— 1994 11 June.

—— 1998, 27 September.

—— 2000a, 16 February.

—— 2000b, 8 March.

—— 2000c, 8 April.

—— 2002, 8 November.

Asaoka Kunio 1987, 'Henrī J Burakku no rainichi jiki', *Kairakutei Burakku kenkyū* 2, 19 September.

—— 1988, 'Burakku hen "danjo seibi" keshōhō ni tsuite' in *Kairakutei Burakku kenkyū* 3, 19 September.

—— 1992, 'Kairakutei Burakku no "Kekkon/Kika" Mondai kō', *Kairakutei Burakku Kenkyū* 6.

Asia Pacific Focus 2004, ABC television, 23 August.

Auslander, P 1997, *From acting to performance*, Routledge, London and New York.

'Australian printmakers in America 1900–1950' 1992, National Gallery of Australia, Canberra, 21 December to 5 April.

Balkenhol, Heinz and Sasaki Miyoko 1979, 'Rakugo: fascination for and popularity of one of the classical Japanese arts of narration' in *Journal of Popular Culture* 13(1).

Barber, S 2002, 'Tokyo's Urban and Sexual Transformations: Performance Art and Digital Cultures' in Lloyd, F (ed), *Consuming bodies: sex and contemporary Japanese art*, Reaktion Books, London.

Barr, P 1967, *The coming of the Barbarians: a story of Western settlement in Japan 1853–1870*, Macmillan, London.

Barthes, Roland 1968, *Empire of the signs*, Routledge & Kegan Paul, London.

Bauman, Z 1998, *Globalization: the human consequences*, Columbia University Press, New York.

Bevege, Margaret 1993, *Behind barbed wire: internment in Australia during World War II*, University of Queensland Press, St Lucia.

Black, Henry 1887, *Yōi dokushū: Eiwa kaiwa hen: easy conversations in English written especially for Japanese wishing to learn English*, Chūgaidō, Tokyo.

Black, John Reddie 1968 [1880], *Young Japan: Yokohama and Yedo, 1858–79*, Oxford University Press, Tokyo and New York.

Boeringer, Pierre N 1895, 'Some San Francisco illustrators—curbstone Bohemia', *Overland Monthly and Out West*, San Francisco, 26(151).

Box of Curios P & P Co Souvenir, 1888–1903: A brief history of the Box of Curios Printing and Publishing Co 1904, Box of Curios Printing and Publishing Co, Yokohama, (unpaginated booklet).

Brehm, M (ed) 2002, *The Japanese experience - inevitable*, Hartje Cantz Verlag, Ostfildern-Ruit.

Broinowski, Alison 1996, *The yellow lady: Australian impressions of Asia*, Oxford University Press, Melbourne.

—— 2003, 'Theatre of body in Japan: Ankoku Butoh (Dance of Darkness)-Gekidan Kaitaisha (Theatre of Deconstruction)', MA thesis, University of Melbourne.

Brown, Bob 2002, press release, 24 June.

Brown, Milton W 1988, *The story of the Armory Show*, second edition, Abbeville Press, New York.

'BT' 2000, *Monthly Art Magazine* 5, May.

Bulletin 1937, 'Nankivell's Etchings', Sydney, 6 October.

Burakku, Eikokujin 1891, *Eikoku Rondon gekijō no miyage*, Nomura Ginzaburō, Tokyo.

Burakku, Henrī Zeemusu (ed) 1886, Lesson 15, *Yōi dokushū: Eiwa kaiwa hen* [*Easy self study—English–Japanese conversation edition*], Chūgaidō, Tokyo.

Burakku, Ishii 1896, *Minashigo* [*The orphan*], Kin'ōdō, Tokyo.

Butler, Roger (no date), 'Nankivell, Frank A', *Prints & printmaking in Australia & the Australasian region*, National Gallery of Australia, www.australianprints.gov.au/Search/DETAIL.cfm?SearchID=1&ArtistID=3367, viewed 15.8.2005.

Campbell, John Francis 1876, *My circular notes: extracts from journals, letters sent home, geological and other notes, written while traveling westwards round the world, from July 6, 1874, to July 6, 1875*, two volumes, Macmillan, London.

Castlemaine Mail 1942, 'The position inside Japan', 5 October.

Castles, Stephen 1996, 'The racisms of globalization' in Vasta, E and S Castles (eds), *The teeth are smiling: the persistence of racism in multicultural Australia*, Allen & Unwin, St Leonards.

Charlesworth, Hilary 1991, 'Australia's accession to the First Optional Protocol to the ICCPR', *Melbourne University Law Review* 18(1).

Chika, Honda 2002, message for a forum organised by the Osaka lawyers, 4th September, www.melbosaka.com.

Chronicle directory for Tokyo, Yokohama, Osaka, Kobe, Nagoya, Kyoto, Shidzuoka, Formosa, Korea, Dairen, Nagasaki, Kyushu, Moji, Hokkaido, Shimonoseki, alphabetical list of residents and list of missionaries in Japan 1940, Japan Chronicle, Kobe.

Chūka Kaikan [Chinese Association] (ed) 2000, *Rakuchi seikon: Kobe kakyō to Shinhan Chūka Kaikan no hyakunen [Roots in a new homeland: a hundred years of Chinese in Kobe–Osaka and their association]*, Kenbun Shuppan, Tokyo.

Clammer, J 2000, 'Received dreams: consumer capitalism, social process, and the management of emotions in contemporary Japan' in Eades, JS, T Gill and H Befu (eds), *Globalisation and social change in contemporary Japan*, Trans Pacific Press, Rosanna.

Clark, John 2000, 'Chronology: Japanese printing, publishing and prints, 1860s–1930s' in Tipton, Elise and John Clark (eds), *Being modern in Japan: culture and society from the 1910s to the 1930s*, University of Hawaii Press, Manoa.

—— 2001, *Japanese exchanges in art 1850s–1930s—with Britain, continental Europe, and the USA*, Power Publications, Sydney.

Clark, Steve 1999, *Travel writing and empire: postcolonial theory in transit*, Zed Books, London.

Clarke, IF 1966, *Voices prophesying war, 1763–1984*, Oxford University Press, London.

Coshocton Tribune 1922, 'Supremacy of white race in Pacific goal of Australia: trade alliance is sought with America in hope of holding off Japan: sees yellow peril: Anglo–Japanese treaty source of fear, says parliamentarian' (evening edition), Coshocton, Ohio, 23 March.

Cottle, Drew 2001, 'The Brisbane Line: an episode in capital history', *Journal of Australian Studies* 69.

County Court, Criminal Jurisdiction 1994, *Before His Honour Judge RPL Lewis, the Queen v Fong Huat Su, Yoshio Katsuno, Masaharu Katsuno, Mitsuo Katsuno, Kiichiro Asami, Chika Honda*, Victoria Government reporting Service, Melbourne.

Courier 1930, 'A brilliant scholar', Ballarat, 12 April.

Courier 1940, 'Mr Russo on Tokio appointment', Ballarat, 28 August.

Courier-Mail 1940a, 'Japan's message to Australia', 16 July.

Courier-Mail 1940b, 'Policy of harmony should be aim', 16 July.

CPD (*Commonwealth Parliamentary Debates*) 1901, Senate and House of Representatives, Commonwealth of Australia.

—— 1971a, Senate, volume 49, 19 August.

—— 1971b, Senate, volume 49, 24 August.

—— 1971c, House of Representatives, volume 73, 25 August.

Creelman, James 1894a, 'Back to barbarism: serious charges against the victorious Japanese Armies: now savage war of conquest', *Middletown Daily Argus*.

—— 1894b, 'The Eastern war', *Sandusky Register*, Sandusky OH, 20 December.

Crow, Arthur H 1883, *Highways and byeways in Japan, the experiences of two pedestrian tourists*, Sampson Low, Marston, Searle, and Rivington, London.

Curthoys, Anne 2000, 'An uneasy conversation: the multicultural and the indigenous' in Docker, J and G Fischer (eds), *Race, colour and identity in Australia and New Zealand*, UNSW Press, Sydney.

Daily News 1922, 'Credit to American rule: affairs in Pago Pago, in the South Seas, declared admirably managed', Frederick, Maryland, 27 October.

Daily Telegraph 1940, 'Minister to Japan favored', 16 July.

Davies, George 2001, *The Occupation of Japan: the rhetoric and the reality of Anglo-Australasian Relations 1939–1952*, University of Queensland Press, St Lucia.

Davis, Pedr 1999, *The long run – Toyota: The first 40 years in Australia*, Type Forty Pty Ltd, Melbourne.

Debord, G 1995, *The society of the spectacle*, Zone Books, New York.

Dening, G and D Kennedy 1993, *Xavier portraits*, Old Xaverian's Association, Melbourne.

Dixon, Robert 1995, *Writing the colonial adventure: race, gender and nation in Anglo-Australian popular fiction, 1875–1914*, Cambridge University Press, Melbourne.

Docker, John 1991, *The nervous nineties: Australian cultural life in the 1890s*, Oxford University Press, Melbourne.

Dower, John 1999, *Embracing defeat: Japan in the aftermath of World War II*, Penguin Books, Ringwood.

Eckersall, P 2000, 'Japan as dystopia: an overview of Kawamura Takeshi's Daisan Erotica', *The Drama Review* 44(1).

—— 2005, 'Theatrical collaboration in the age of globalisation: the Gekidan Kaitaisha–NYID Collaboration Project' in Um, H-k (ed), *Diasporas and interculturalism in Asian performing arts*, Routledge Curzon, London.

—— 2004, 'Trendiness and appropriation? On Australia–Japan contemporary theatre exchange' in Eckersall, P, T Uchino and N Moriyama (eds), *Alternatives: debating theatre culture in the age of confusion*, PIE Peter Lang, Brussels.

Eckersall, P, T Uchino and N Moriyama (eds) 2004, *Alternatives: debating theatre culture in the age of confusion*, PIE Peter Lang, Brussels.

Encyclopaedia Britannica 1911, 'Caricature', New York.

Faine, Jon 2005, ABC radio, 774 Melbourne, 1 June.

Ferargil Galleries 1929, 'Color etchings by Frank A Nankivell', pamphlet, New York.

Frei, H 1984, 'Japan discovers Australia: the emergence of Australia in the Japanese world-view, 1540s–1900s', *Monumenta Nipponica, Studies in Japanese Culture* 39(1), Sophia University, Tokyo.

—— 1991, *Japan's southward advance and Australia from the sixteenth century to World War II*, Melbourne University Press, Carlton.

Gepp, HW 1932, *Report on trade between Australia and the Far East*, 1932, Government Printer, Canberra.

George, Gilbert 1987, 'Letter to me' 3/1/26-87T, ZT-II (L0723) 12 August, Harold S Williams Collection, National Library of Australia.

Gluck, Carol 1985, *Japan's modern myths*, Princeton University Press, Princeton.

—— 1998, 'The invention of Edo' in Vlastos, Stephen (ed), *Mirror of modernity*, University of California Press, Berkeley and Los Angeles.

Green, Dorothy 1973, 'Poet's progress', *Hemisphere* 17(12).

—— 1981, 'A candle in the sun', *The Eastern Buddhist* 14(2).

Green, Shane 2002a, 'After 10 years in jail, a new fight for innocence', the *Age*, 17 August.

—— 2002b, 'Deportation ends 10 years of purgatory', the *Age*, 19 November.

Greenblatt, Stephen 1980, *Renaissance self-fashioning: from More to Shakespeare*, University of Chicago Press, Chicago.

Grimshaw, P et al 1994, *Creating a nation*, McPhee Gribble, Ringwood.

Guénon, René 1941, *East and West*, Luzac, London.

—— 1943, *The crisis of the modern world*, Luzac, London.

Haese, Richard 1988, *Rebels and precursors: the revolutionary years of Australian art*, Penguin, Ringwood.

Hage, G 2003, *Against paranoid nationalism: searching for hope in a shrinking society*, Pluto Press, Sydney.

Hall, Stuart 1996, 'Introduction: who needs identity?' in Hall, Stuart and Paul du Gay (eds), *Questions of Cultural Identity*, Sage, London, 1996.

Hall, S and P du Gay (eds) 1996, *Questions of cultural identity*, Sage, London.

Hanazono Kanesada 1926, 'JR Black' in *Journalism in Japan and its early pioneers*, Osaka Shuppansha, Osaka.

Hara, Takeshi 1997, 'Historical material on the Japanese Army that relate to Australia in the Second World War', *Journal of the Australian War Memorial* 30, www.awm.gov.au/journal/j30/hara.htm.

Hardt, M and A Negri 2000, *Empire*, Harvard University Press, Cambridge.

Harootunian, HD 1993, 'America's Japan/Japan's Japan' in Miyoshi, M and HD Harootunian (eds), *Japan in the world*, Duke University Press, Durham and London.

Herald 1905, 12 June.

—— 1930, 'Mollison Scholarship winner', 8 April.

—— 1935a, 'Japan's eyes not set on Australia', 16 July.

—— 1935b, 'Japan clings to spirit of old traditions', 17 July.

Herald-Sun 1992, 22 June.

Hetherington, John 1960, 'The impious crusader' in *Australians: nine profiles*, Cheshire, Melbourne.

Heyward, Michael 1993, *The Ern Malley affair*, University of Queensland Press, St Lucia.

Hirodo, Kenji 2004–05, recorded interviews with Graham Eccles, Black Rock, Victoria and by telephone.

Hjalmarson, Birgitta 1999, *Artful players: artistic life in early San Francisco*, Balcony Press, Los Angeles.

Hoare, JE 1994, *Japan's treaty ports and foreign settlements—the uninvited guests 1858–1899*, Japan Library, Kent.

Hollinsworth, David 1998, *Race and racism in Australia*, Social Science Press, Katoomba.

'Homage to the Square: picturing Washington Square, 1890–1965' 2001, Berry-Hill Galleries, New York, 23 May to 13 July.

Hope, A D 1948, Review of *Phoenix wings*, *Meanjin* 7(4).

Howe, C 1996, *The origins of Japanese trade supremacy: development and technology in Asia from 1540 to the Pacific War*, Crawford House Publishing, Bathurst.

Illustrated Monthly of the Box of Curios 1892, no 2, Yokohama, May.

Irokawa Daikichi 1985, *The culture of the Meiji period*, Jansen, Marius B (ed & trans), Princeton University Press, Princeton.

Itō Hisako 1987, 'Shiryō yomoyama-banashi: Gekkan bokkusu obu kyuriosu' [chatting about archival materials: monthly box of curios], *Yokohama Kaikō Shiryō-kan Kanpō* [Yokohama Archives of History News] 20, 1 August.

—— 1995, 'EV Sōn: Kokkei shinbun, zasshi o hakkō' [EV Thorn: the publication of a humourous newspaper] in Yokohama Kaikō Shiryō kan (ed), *Yokohama jinbutsu-den: rekishi o totta 50 nin* [Yokohama biographies: 50 people who took hold of history], Kanagawa Shinbun, Yokohama.

Jansen, Marius B 1995, 'The Meiji restoration' in Jansen, Marius B (ed), *The emergence of Meiji Japan*, Cambridge University Press, Cambridge.

Japan Chronicle 1908, 28 August.

Japan Daily Herald 1880, 28 April, quoted from the *Kinji Hioron* [sic] No 263, 28 April 1880.

Japan Gazette (ed) 1893, *Japan Directory 1893*, Yokohama.

—— 1894, *Japan Directory 1894*, Yokohama.

Japan Punch 1873, September.

Japan Weekly Mail 1885, 30 May.

—— 1889, 'A new journal in Yokohama', 28 December.

—— 1892, 3 September.

Johnson, Sheila K 1988, *The Japanese through American eyes*, Stanford University Press, Stanford.

Jones, HJ 1985, 'The Griffis thesis and Meiji policy toward hired foreigners' in Burks, Ardath W (ed), *The modernizers: overseas students, foreign employees, and Meiji Japan*, Westview Press, Boulder.

Jones, Noreen 2002, *Number 2 home: a story of Japanese pioneers in Australia*, Fremantle Arts Press, Fremantle.

Jones, P 2001, 'Racial character and Australia and Japan in the 1930s' in Jones, P and P Oliver, *Changing histories: Australia and Japan*, Monash University Press, Clayton.

Jones, Paul and Pam Oliver (eds) 2001, *Changing histories: Australia and Japan*, Monash University Press, Clayton.

Jung CG 1931, *The secret of the golden flower: a Chinese book of life*, Routledge & Kegan Paul, London.

Kaitaisha (ed) 2001, *Theatre of deconstruction*, Gekidan Kaitaisha, Tokyo.

Kanai Madoka 1967, 'Eijin Burakku to Nihon', *Kokusai bunka* 162.

Karatani, Kōjin 1993, *Origins of modern Japanese literature*, Brett de Bary (ed), Duke University Press, Durham and London.

Katsura Beichō 1976, *Rakugo to watashi*, Popurasha, Tokyo.

Kawamura, T 2004, interview with author, Tokyo, 13 January.

KBS Quarterly 1935 1(1).

Kirton, Walter 1908, 'A Jap school for spies', *Lone Hand*, September.

Kitazawa Rakuten 1928, 'Manga-kai mukashi-banashi' [Old tales from the comic art world], *Chūō Bijutsu* [Central Art] 14(2).

—— 1936, 'Meiji jidai no manga; tokyo pakku o chushin to seru' [*Cartoons of the Meiji period: focusing on* Tokyo Puck], *Tōyō* [Eastern Sun], October.

—— 1952, 'Manga Taiheiki' [Comic art war tales], *Warai no izumi* [*Wellspring of laughs*], July.

Kobe Weekly Chronicle 1901a, 9(234).

—— 1901b, 24 December.

Kōdan zasshi 1897, 'Kōdan yose no kairyō wo nozomu', 5 March.

Kurata Yoshihiro 1980a, *Meiji Taishō minshū goraku*, Iwanami Shinsho, Tokyo.

—— (ed) 1980b, *Meiji no engei*, volume 1, Kokuritsu Gekijō, Tokyo.

—— 1981 *Meiji no engei*, volume 2, Kokuritsu Gekijō, Tokyo.

—— 1982 *Meiji no engei*, volume 3, Kokuritsu Gekijō, Tokyo.

—— 1984 *Meiji no engei*, volume 5, Kokuritsu Gekijō, Tokyo.

—— 1985 *Meiji no engei*, volume 6, Kokuritsu Gekijō, Tokyo.

—— 1987, *Meiji no engei*, volume 8, Kokuritsu Gekijō, Tokyo.

La Nauze, JA 1965, *Alfred Deakin, a biography* volume 1, Melbourne University Press, Carlton.

Laster, Kathy and Veronica L Taylor 1994, *Interpreters and the legal system*, Federation Press, Sydney.

Leiter, Samuel L 1979, *New kabuki encyclopedia*, Greenwood Press, Westport.

Lindsay, Norman 1987, *The comic art of Norman Lindsay* (selected by Keith Wingrove), Angus & Roberstson, North Ryde.

—— 1976, *My mask*, Angus & Robertson, Sydney.

Lingis, Alphonso 1994, *Foreign bodies*, Routledge, New York.

Lo, J and Gilbert, H 2002, 'Toward a topography of cross-cultural theatre praxis', *The Drama Review* 46(3).

Mackie, Vera 2000, 'Sexual violence, silence, and human rights discourse: the emergency of the military prostitution issue' in Hilsdon, Anne Marie et al (eds), *Human rights and gender politics: Asia Pacific perspectives*, Routledge, London.

Mackie, Vera and Paul Jones (eds) 2001, *Relationships: Japan and Australia, 1870s–1950s*, History Department, University of Melbourne, Parkville.

Mahood, Marguerite 1973, *The loaded line: Australian political caricature 1788–1901*, Melbourne University Press, Carlton.

Mainichi Shinbun 1971, 4 April.

—— 1987, 16 February.

—— 1999, 30 October.

—— 2002, 8 November.

Malik, Kenan 1996, *The meaning of race, race, history and culture in Western society*, New York University Press, New York.

Marschall, Richard E 1980a, 'A history of *Puck*, *Judge* and *Life*' in Horn, M (ed) *The world encyclopedia of cartoons*, Chelsea House, New York.

—— 1980b, 'Nankivell, Frank Arthur (1869–1859)' in Horn, M (ed) *The world encyclopedia of cartoons*, Chelsea House, New York.

McCullagh, Francis 1902, 'The story-teller in Japan', *East of Asia Magazine* 1.

McCutcheon, Peter 2005, *The 7:30 Report*, ABC television, 21 June.

McMullin, Ross 1984, *Will Dyson: cartoonist, etcher and Australia's finest war artist*, Angus & Robertson, Sydney.

Meaney, N 1976, The *search for security in the Pacific, 1901–14*, Sydney University Press, 1976.

—— 1996, *Fears and phobias: EL Piesse and the problem of Japan, 1909–39*, National Library of Australia, Canberra.

—— 1999, *Towards a new vision: Australia and Japan through 100 years*, Kangaroo Press, East Roseville.

Megaw, Ruth 1973, 'The Australian Goodwill Mission to the Far East in 1934: its significance in the evolution of Australian foreign policy', *Journal of the Royal Australian Historical Society* 59, December.

Melbourne Jiken Bengodan (ed) 2002, *Tōku Ōsutoraria no Chi kara Mujitsuo Sakebistuzukeru Gonin no Nihonjinn* [*The five Japanese who keep crying innocence from far away Australia*], Melbourne Jiken Bengodan, Osaka.

Menpes, Dorothy 1904, 'Mortimer Menpes, colorist', *The Booklovers Magazine* 3, January.

Mese, Minoru 1968, *Memoirs of Shigeyoshi Hirodo*, privately printed, Kobe, copy held by Kenji Hirodo.

Middletown Daily Argus 1894, 'Back to Barbarism: serious charges against the victorious Japanese armies: now savage war of conquest', 20 December .

Miller, J Scott 1997, 'Tale as text: *Sokkibon* in the Diet Library collection' in Hardacre, Helen (ed), *New directions in the study of Meiji Japan*, Brill, Leiden, New York, Köln.

Minamitari, Akimasa 1990, 'Hamlet in Japan', *Japan Quarterly*, April–June.

Minoru, Mese 1968, *Memoirs of Shigeyoshi Hirodo*, privately printed, Kobe.

Miyako Shinbun 1920, 'Tensa Rōza koi monogatari', 30 July.

Miyamoto Hirohito 1995, 'Manga izen kara: Bakumatsu, Meijiki no 'mangateki' shohyōgen no kōsei o megutte' [From pre-manga: regarding the structure of all comic/cartoon-like expression of the Bakumatsu and Meiji periods], MA dissertation, Tsukuba University.

'Miyatake Gaikotsu' 1993, *Japan: an illustrated encyclopedia*, Kodansha, Tokyo.

Moore, Ronald 1994, The management of the Western Australian pearling industry, 1860 to the 1930s', *Great Circle* 16(2).

Moore, W 1980 [1934], *The story of Australian art*, volume 2, Angus & Robertson, London and Sydney.

Morioka, Heinz and Miyoko Sasaki 1983, 'The blue-eyed storyteller: Henry Black and his *rakugo* career', *Monumenta Nipponica* 38(2).

—— 1986, *Kairakutei Burakku no 'Nippon'*, PHP Kenkyujo, Tokyo.

—— 1990, *Rakugo, the popular narrative art of Japan*, Council on East Asian Studies, Harvard University, Cambridge.

Morris. HH 1940, letter to editor, *Argus*, 7 October.

Morris-Suzuki, Tessa 1998, *Re-inventing Japan: time, space, nation*, ME Sharpe, New York.

—— 2003, 'Histerī no Seijigaku' [Politics of hysteria]', *Sekai*, February.

Morrow, BF 1931a, 'The etching technique of Nankivell', *Prints*, 2(1).

—— 1931b, 'Frank A Nankivell, the master', *Prints*, 1(5).

—— 1947, 'Forward' in Nankivell, Frank A 1945–7, 'A bowl of rice and other grains', unpublished manuscript.

Murakami, Y 2001, 'Australia's immigration legislation, 1893–1901: the Japanese response' in Mackie, Vera and Paul Jones (eds), *Relationships: Japan and Australia, 1870s–1950s*, History Department, University of Melbourne, Parkville.

Murphet, R 2001, 'David Pledger: the danger zone', *Real Time 44*, Open City 2005, Sydney.

Murphy, PB 1980, 'Australia and Japan in the nineteen thirties', *Journal of the Royal Australian Historical Society* 65(4).

Nagata, Yuriko 1996, *Unwanted aliens: Japanese internment in Australia*, University of Queensland Press, St Lucia.

—— 1999, 'Japanese-Australians in the post-war Thursday Island community', Queensland Review 6(2).

—— 2001, 'Lost in space: ethnicity and identity of Japanese-Australians, 1945 to the 1960s' in Jones, P and P Oliver, *Changing histories, Australia and Japan*, Monash University Press, Clayton.

Nakagomi Shigeaki 1998, 'Rakugo "furoshiki" saikō', *Bulletin of Graduate Studies* 40, Hōsei University, Tokyo.

Nankivell, Frank A 1945–7, 'A bowl of rice and other grains', unpublished manuscript, Nankivell family document.

Nettlefold, AJ 1940, letter to editor, *Argus*, 25 October.

The new idea: a women's home journal for Australasia 1903–11, TS Fitchett, Melbourne.

New York Times 1959, 'Frank Nankivell, an artist, was 89: ex-newspaper illustrator is dead – Puck cartoonist, had works in museums', 8 July.

Nichigo Press 2002, December.

Nish, I (ed) 1982, *Anglo-Japanese alienation, 1919–1952*, Papers of the Anglo-Japanese Conference of the History of the Second World War, Cambridge University Press, New York and Cambridge.

Nishidō, K 2004, 'The journey to con-fusion: between Australia and Japan' in Eckersall, P, T Uchino and N Moriyama (eds), *Alternatives: debating theatre culture in the age of confusion*, PIE Peter Lang, Brussels.

Nishiyama Matsunosuke 1997, *Edo culture: daily life and diversions in urban Japan, 1600–1868*, University of Hawaii Press, Manoa.

Nishūbashi Sei 1905, 'Kairakutei Burakku', *Shinsen: rakugo daizen (bungei kurabu teiki zōkan)* 11(14), Bungei kurabu, Tokyo.

Nobuhiro, Shinji 1986, *Rakugo wa ikani shite keisei saretaka*, Heibonsha, Tokyo.

Notman, Otis 1907, 'A talk with illustrators.' *New York Times*, 22 June.

Novograd, Paul 1974, 'Rakugo: the storyteller's art', *Japan Quarterly* 21(2).

Nyorai An 1896a, 'Shunpū kanwa: Kairakutei Burakku', *Yomiuri Shinbun*, 30 April.

—— 1896b, 'Shunpū kanwa: Kairakutei Burakku', *Yomiuri Shinbun*, 1 May.

—— 1896c, 'Shunpū kanwa: Kairakutei Burakku', *Yomiuri shinbun*, 2 May.

—— 1896d, 'Shunpū kanwa: Kairakutei Burakku', *Yomiuri shinbun*, 4 May.

Nyūsupaaku (ed) 2003, *Shinbun no me- hito, seiji, shakai* [The gaze of newspaper manga—people, politics and society], Nyūsupaaku [Newspark, Japan Newspaper Muesum], Yokohama.

Oakland Daily Evening Tribune 1894, 'Literary notes', Oakland, 18 December.

O'Herne, Jan R 1994, *50 years of silence*, ETT Imprint, Sydney.

Oizuru Yoshiya 1986, '*Chōya shinbun*: kōkoku ran ni miru Burakku' in *Kairakutei kenkyū* 1, 19 September.

Okamoto Ippei 1929, 'Hebo kyūri' in *Ippei zenshū*, volume 3, Senshinsha, Tokyo.

Oliver, PM 2001, 'Japanese immigrant merchants and the Japanese trading company network in Sydney, 1880s to 1941' in Jones, P and P Oliver, *Changing histories, Australia and Japan*, Monash University Press, Clayton.

—— 2002, 'Who is one of us? (Re)discovering the inside-out of Australia's Japanese immigrant communities, 1901–57', *Japanese Studies*, December.

—— 2003a, 'Espionage and paranoia: assessing Australian responses to 'Japanese activities' 1870–1947' in *Ritsumeikan Journal of Asia Pacific Studies* 11, University of Tokyo, March.

—— 2003b, 'Interpreting Japanese activities in Australia—1880–1945' in *Ritsumeikan Journal of Asia Pacific Studies*, University of Tokyo, March.

—— 2004, *Allies, enemies, trading partners: records on Australia and the Japanese*, National Archives of Australia, Canberra.

—— 2006, 'Finding Dame Nellie Melba's butler: the hidden history of Victoria's Japanese immigrants 1869–1943', lecture delivered at the Immigration Museum, Melbourne, 9 April, text available from Institute of Public History, Monash University, www.arts.monash.edu.au/public-history-institute/index.html.

Ōmiya-shi Keikakubu Kokusai Bunka-ka (ed) 1991, *Kindai Manga no Sō 'Kitazawa Rakuten' zuroku*: *Kitazawa Rakuten, founder of the modern Japanese cartoon*, International and Cultural Section, Planning Department, City of Omiya.

'Order and disorder: architectural transactions in print and photographs' 1999, New York Public Library, New York, 30 January to 3 April.

Ōta Hiroshi 1998, *Rakugo to kabuki: ikina naka*, Heibonsha, Tokyo.

Ōta, S 1990, 'The water station', *Asian Theatre Journal* 7(2).

Overland Monthly and Out West 1894, 'Book reviews', San Francisco, 24(144).

Park, Kenneth W 1998, correspondence, and extract from the Wesley College entry book, 27 October.

Pearson, CH 1893, *National life and character: a forecast*, Macmillan, London.

Perlman, Bennard B 1999, *The lives, loves, and art of Arthur B Davies*, State University of New York Press, Albany.

Pflugfelder, Gregory M 1999, *Cartographies of desire: male–male sexuality in Japanese discourse*, 1600–1950, University of California Press, Berkeley.

Powell, TB (ed) 1999, *Beyond the binary: reconstructing cultural identity in a multicultural context*, Rutgers University Press, New Brunswick.

Puck 1905, 18 January.

—— 1906, 16 August.

—— 1907, 13 March.

Punshon, EM 1987, *Monte-san: the times between, life lies hidden*, Kobe Japan–Australia Society, Kobe.

Purcell, WR 1980, 'The nature and extent of Japanese commercial and economic interests in Australia 1932–1941', PhD thesis, University of New South Wales, Sydney.

Pyle, Kenneth B 1969, *The new generation in Meiji Japan: problems of cultural identity, 1885–1895*, Stanford University Press, Stanford.

Registrar of Births, Deaths & Marriages 1992, 'Victorian pioneers index c1837–1888: index to births, deaths and marriage records held by Registry of Births, Deaths & Marriages', Melbourne.

Rix, A 1998, *The Australia–Japan political alignment, 1952 to the present*, Routledge, London and New York.

Rolf, R 1992a, 'Japanese theatre from the 1980s: the Ludic conspiracy', *Modern Drama* 34(1).

Rule, Andrew 2002, 'How four suitcases of heroin turned a five-day dream holiday into 10 years behind bars', the *Age*, 'Insight' section, 17 August.

Rundle, G 2001, *The opportunist: John Howard and the triumph of reaction*, Black Inc, Melbourne.

Russo, Peter V 1936, 'The Australian in Japan', *Herald*, 5 September.

—— 1943, *Spoken Japanese simplified*, Robertson and Mullens, Melbourne.

—— 1945a, 'Make Hirohito denounce Japan's war crimes', *Herald*, 11 September.

—— 1945b, 'Konoye failed in great trust', *Argus*, 17 December.

—— 1948a, 'Honourable Information', Twelfth Arthur Norman Smith Memorial Lecture in Journalism, University of Melbourne, August.

—— 1948b, 'Then and now', *British Commonwealth Occupation News* (*BCON*), Christmas souvenir issue, 25 December.

S, C 1900, 'Frank A Nankivell', *The poster*, October.

Said, Edward W 1985, *Orientalism*, Penguin, Harmondsworth.

Saxonhouse, G 1974, 'A tale of Japanese technological diffusion in the Meiji Period', *Journal of Economic History* (34).

Sessions, Jane 1896, 'Nankivell: the talented cartoonist of the Pacific slope', *Colorado Springs Gazette*, 10 January.

Shearston May, AK 1911, 'New Caledonia: a menace to white Australia', *Lone Hand*, June.

Shimizu Isao 1984, *Bigō Nihon sobyō-shū* [*Bigot's Japanese sketch collection*], Iwanami, Tokyo.

Shimizu, S 1996, interview with author, Tokyo, 17 October.

Shively, Donald H 1971, 'The Japanization of the middle Meiji' in Shively, Donald H (ed), *Tradition and modernization in Japanese culture*, Princeton University Press, Princeton.

Shogei Konwakai (ed) 1977, *Kairakutei Burakku kankei bunken mokuroku*, Shogei Konwakai, Yokohama.

Silvester, John 1994, 'Customs picks the "mules" among tourists', *Sunday Age*, 29 May.

Sissons, DCS 1956, 'Attitudes to Japan and defence 1890–1923', MA thesis, University of Melbourne.

—— 1972, 'Australian fears of Japan as a defence threat', Australia, Senate Standing Committee on Foreign Affairs and Defence - Reference: Japan, Official Hansard Report, 28 April.

—— 1975, 'Private diplomacy in the 1936 trade dispute with Japan', *Australian Journal of Politics and History* 27(2).

—— 1976, 'Manchester v Japan: the imperial background of the Australian trade diversion dispute with Japan, 1936', *Australian Outlook* 30(3).

—— 1977, 'Japanese in the Northern Territory 1884–1902', *South Australiana* 16(1).

—— 1979a, 'The Japanese in the Australian pearling industry', *Queensland Heritage* 3(10).

—— 1979b, 'A selector and his family', *Hemisphere* 25.

—— 1988, 'Australian contact with Japan in the nineteenth century', Japan Foundation Papers 7.

SMH [*Sydney Morning Herald*] 1935, 'Japan's culture', 15 July.

Smith, Henry D II 1978, 'Tokyo as an idea: an exploration of Japanese urban thought until 1945', *Journal of Japanese Studies* 1(1).

Sono, Takeo 2000, *Photographic history of Japanese society in Australia 1927–1942*, printed privately.

Southern Sky 2002, December.

Sterry, Lorraine 2003, 'Constructs of Meiji Japan: the role of writing by Victorian women travellers', *Japanese Studies* 23(2).

Stewart, Harold 1934, 'Betrayal', *Fortian*, December.

—— 1941, '"Modern" "Australian" "Art"', *Arna*.

—— 1960, *A net of fireflies*, CE Tuttle, Tokyo.
—— 1969, *A chime of windbells*, CE Tuttle, Tokyo.
—— 1975, 'A fair and temples', *Hemisphere* 19.
—— 1977, 'A retreat of *Rakan*', *Hemisphere* 21.
—— 1979a, 'A walk in old Kyoto', *Hemisphere* 23.
—— 1979b, 'A walk in old Kyoto, Part II', *Hemisphere* 23.
—— 1981, *By the old walls of Kyoto*, CE Tuttle, Tokyo.
Stewart, Ron 2003, 'Furanku A Nankiberu: Nihon no manga-shi no kyakuchū' [Frank A Nankivell: footnote to Japanese cartoon histories], *Manga Kenkyū* [*Manga Studies*] 3, March.
Stoddard, Lothrop 1920, *The rising tide of color against white world-supremacy*, Charles Scribner's Sons, New York.
Strickland, Miriam F 1970 [1939], 'Frank Arthur Nankivell—painter and graver' in Research Institute of the College of Art Association (ed), *Index of twentieth-century artists, 1933–1937*, Arno Press, New York.
Sun 1940, 'Japan as neighbour', 16 July.
Sun News-Pictorial 1932, 'Landed linguistic job', 21 April.
Sunday Mainichi 2000, 2 January.
Tait, P 2001, 'Scenes of the beginning from the end', *Real Time 43*, Open City 2005, Sydney.
Takagi, Kazuo 2000, *Rakuen Osen* [*Polluting Paradise*], Kyōiku Shiryō Shuppan Kai, Tokyo.
Tamura, Keiko 2003, 'Meeting, committing and adapting: Japanese war brides and the experience of migration', *Ritsumeikan Journal of Asia Pacific Studies* 11.
—— 2005, 'Mary Kawatani Kirby: a woman of two worlds', *National Library of Australia News* 15(7).
Taylor, Thomas 1992, 'Yakuza link suspected in tourist heroin haul', the *Age*, 22 June.
Terada, Takahashi 2001, 'Nagano Shigeo: business leadership in the Asia Pacific region of the Pacific Basin Economic Council', *Australian Journal of Politics and History*, January.
Thompson, RC 1980, *Australian imperialism in the Pacific the expansionist era 1820–1920*, Melbourne University Press, Carlton.
Thornton, Bob 1988, *An index to Victorian railway employees of the 19th century*, Library Council of Victoria, Melbourne.
'Tokio aiding Japs in drive to seize California without hitting a blow, Phelan says' 1920, *Woodland Daily Democrat*.
Torney-Parlicki, Prue 2000, *Somewhere in Asia: war, journalism and Australia's neighbours 1941–75*, UNSW Press, Sydney.

—— 2001, 'Selling goodwill: Peter Russo and the promotion of Japan–Australia relations 1935–1941', *Australian Journal of Politics and History* 46(3).

—— 2005, *Behind the news: a biography of Peter Russo*, University of Western Australia Press, Crawley.

Treat, John Whittier 1999, *Great mirror shattered: homosexuality, Orientalism, and Japan*, Oxford University Press, New York and Oxford.

Tsokhas, K 1989, 'The wool industry and the 1936 trade diversion dispute between Australia and Japan', *Australian Historical Studies* 23(93).

—— 1992, 'The Eastern & Australian Steamship Company and the shipping dispute between Australia and Japan, 1936–9', *Business History* 34(2).

Tweedie, S 1994, *Trading partners: Australia and Asia, 1790–1993*, NSW University Press, Sydney.

Uchino, T 1999, 'Deconstructing "Japaneseness": towards articulating locality and hybridity in contemporary Japanese performance', *Disorientations Cultural Praxis in Theatre: Asia, Pacific, Australia*, Fensham, R and P Eckersall, Monash Theatre Papers, Clayton.

—— 2000, 'Images of Armageddon: Japan's 1980s theatre culture', *The Drama Review* 44(1).

—— 2006, Mapping/zapping 'J' theatre at the moment', *Performance Paradigm* 2, www.performanceparadigm.net.

Utsumi, A and H Nagai (eds) 1999, *Tokyo saiban shiryō: Furyo Jōhōkyoku kankei bunsho* [*Material related to the Tokyo trials: documents related to the Prisoner of War Information Bureau*], Gendai shiryō shuppan, Tokyo.

Walker DR 1999, *Anxious nation: Australia and the rise of Asia, 1850–1939*, University of Queensland Press, St Lucia.

Waswo, Ann 1996, *Modern Japanese society 1868–1994*, Oxford University Press, Oxford.

Weatherstone, EM 2004, telephone interview with Graham Eccles, Australian Capital Territory, 9 December.

Weinberg, Gerhard L 1994, *A world at arms: a global history of World War II*, Cambridge University Press, New York

Weitenkampf, Frank 1924, *American graphic art*, Macmillan, New York.

West, Richard S 1988, *Satire on stone: the political cartoons of Joseph Keppler*, University of Illinois Press, Urbana.

White, Arnold 1911, 'Defence of Australia', *Lone Hand*, 1 November.

White, Judy 1981, *The White family of Belltrees: 150 years in the Hunter Valley*, Seven Press, Sydney.

Who's who in America 1912–13, volume 7, Marquis, Chicago.

Williams, Harold S 1958a, *Tales of the foreign settlements in Japan*, CE Tuttle, Tokyo.

—— 1958b, 'Those Australians' in *Tales of the Foreign Settlements in Japan*, CE Tuttle, Tokyo.

—— 1959, *Shades of the past or indiscreet tales of Japan*, CE Tuttle, Tokyo.

—— 1963, *Foreigners in Mikadoland*, CE Tuttle, Tokyo.

—— 1968, *The story of Holme Ringer & Co Ltd*, CE Tuttle Company, Tokyo.

—— 1970, *Kobe Regatta & Athletic Club: the first hundred years*, Kobe Regatta & Athletic Club, Kobe.

—— 1975, *The Kobe Club*, Kobe Club, Kobe.

—— 1975, 'Two remarkable Australians of old Yokohama', *Transactions of the Asiatic society of Japan* 3(12).

—— 1984, *The story of Shioya, of the James Estate, of James Yama and of the Shioya Country Club*, International Committee of the Kansai, Osaka.

Williams, Harold S and Jean 1996, *West meets East: the foreign experience of Japan*, Halstead Press Publishers, Rushcutters Bay.

Williams, Jean 1989, Interview with Gertrude (Jean) Williams, sound recording, interviewed by Jennifer Gall, Oral History Collection, National Library of Australia, Canberra.

Williams, Peter John 2003, Interview with Peter Williams, sound recording, interviewed by Keiko Tamura. Oral History Collection, National Library of Australia, Canberra.

Wilson, Paul 1991, 'Miscarriages of justice in serious criminal cases in Australia' in Carrington, Kerry, Maryanne Dever, Russell Hogg, Jenny Bargen and Andrew Lohrey (eds), *Travesty*, Pluto Press, Leichhardt.

Woodland Daily Democrat 1920, 'Tokio aiding Japs in drive to seize California without hitting a blow, Phelan says', reproduced from the *San Francisco Examiner*, Woodland, 8 October.

Woodward, Kathryn 1997, 'Introduction' in *Identity and Difference*, Sage Publications, London.

WPA Federal Art Project 1938, 'The Works Program US Works Progress Administration; for immediate release: Frank A Nankivell to show prints at Smithsonian in Washington', two page press release, Department of Information, 25 April.

Wray, WD 1984, *Mitsubishi and the NYK, 1870–1914: business strategy in the Japanese shipping industry*, Council on East Asian Studies, Harvard University, Cambridge.

The Xaverian 1898 St Francis Xavier College, Kew.

—— 1910, St Francis Xavier College, Kew.

Yamamoto, Shōgetsu 1936, 'Hana peko no yaegaki hime' in *Meiji sesō hyakuwa*, Dai-ichi shobō, Tokyo.

Yonetani, J 2004, 'The 'history wars' in comparative perspective: Australia and Japan', *Cultural Studies Review* 10(2).

'Yume (dream) the year 2000 they dreamed of' 1999, Mikimoto Hall, Mikimoto Jewellery Store, Ginza, Tokyo, 6–20 December.

Zainu'ddin, AGT 1985, 'Rose Inagaki: is it a crime to marry a foreigner?' in Kelly, F and M Lake (eds), *Double time: women in Victoria's 150 years*, Penguin Books, Ringwood.

Zipper, B 2001, 'Scenes of the beginning from the end', *Stage Left*, Stage Left 2003, Melbourne.

Archival material

Australian Defence Force Academy (ADFA)

MS G233, Stewart papers, letters to Dorothy Green, 23 June 1973; 28 August 1974; 16 May 1975; 8 July 1980.

Australian War Memorial (AWM)

AWM83 251, *United States of America versus Hiroshi Tamura Military Tribunal, SCAP Tokyo, Japan, 29 October 1948–23 February 1949* 5754.

AWM54 779/1/1, Report on investigations in Manila and Japan regarding Prisoners of War and civilians, by Major HS Williams LO 1 Australian PW Contact and Enquiry Unit.

AWM MSS 1641, Beverley Durant, '2 Australian War Crimes Section'.

Battye Library, State Library of Western Australia

MN1216 ACC 1019A/1-52, Muramats

MN1216 ACC2628A/1-12. Muramats

MN1216 ACC 3700A, Muramats

Belltrees archives

Letterbooks, volume 18, letter from HL White, 1908.

National Archives of Australia (NAA)

Australian Capital Territory

A1/15, 1911/16228, Japanese named Nakashiba wishes to take his alleged adopted child to Japan.

A1/15, 1921/24449, B Nakashiba Exemption Certificate.

A10078/1, 1923/10, Muramats Jiro versus WAY, H R Commonwealth Electoral Officer for the State of Western Australia.

A1379/1, EPJ122

A1379/1, EPJ1396, Muramats, Jiro - deceased internee.

A367/1, C65778, Russo. Deter.Martyr Graham. Thomas, AF. Pickering, EH. Nakashiba (Peter also called Nash, Peter).

A367/1, C68609, Nakashiba Samuel.

A3688/48, Volumes of Proceeding and Exhibits of a Court of Inquiry at No 12 Prisoner of War Group – Cowra, 5 August 1944.

A406/62, E1945/1, part 1 attachment, Jiro Muramats - A native of Japan. Disqualification under Section 39 (S). Appeal before High Court of Australia.

A433/1, 1940/2/2351, Japanese merchants and their families resident in Australia.

A433/1, 1941/2/2244, Muramats JT, pearling applications Cossack, WA and Darwin NT.

A461/8, 748/1/569, letter from AG Hard to secretary, Prime Minister's Department, 6 July 1940.

A461/8, 748/1/569, 'Message from Prince Fumimaro Konoye to the people of Australia', 1 July 1940.

A6119/79, 1256, letter from R Flower to Prime Minister, 21 October 1940.

A712/1, 1899/K6473, Muramats Jiro -naturalisation

A7359/101, 9, J & T Muramats - pearlers

New South Wales

C123, WOS, World War 2 Security Investigation Dossiers.

C443/P1, J20, letter from Masatoshhi Akiyama to Peter Russo, 3 October 1940.

SP1096/6, Box 5, Mitsui Melbourne sales journals 1931 to 1941.

SP1098/12, boxes 2,12,13, miscellaneous records of Nosawa & Co.

SP11/4, Japanese A–Z.

SP1714/1, N40344, Japanese Activities in Australia.

SP1714/1, N45868, letter from WH Barnwell to Inspector, Commonwealth Investigation Branch, 26 August 1940.

SP1714/1, N45868, report by Lieutenant G Caiger, Intelligence Section, Eastern Command, 17 July 1940.

SP1714/1, N45868, report by Lieutenant G Caiger, 18 April 1941.

SP1714/1 N45868, 'Far Eastern News Letter no1', Peter V Russo, 1 January 1941, typescript.

SP1714/1 N45868, 'Far Eastern News Letter no 2', Peter V Russo, 1 February 1941, typescript.

SP1714/1 N45868, report by Major WJR Scott, Director of Military Operations and Intelligence, Department of the Army, 5 August 1940.

SP1714/1 N45868, report by Major WJR Scott, 21 August 1940.

Northern Territory

F1/0, 1936/271, Purchase of patrol launches, sea plane for control of Pearl shell poaching etc. Correspondence with HWH Stevens re vessel.

F1/0, 1938/402, Gregory AC & Co pearlers.

Queensland

BP242/1, Q24264, Nakashiba Peter alias Nash - Queensland investigation case file [with photograph and negative].

Victoria

B13/0, WOS, Customs records.

MP1103/2, DJ18118, List of Jiro Muramats assets 1/12/35.

MP124/6, 462/201/753, Lecture, Japan and her Navy, 1933.

MP529/3, Tribunal 4/117, transcript of evidence of objection by M Inagaki, Japanese internee, Tatura 11/2/1942, continued in Melbourne 24/2/42, 5/3/42.

MP729/6, 63/401/518, Nakashiba [internment of family].

MT33/1, WOS, Aliens Registration Forms.

Western Australia

PP302/1, WA17964, Jiro [Giro] MURAMATS.

National Library of Australia (NLA)

MS 1009, series 58, item 62, Peter V Russo, letter to Joseph Bainbridge, 1934.

MS 1009 series 65, item 83, Peter V Russo, letter to Latham, 19 August 1940.

MS3925 series 2, box 7, HM Green papers, letter, 17 April 1943.

MS3925 series 2, box 7, Hope Papers, letter to AD Hope, 'Friday 17th'.

MS 6681, HS Williams, letter to Alan Fleming, 1 October 1973.

MS 6681, series 1/30b, HS Williams, letter to DCS Sissons, 18 December 1975.

MS 8202, Sim, Senator Peter, chairman, Standing Committee on Foreign Affairs and Defence, letter to Russo, 29 February 1972.

MS 8202, series 1, box 1, Murdoch letter to Russo, 16 February 1941.

MS 8202, series 6, box 11, GS Browne, letter to Russo, 18 October 1937.

MS 8202, series 6, box 11, KS Cunningham, letters to Peter V Russo, 4 May 1936 and 20 July 1936.

MS 8202, series 6, box 11, Peter V Russo, 'Kokusai Bunka Shinkokai – then and now', *KBS Bulletin*, 57, November–December 1962, p.3.

MS 8202, series 6, box 11, folder 1, Count Ayske Kabayama, letter to Russo, 20 December 1935.

MS 8202, series 6, box 11, folder 8, official notification of appointment.

MS 8202, series 6, box 12, Peter V Russo, letter to Peter Sim, 5 March 1972.

MS 8202, series 7, box 16, itinerary of Japanese goodwill mission to Australia and New Zealand.

MS8973, series 1, box 1, letter to Marion Riley, 6 June 1966.

MS8973, series 1, box 1, letter to Marion Riley, 12 April 1967.

MS8973, series 3, box 6, letter to Stewart from Carmen Blacker, 25 September 1975.
MS8973, series 5, box 3, travel diaries 1966–69.
MS8973, series 6, box 1, Stewart papers, notebook.
MS8973, series 7, haiku translations.
MS8973, series 10, 'New phoenix wings'.
MS8973, series 11, 'Autumn landscape roll: a divine panorama'.
MS8973, series 13, box 2, Stewart papers.
MS8973, series 16, box 1, letter to Peter Muller, 12 December 1958.
MS8973, series 16, box 6, letter to Gwen Smith, 20 December 1966.
MS8973, series 16, box 6, letter to Kurt Forrer, 10 September 1967.
MS8973, series 16, box 6, letter to Gwen Smith, 6 November 1982.
MS8973, series 16, box 6, letter to Gwen Smith, 12 May 1989.
MS8973, series 16, box 34, letter to Peter Kelly, 1 April 1994.

Norma McAuley Collection

Most of the papers of Norma McAuley are in a private collection. Some have been passed on to the Mitchell Library at the State Library of New South Wales, where they are subject to a long embargo.

Riley Collection

This private collection contains books and papers of Harold Stewart that he left in the care of his sister, Marion Riley. Now in the possession of Lee Riley, the collection may be contacted through the National Library of Australia.

St Francis Xavier College Archives, Kew Victoria

Ledger begun February 1886:195–6.